Promises of the Past

Promises of the Past

A History of Indian Education in the United States

David H. DeJong

North American Press
a division of Fulcrum Publishing
Golden, Colorado

Library of Congress Cataloging-in-Publication Data

David H. DeJong
    Promises of the past : a history of Indian education in the United States / David H. DeJong.
        p.   cm.
    Includes bibliographical references and index.
    ISBN 1-55591-905-7
    1. Indians of North America–Education–History.   I. Title.
    E97.D45   1993
    371.97'97–dc20   93-10469
                                                                                        CIP

Cover design by Sarah Chesnutt

Printed in the United States of America

0 9 8 7 6 5 4 3 2 1

North American Press
a division of
Fulcrum Publishing
350 Indiana Street, Suite 350
Golden, Colorado 80401-5093

CONTENTS

FOREWORD

...We see the function of the Indian controlled schools as two-fold. First, it gives us ... a chance to express our concern for our children and to help them in their education. Further, it is a place for us to learn and to make a contribution. ... Of course, our main concern is for our children's education. We want to help the school develop the student into a person who ... has respect for himself and all men. We would like to see our children finish their formal education exemplifying those personal qualities we hold most dear—courage, generosity, wisdom, humility. On the other hand, we want our children to have the best of training in academic skills; to be prepared to choose a career in the professional, technical, vocational, or the creative arts arenas. Most of all, we want our schools to help our children fulfill themselves as individual human beings. ...

We Indian adults do not need to read the mountains of scholarly studies on Indian education to know how badly the schools of the past have failed us. We know it only too well from personal experience. ... All too often, schools were used as a weapon against Indians to destroy what we hold most dear—our culture and our civilization. Instead of building on what we were as a people so that we became educated in Western ways, as it is normally done, we were almost demoralized by this attack on our very being as individuals.

It is a miracle that we have survived as well as we have, and it is no wonder that we have not been able to use the school in the past as a vehicle for our improvement. We feel we must now step forward to act in our own behalf and in our children's behalf. We cannot act on our behalf in the educational realm unless we have Indian controlled schools. ...

We want our children to take their rightful place in the destiny of America as have the children of so many people. ... We know that if Indian people are allowed to create a bicultural education for our children which will regain our greatness as a people ... our children [will] take their place in the American sun.

—*Coalition of Indian Controlled Schools*

PREFACE

SEVERAL YEARS AGO a Choctaw man explained to me his view of the far-reaching consequences of the Bureau of Indian Affairs system of education. He explained that in his experience federal Indian schools had become an "institutional parent" for the children that attended such facilities. "My parents were the Bureau of Indian Affairs," he admitted. The consequences of such an upbringing—personal, familial, and social—have been well documented. Students of government Indian schools have become adults who struggle to develop interpersonal relationships with their children. The reason for this struggle is that, as children, these Indians had been taken away from their families and sent to federal Indian schools. Under normal circumstances (community schools), these children would have had the benefit of a caring and supportive family that would have nurtured and accepted them. Because they were sent to boarding schools, often away from home for years at a time, these students were denied the comfort and support of a home environment, which is essential in the development of children. In addition, because generations of boarding school students have grown up without parental role models, they have been denied the opportunity to learn how to relate with their own children. Many of these children in turn have been denied parental role models; thus, the cyclical process of institutional-ized children is perpetuated.

The wide-ranging social ramifications of institutionalized education have come to haunt many American Indians. Some cannot communicate with their children; others are abusive. Undoubtedly, the process of taking Indian children out of their communities to place them in institutions has broken up the family life of many Indians and has also weakened parental responsibility. These patterns have been passed down to the next genera-tion of Indian children, who, whether or not they attend a boarding school, are affected by their familial environment, and the problem is exacerbated. The boarding school experience is just one example of how the educational system has not met the needs of American Indians.

Today, though no longer forced to attend boarding schools, Indian students still face many cultural challenges, the most important of which may be preserving their Indian identities. One Alaska native described the importance of identity as follows:

> I can't predict how I should educate my children. I can't predict how they should be educated, but one thing I do know is, if my children are proud, if my children have identity, if my children know who they are and if they are proud of who they are, they'll be able to encounter anything in life. ... I say that a man without identity—if a man doesn't know who he is—might as well be dead. [1]

Gerald Wilkenson, in his article in "Educational Problems in the Indian Community," noted:

> Education is the great massifier of America. Its goal is to break down distinctions between people, to teach people to live in a rootless society, and to foster communication among strangers. Socialization is more important (in this type of education) than providing content. ... [Education] seeks not to make the individual into a better member of his town, village, ethnic group or tribe, but to socialize him so that he can take his place in a corporate niche. The effort is to massify the society. [2]

In the words of a Ponca testifying before the 1969 hearings on Indian education: "School is the enemy." [3]

This book presents a broad historical overview of Indian education. The readings, taken from both government and private studies, point to the fact that too often education has been used as a tool to acculturate Indians. To this end, the educational system has sought to replace what American Indians hold most dear: self-identity. As the Kennedy Report noted in 1969, educational institutions are often seen as battlegrounds by American Indian children and parents; schools pit self-identity and cultural values against a foreign identity and values. [4]

Educational efforts that seek not to instruct but to assimilate constitute educational malpractice. Until the educational process reflects the values and needs of the Indian community, it may well remain a battleground for American Indians.

ACKNOWLEDGMENTS

I WISH TO acknowledge the assistance of several people who helped make this book possible. Foremost, I would like to express my gratitude to Vine Deloria, Jr., for his assistance and encouragement. It was with Vine's support that I undertook the arduous task of assembling this reader. I would also like to acknowledge the contributions of the late Robert K. Thomas, whose wisdom and insight were of great help. I would be remiss if I did not acknowledge the contributions of Laura, Rick, Brad, Vivian, and Phil. Finally, I must acknowledge the support of my wife, Cindy. Without her support and understanding this anthology never could have been written.

INTRODUCTION
Vine Deloria, Jr.

IN THE FIRST century of European discovery of North America, the French along the St. Lawrence made it a practice to exchange young children with the Indian nations in the hope that better relations could be established as the generations passed. This interchange was probably the first effort to change the manner in which American Indians educated their children. The English and Spanish were not nearly as benign, virtually kidnapping Indian children and indoctrinating them in the rigors of English culture or the complexities of Spanish theology. Not much has changed in the intervening centuries since the Americans seem to have sporadically adopted both approaches in trying to come to grips with Indian people.

The education section of the Bureau of Indian Affairs budget is substantial. With the additional funds spent by the Department of Education and various federal agencies involved with economic development and health, the United States Government must spend in the neighborhood of $1 billion a year on some form of Indian education—with the sparsest results. From Alice Fletcher's report on Indian education in the closing years of the last century up to the present, we can find dozens, if not hundreds, of government reports and investigations of Indian education and an imposing list of proposed reforms. Unfortunately, all too often both needs and solutions remain identical and it is simply the lack of resources that prevents growth and resolution of educational problems.

In the last three decades there has been a tremendous expansion of educational programs for American Indians. Federal programs reach out into many reservations and cities, to most universities and colleges, and into a variety of adult training programs so that if Indians cannot find resources for other areas of their lives, it is certain that they can attach themselves to an educational program that will help them move along in better fashion in this complex industrial world.

Two things greatly inhibit Indian education today. No federal agency ever takes seriously the exploding population in the Indian community. The majority of American Indians today are under eighteen years of age, and the average age of Indians seems to be dropping. When this condition is matched with the declining appropriations for supporting educational programs, it is not difficult to see that catastrophe is approaching. The federal programs that do exist are now complicated beyond understanding by rules and regulations that are designed to make programs more efficient but in fact consist of a few general rules and hundreds of waivers. Tribes, community colleges, and reservation schools must wade through a forest of exceptions and reclassifications in order to get programs funded, and educational committees of tribes have not developed an expertise in traversing complex federal administrative law.

Indian educational conferences are not as numerous as they once were but they still pose a formidable barrier to people wishing to remain at home and operate programs. Unless an educator is current on present interpretation of program eligibility rules, he or she has no idea what is changing in Indian education or why. Consequently, educational conferences feature a series of speakers who valiantly attempt to update people on the various new twists and turns of educational exegesis. One can attend an educational conference and never once hear the word "children" or "student" pass anyone's lips. It would not be unfair to observe that everything *except* education is discussed at Indian educational meetings and that children, the ultimate beneficiaries of education, seem to be the missing ingredient in an otherwise busy network of activity.

Some years ago I taught a graduate seminar in Indian Education Legislation at the University of Arizona. Seeking to overcome the extreme concentration on laws and regulations to the exclusion of students and children, I compiled a basic list of readings for my students. David DeJong was tremendously excited about the documents and resource materials that existed in this field. He took the basic readings and began a tedious, exhausting, and systematic search of federal records in an effort to create an educational reader that would give a fair representation of what has happened in Indian education from contact through the modern statements and meetings that we see today.

I was quite overwhelmed when David gave me the first draft of his collection because it seemed as if he had included everything that had ever been said or recorded on Indian education. So the collection had to be pared down to provide an overview of the subject that would give the flavor of what has been happening in Indian education. The result is a splendid historical documentary survey of the events, policies, and most of all the people who have been the subject of educational efforts over the years. Here we meet the determination of administrators and the bewilderment of Indians who cannot fathom the task of acquiring knowledge that seemingly has no useful purpose.

This collection should be used in classrooms so Indians can understand the suffering and confusion of past generations and recognize in current efforts that there are continuing problems that each generation must face and resolve. At the graduate level this collection can be the introduction to the larger set of documents from which these selections are taken. Gaining an insight into the bureaucratic mind through a reading of an excerpt should inspire older students to return to the original sources and immerse themselves in the policy deliberations of the past. Only in that way will they be able to detect the flaws in the present configuration of educational programs now offered to Indian tribes.

The general theme of all these selections is the deep belief, not surrendered today, that somehow Indians must accommodate themselves to the larger society, learns its truths and values, and come to grips with its method of functioning. This attitude surfaces again and again in federal pronouncements on education; it changes clothes frequently and uses masks and much costuming but it remains the same in intent and direction. Only by being able to identify it can we move Indian education beyond its present impasse and create an educational system that truly answers the needs of our students.

It is my hope, and I know it is David's hope, that people who read these selections will take them to heart, think deeply about the turmoil which Indian children have suffered, and deal with the larger ideology that demands that Indians accept the dictates of the larger society before they have completely understood their own traditions. Indian customs and methods of teaching have much to tell the world of education, but Indians cannot impart this knowledge until they are able to rise above the tidal wave of Anglo cultures, master its theoretical/philosophical basis, and articulate philosophies of their own. Discovering, through this book, what has gone before is the first step in accomplishing such a transformation.

Promises of the Past

1

TRADITIONAL INDIAN EDUCATION

WITH FEW EXCEPTIONS the written history of Indian education relates attempts to apply a white man's education and educational processes to the American Indian. Most federal and state initiatives focused on changing the Indian without allowing for cultural differences or taking into account traditional Indian patterns and practices.

It is important to note that every human society has its own means of preparing children for adult participation in that society. Prior to the coming of the white man and the imposition of the Euro-American educational system, the many Indian nations had their own very diverse educational systems, but all were geared to giving education informally through parents, relatives, elder members of the tribe, and religious and social groups.

According to George Bird Grinnell, people too often think of the Indian as a warrior only.

> They do not realize that this phase of life occupies but a small part of his existence, or that aside from this he has a communal and family life on which his well-being depends. He has a wife and little ones whom he loves as we do ours; parents and grandparents whom he respects for their experience and the wisdom derived from it; chiefs and rulers to whose words he listens and whose advice he follows, and spiritual directors, who tell him about the powers which rule the earth, the air, and the waters, and advise him in his relation to the forces of the unseen world. In other words, his is a complex life, not devoted solely to one pursuit, but full of varied and diverse interests. He must provide food for his family, must maintain his position in the camp, and must uphold the standing of the tribe in its relations to other peoples. All these duties call for the exercise of discretion and self-restraint in his living which can be acquired only as a result of some system of education.[1]

The readings in this chapter describe the traditional methods used to teach Indian children the rules, roles, values, and world view of their society. The traditional method of education was an informal community effort; each member of the community had a function in the transmission of knowledge. For example, elders instructed children in kinship roles and the social values of the community. As part of the community each child learned to assume the responsibilities of adulthood, one of which was providing for his or her family. Among the Gila River Pima, for example, boys gained intimate knowledge of plants, seasons, irrigation, and agricultural practices. Pima girls learned to prepare food, take care of the family, and make household items. But perhaps the most significant aspect of traditional Indian education is that each child was treated as a distinct person rather than as an interchangeable piece in a puzzle.

Disparate Educational Philosophies

Differences in the Euro-American and traditional Indian approaches to education amount to more than method or emphasis; they reflect disparate philosophies. No one captured this truth better than Big Soldier, an Osage who expressed his views to George C. Sibley, the factor of Fort Osage in 1820.

> I see and admire your manner of living, your good warm houses, your extensive fields of corn, your gardens, your cows, oxen, workhorses, wagons, and a thousand machines that I know not the use of. I see that you are able to clothe yourselves, even from weeds and grass. In short you can do almost what you choose. You whites possess the power of subduing almost every animal to your use. You are surrounded by slaves. Everything about you is in chains, and you are slaves yourselves. I fear if I should exchange my pursuits for yours, I too should become a slave. Talk to my sons, perhaps they may be persuaded to adopt your fashions, or at least to recommend them to their sons; but for myself, I was born free, was raised free, and wish to die free.[2]

The Euro-American education binds its students to the possessions it helps them attain; students become slaves to the very goods they seek. The more the educated person accumulates, the more real freedom is lost as he falls into the trap of materialism.

Big Soldier was not alone in spurning Euro-American education. At the 1744 Treaty of Lancaster, the Virginia legislature invited the Six Nations to send six youths to be educated at the College of William and Mary. Speaking for the Iroquois, Canassatego refused, amplifying the differences between traditional Indian and Euro-American ideas of education.

> We know you highly esteem the kind of learning taught in these Colleges, and the maintenance of our young Men, while with you, would be very expensive to you. We are convinced therefore, that you mean to do us Good by your

Proposal; and we thank you heartily. But you who are so wise must know that different Nations have different Conceptions of things; and you will not therefore take it amiss if our Ideas of this kind of Education happens not to be the same with yours. We have had some experience of it. Several of our young People were formerly brought up in the Colleges of the Northern Provinces; they were instructed in all your Sciences; but, when they came back to us, they were bad Runners, ignorant of every means of living in the woods, unable to bear either Cold or Hunger, knew neither how to build a Cain, take a deer, or kill an enemy, spoke our language imperfectly, were therefore neither fit for Hunters, Warriors, nor Counsellors; they were totally good for nothing. We are however not the less obliged for your kind Offer, tho' we decline accepting it; and to show our grateful Sense of it, if the Gentlemen of Virginia shall send us a Dozen of their Sons, we will take great care of their Education, instruct them in all we know, and make Men of them.[3]

Mescalero Apache Chief Cadete was well aware of the gulf between the Euro-American and traditional Indian educational philosophies. Speaking to Captain John C. Cremony in the mid-nineteenth century, Cadete explained,

You desire our children to learn from books, and say, that because you have done so, you are able to build all those big houses, and sail over the sea, and talk with each other at any distance, and do many wonderful things; now let me tell you what we think. You begin when you are little to work hard, and work until you are men in order to begin fresh work. You say that you work hard in order to learn how to work well. After you get to be men, then you say, the labor of life commences; then too, you build big houses, big ships, big towns, and everything else in proportion. Then, after you have got them all, you die and leave them behind. Now we call that slavery. You are slaves from the time you begin to talk until you die; but we are free as air. We never work, but the Mexicans and others work for us. Our wants are few and easily supplied. The river, the wood and plain yield all that we require, and we will not be slaves; nor will we send our children to your schools, where they only learn to become like yourselves.[4]

What, then, was a traditional Indian education? One answer does not suffice for all tribes; each tribe had its own ideas and perceptions of what was important. However, several characteristics were common among most tribes. Indian children learned by application and imitation rather than memorization of principles. Great value was placed on sharing and coopera-tion, which contrasts sharply with the American values of competition and individualism. Indeed, in tribal societies the individual was subordinate to the tribal group; thus, tribal needs were given priority over individual needs.

Traditional Indian education covered tribal history, including ori-gin and great deeds; physical science, as seen in the Indian's love and care of the natural world; physical education and athletic ability; etiquette, including respect for elders; hunting or learning to provide for one's family; religious training and fasting, which connotes self discipline; and diet and health care. In short, traditional Indian education provided the skills needed for any society to function.

In *Indian Boyhood*[5] Charles Eastman, or Hakadah, describes his traditional Santee Sioux education and the role that his grandmother and uncles played in it. Reared by his grandmother, Hakadah learned the cultural attributes and skills that he would need to survive as an adult Sioux. At the age of fifteen Hakadah was reunited with his father, who had been imprisoned for his alleged role in the 1862 Sioux uprising in Minnesota and who was believed to have been killed by whites. His father took Hakadah to Flandreau, South Dakota, where his formal education began. Doctor Charles Eastman later earned advanced degrees at Dartmouth and the Boston University School of Medicine.

An Indian Boy's Training

It is commonly supposed that there is no systematic education of the children among the aborigines of this country. Nothing could be farther from the truth. All the customs of this primitive people were held to be divinely instituted, and those in connection with the training of children were scrupulously adhered to and transmitted from one generation to another.

The expectant parents conjointly bent all their efforts to the task of giving the new-comer the best they could gather from a long line of ancestors. A pregnant Indian woman would often choose one of the greatest characters of her family and tribe as a role model for her child. This hero was daily called to mind. She would gather from tradition all of his noted deeds and daring exploits, rehearsing them to herself when alone. In order that the impression might be more distinct, she avoided company. She isolated herself as much as possible, and wandered in solitude, not thoughtlessly, but with an eye to the impress given by grand and beautiful scenery.

Scarcely was the embryo warrior ushered into the world when he was met by lullabies that speak of wonderful exploits in hunting and war. Those ideas which so fully occupied his mother's mind before his birth are now put into words by all about the child, who is as yet quite unresponsive to their appeals to his honor and ambition. He is called the future defender of his people, whose lives may depend upon his courage and skill. If the child is a girl, she is at once addressed as the future mother of a noble race.

Very early, the Indian boy assumed the task of preserving and transmitting the legends of his ancestors and his race. Almost every evening a myth, or a true story of some deed done in the past, was narrated by one of the parents or grandparents, while the boy listened with parted lips and glistening eyes. On the following evening, he was usually required to repeat it. If he was not an apt scholar, he struggled long with his task; but as a rule, the Indian boy is a good listener and has a good memory, so that the stories were tolerably well mastered. The household became his audience, by which he was alternately criticized and applauded.

This sort of teaching at once enlightens the boy's mind and stimulates his ambition. His conception of his future career becomes a vivid and irresistible force. Whatever there is for him to learn must be learned; whatever qualifications are necessary to a truly great man he must seek at any expense of danger and hardship. Such was the feeling of the imaginative and brave young Indian. It became apparent to him early in life that he must accustom himself to rove alone and not to fear or dislike the impression of solitude.

It seems to be a popular idea that all the characteristic skill of the Indian is instinctive and hereditary. This is a mistake. All the stoicism and patience of the Indian are acquired traits, and continual practice alone make him master of the art of woodcraft. Physical training and dieting were not neglected. I remember that I was not allowed to have beef soup or any warm drink. The soup was for the old men. General rules for the young were never to take their food very hot, nor to drink much water.

My uncle, who educated me up to the age of fifteen years, was a strict disciplinarian and a good teacher. When I left the teepee in the morning, he would say: "Hakadah, look closely to everything you see;" and at evening, on my return, he used often to catechize me for an hour or so.

"On which side of the trees is the lighter-colored bark? On which side do they have most irregular branches?"

It was his custom to let me name all the new birds that I had seen during the day. I would name them according to the color or the shape of the bill or their song or the appearance and locality of the nest—in fact, anything about the bird that impressed me as characteristic. I made ridiculous errors, I must admit. He then usually informed me of the correct name. Occasionally I made a hit and this he would warmly commend.

He went much deeper into this science when I was a little older, that is, about the age of eight or nine years. He would say, for instance: "How do you know that there are fish in yonder lake?" "Because they jump out of the water for flies at mid-day." He would smile at my prompt but superficial reply.

"What do you think of the little pebbles grouped together under the shallow water? and what made the pretty curved marks in the sandy bottom and the little sand-banks? Where do you find the fish-eating birds? Have the inlet and the outlet of a lake anything to do with the question?" He did not expect a correct reply at once to all the voluminous questions that he put to me on these occasions, but he meant to make me observant and a good student of nature.

"Hakadah," he would say to me, "you ought to follow the example of the shunktokecha (wolf). Even when he is surprised and runs for his life, he will pause to take one more look at you before he enters his final retreat. So you must take a second look at everything you see.

"It is better to view animals unobserved. I have been a witness to their courtships and their quarrels and have learned many of their secrets in this way. I was once the unseen spectator of a thrilling battle between a pair of grizzly bears and three buffaloes—a rash act for the bears, for it was in the moon of the strawberries, when buffaloes sharpen and polish their horns for bloody contests among themselves.

"I advise you, my boy, never to approach a grizzly's den from the front, but to steal up behind and throw your blanket or a stone in front of the hole. He does not usually rush for it, but first puts his head out and listens and then comes out very indifferently and sits on his haunches on the mound in front of the hole before he makes any attack. While he is exposing himself in this fashion, aim at his heart. Always be as cool as the animal himself." Thus he armed me against the cunning of savage beasts by teaching me how to outwit them.

"In hunting," he would resume, "you will be guided by the habits of the animal you seek. Remember that a moose stays in swampy or low land or between high mountains near a spring or lake, for thirty to sixty days at a time. Most large game moves about continually, except the doe in the spring; it is then a very easy matter to find her with the fawn. Conceal yourself in a convenient place as soon as you observe any signs of the presence of either, and then call with your birch doe-caller.

"Whichever one hears you first will soon appear in your neighborhood. But you must be very careful, or you may be made a fawn of by a large wild-cat. They understand the characteristic call of the doe perfectly well.

"When you have any difficulty with a bear or a wild-cat—that is, if the creature shows signs of attacking you—you must make him fully understand that you have seen him and are aware of his intentions. If you are not well equipped for a pitched battle, the only way to make him retreat is to take a long sharp pointed pole for a spear and rush toward him. No wild beast will face this unless he is cornered and already wounded. These fierce beasts are generally afraid of the common weapon of the larger animals—the horns, and if these are very long and sharp, they dare not risk an open fight.

"There is one exception to this rule—the grey wolf will attack fiercely when very hungry. But their courage depends upon their numbers; in this way they are like white men. One wolf or two will never attack a man. They will stampede a herd of buffaloes in order to get at the calves; but they are always careful about attacking man."

Of this nature were the instructions of my uncle, who was widely known at that time as among the greatest hunters of his tribe.

All boys were expected to endure hardship without complaint. In savage warfare, a young man must, of course, be an athlete and used to undergoing all sorts of privations. He must be able to go without food and water for two or three days without displaying any weakness, or to run for a day and a night without any rest. He must be able to traverse a pathless and wild country without losing his way either in the day or night time. He cannot refuse to do any of these things if he aspires to be a warrior.

Sometimes my uncle would waken me very early in the morning and challenge me to fast with him all day. I had to accept the challenge. We blackened our faces with charcoal, so that every boy in the village would know that I was fasting for the day. Then the little tempters would make my life a misery until the merciful sun hid behind the western hills.

I scarcely can recall the time when my stern teacher began to give sudden war-whoops over my head in the morning while I was sound asleep. He expected me to leap up with perfect presence of mind, always ready to grasp a weapon of some sort and to give a shrill whoop in reply. If I was sleepy or startled and hardly knew what I was about, he would ridicule me and say that I need never expect to sell my scalp dear. Often he would vary these tactics by shooting off his gun just outside of the lodge while I was yet asleep, at the same time giving blood-curdling yells. After a time I became used to this.

When Indians went upon the warpath, it was their custom to try the new warriors thoroughly before coming to an engagement. For instance, when they were near a hostile camp, they would select the novices to go after water and make them do all sorts of things to prove their courage. In accordance with this idea, my uncle used to send me off after water when camped after dark in a strange place. Perhaps the country was full of wild beasts, and, for aught I knew, there might be scouts from hostile bands of Indians in that very neighborhood.

Yet I never objected, for that would show cowardice. I picked my way through the woods, dipped my pail in the water, and hurried back, always careful to make as little noise as a cat. Being only a boy, my heart would leap at every crackling of a dry twig or distant hoot of an owl, until at last, I reached our teepee. Then my uncle would perhaps say: "Ah, Hakadah, you are a thorough warrior," empty out the precious contents of the pail, and order me to go a second time.

Imagine how I felt! But I wished to be a brave man as much as a white boy desires to be a great lawyer or perhaps even President of the United States. Silently I would take the pail and endeavor to retrace my footsteps in the dark.

With all this, our manners and morals were not neglected. I was made to respect the adults and especially the aged. I was not allowed to join in their discussions, nor even to speak in their presence, unless requested to do so. Indian etiquette was very strict, and among the requirements was that of avoiding the direct address. A term of relationship or some title of courtesy was commonly used instead of the personal name by those who wished to show respect. We were taught generosity to the poor and reverence for the "Great Mystery." Religion was the basis of all Indian training.

I recall to the present day some of the kind warnings and reproofs that my good grandmother was wont to give me. "Be strong of heart— be patient!" she used to say. She told me of a young chief who was noted for his uncontrollable temper. While in one of his rages he attempted to kill a woman, for which he was slain by his own band and left unburied as a mark of disgrace— his body was simply covered with green grass. If I ever lost my temper, she would say: "Hakadah, control yourself, or you will be like that young man I told you of, and lie under a blanket!"

In the old days, no young man was allowed to use tobacco in any form until he had become an acknowledged warrior and had achieved a record. If a youth should seek a wife before he had reached the age of twenty-two or twenty-three, and been recognized as a brave man, he was sneered at and considered an ill-bred Indian. He must also be a skillful hunter. An Indian cannot be a good husband unless he brings home plenty of game.[6]

As Eastman suggests, Indian children were taught how things behave so that the children could analyze other similar behavior. The child's relationship with the natural world was fostered by his parents and elders with ever-increasing sophistication; knowledge and understanding came not by intuition but by training.

Education was by imitation and direct application. It provided the child with the essential qualities needed to exist within the tribal social structure. The home provided a forum in which to practice his newly learned skills; relatives provided discipline, morals, manners, and generosity. Religion was the center of all Indian educational undertakings. The following selection, from *Sun Chief: The Autobiography of a Hopi Chief*, illustrates the informality and experiential emphasis of traditional Indian educational methods.

Learning to work was like play. We children tagged around with our elders and copied what they did. We followed our fathers to the fields and helped plant and weed. The old men took us for walks and taught us the use of plants and how to collect them. We joined the women in collecting rabbitweed for baskets, and went with them to dig clay for pots. We would taste this clay as the women did to test it. We watched the fields to drive out the birds and rodents, helped pick peaches to dry in the sun, and gather melons to lug up the mesas. We rode the burros to harvest corn, gather fuel, or herd sheep. In house-building we helped a little by bringing dirt to cover the roofs. In this way we grew up doing things. All the old people said that it was a disgrace to be idle and that a lazy boy should be whipped.[7]

Another short selection from *Indian Boyhood* illustrates Indian children's interest in the physical environment and their attentiveness to oratory skills. The selection showcases the descriptive skills of the children.

At another time, when I was engaged in a similar discussion with my brother Chatanna, Oesedah came to my rescue. Our grandmother had asked us: "What bird shows most judgment in caring for its young?"

Chatanna at once exclaimed: "The eagle!" but I held my peace for a moment, because I was confused—so many birds came into my mind at once. I finally declared: "It is the oriole!"

Chatanna was asked to state all the evidence that he had in support of the eagle's good sense in rearing its young. He proceeded with an air of confidence: "The eagle is the wisest of all birds. Its nest is made in the safest possible place, upon a high and inaccessible cliff. ...

"Being exposed to the inclemency of the weather the young eaglets are hardy. They are accustomed to hear the mutterings of the Thunder Bird and the sighings of the Great Mystery. Why, the little eagles cannot help being as noble as they are, because their parents selected for them so lofty and inspiring a home! How happy they must be when they find themselves above the clouds, and behold the zig-zag flashes of lightning all about them! It must be nice to taste a piece of fresh meat up in their cool home, in the burning summer-time! Then when they drop down the bones of the game they feed upon, wolves and vultures gather beneath them, feeding upon their refuse. That alone would show them their chieftainship over all other birds. Isn't that so, grandmother?" Thus triumphantly he concluded his argument. I was staggered at first by the noble speech of Chatanna, but I soon recovered from its effects. The little Oesedah came to my aid by saying: "Wait until Ohiyesa tells of the loveliness of the beautiful Oriole's home!" This timely remark gave me courage and I began:

"My grandmother, who was it said that a mother who has a gentle and sweet voice will have children of a good disposition? I think the oriole is that kind of parent. It provides both sunshine and shadow for its young. Its nest is suspended from the prettiest bough of the most graceful tree, where it is rocked by the gentle winds; and the one we found yesterday was beautifully lined with soft things, both deep and warm, so that the little featherless birdies cannot suffer from the cold and wet."

Here Chatanna interrupted me to exclaim: "That is just like the white people—who cares for them? The eagle teaches its young to be accustomed to hardships, like young warriors!"

Ohiyesa was provoked; he reproached his brother and appealed to the judge saying that he had not finished yet.

"But you would not have lived, Chatanna, if you had been exposed like that when you were a baby! The oriole shows wisdom in providing for its children a good, comfortable home! A home upon a high rock would not be pleasant— it would be cold! We climbed a mountain once and it was cold there; and who would care to stay in such a place when it storms? What wisdom is there in having a pile of rough sticks upon a bare rock, surrounded with ill smelling bones of animals, for a home? Also, my uncle says that the eaglets seem always to be on the point of starvation. You have heard that whoever lives on game killed by someone else is compared to an eagle. Isn't that so, grandmother?

"The oriole suspends its nest from the lower side of a horizontal bough so that no enemy can approach it. It enjoys peace and beauty and safety."

Oesedah was at Ohiyesa's side during the discussion, and occasionally whispered into his ear. Uncheedah decided this time in favor of Ohiyesa.[8]

Traditional Educational Methods

John Heckewelder's nineteenth-century study of Indian education high-lights the significance of religion as well as community involvement, respect for elders, and the use of positive and negative reinforcement. Heckewelder observed an ongoing education process that knew neither hour nor day but was given the utmost attention by the entire community throughout the year.

The first step that parents take towards the education of their children is to prepare them for future happiness, by impressing upon their tender minds, that they are indebted for their existence to a great and benevolent Spirit, who not only has given them life, but has ordained them for certain great purposes. That he has given them a fertile extensive country well stocked with game of every kind for their subsistence, and that by one of his inferior spirits he has also sent down to them from above corn, squashes, beans and other vegetables for their nourishment; all which blessings their ancestors have enjoyed for a great number of ages. That this great Spirit looks down upon the Indians, to see whether they are grateful to him and make him a due return for the many benefits he has bestowed, and therefore that it is their duty to show their thankfulness by worshipping him, and doing that which is pleasing in his sight.

They are then told that their ancestors, who received all this from the hands of the great Spirit, and lived in the enjoyment of it, must have been informed of what would be most pleasing to this good being, and of the manner in which his favor could be most surely obtained, and they are directed to look up for instruction to those who know all this, to learn from them, and revere them for their wisdom and the knowledge which they possess; this creates in the children a strong sentiment of respect for their elders, and a desire to follow their advice and example. Their young ambition is then excited by telling them that they were made the superiors of all creatures, and are to have power over them; great pains are taken to make this feeling take an early root, and it becomes in fact their ruling passion through life; for no pains are spared to instill into them that by following the advice of the most admired and extolled hunter, trapper or warrior, they will at a future day acquire a degree of fame and reputation, equal to that which he possesses; that by submitting to the counsels of the aged, the chiefs, the men superior in wisdom, they may also rise to glory, and be called Wisemen, an honourable title, to which no Indian is indifferent. They are finally told that if they respect the aged and infirm, and are kind and obliging to them, they will be treated in the same manner when their turn comes to feel the infirmities of old age.

When this first and most important lesson is thought to be sufficiently impressed upon the children's minds, the parents next proceed to make them sensible of the distinction between good and evil; they tell them that there are good actions and bad actions, both equally open to them to do or commit; that good acts are pleasing to the good Spirit which gave them their existence, and that on the contrary, all that is bad proceeds from the bad spirit who has given them nothing, and who cannot give them anything that is good, because he has it not, and therefore he envies them that which they have received from the good Spirit, who is far superior to the bad one.

This introductory lesson, if it may be so called, naturally makes them wish to know what is good and what is bad. This the parent teaches him in his own way, that is to say, in the way in which he was himself taught by his own parents. It is not the lesson of an hour nor a day, it is rather a long course more of practical than theoretical instruction, a lesson, which is not re- peated at stated seasons or times, but which is shewn, pointed out, and demonstrated to the child, not only by those under whose immediate guardianship he is, but by the whole community, who consider themselves alike interested in the direction to be given to the rising generation.

If the child is sent from his father's dwelling to carry a dish of victuals to an aged person, all in the house will join him in calling him a good child. They will ask whose child he is, and on being told, will exclaim: what! has the Tortoise, or little Bear (as the father's name may be) got such a good child? If the child is seen passing through the streets leading an old decrepit person, the villagers will in his hearing, and to encourage all the other children who may be present to take example from him, call on one another to look on and see what a good child that must be. And so, in most instances, this method is resorted to, for the purpose of instructing children in things that are good, proper, or honourable in themselves; while, on the other hand, when a child has committed a bad act, the parent will say to him: "Oh! how grieved I am that my child has done this bad act! I hope he will never do so again." This is generally effectual, particularly if said in the presence of others. The whole of the Indian plan of education tends to elevate rather than depress the mind, and by that means to make determined hunters and fearless warriors.

In this indirect manner, instruction on all subjects is given to the young people. They are to learn the arts of hunting, trapping and making war, by listening to the aged when conversing together on those subjects, each, in his turn, relating how he acted, and opportunities are afforded to them for that purpose. By this mode of instructing youth, their respect for the aged is kept alive, and it is increased by the reflection that the same respect will be paid to them at a future day when young persons will be attentive to what they shall relate.

Thus has been maintained for ages, without convulsions and without civil discords, this traditional government, of which the world, perhaps, does not offer another example; a government in which there are no positive laws, but only long established habits and customs, no code of jurisprudence, but the experience of former times, no magistrates, but advisors, to whom the people, nevertheless, pay a willing and implicit obedience, in which age confers rank, wisdom gives power, and moral goodness secures a title to universal respect. All this seems to be effected by the simple means of an excellent mode of education, by which strong attachment to ancient customs, respect for age, and love of virtue are indelibly impressed upon the minds of youth, so that these impressions acquire strength as time pursues its course, and as they pass through successive generations.[9]

Informal and indirect as it was, Indian education was by no means haphazard. The Cherokee, for example, who practiced an absence of restraint to the point that parents were unwilling to exercise authority over their children, nevertheless had definite ideas as to the need and purpose of education. Education was a clan directive; legends, precepts, example, and imitation were the means of educating youth. Sanctions also played a corrective role in the educational process. Abraham E. Knepler, in "Education in the Cherokee Nation," explains how children were directed without authoritarianism.

Contemporary observers of Native American customs generally agree that the manner of rearing children has been characterized, as a rule, by the absence of harsh methods. Parents, the mothers especially, were "most kind and indulgent" to their children.

Among the Cherokees the unwillingness to exercise authority in dealing with their children was but a natural consequence of their intense love of liberty. The concept of liberty pervaded the whole of Cherokee life, and constituted the essence of Cherokee political and social organization.

With a point of view that sounds surprisingly modern, the Cherokees opposed strong disciplinarian measures for their children. They were motivated by the belief that "reason will guide their children, when they become use to it, and before that time they cannot commit faults. To chastise them would be to debase the mind, and blunt the sense of honor, by the habit of a slavish motive to action."

The Cherokee concept of freedom did not terminate with childhood. For the male it was constant. In manhood, according to one authority, "Command, subordination, dependence were equally unknown; and by those who wish to possess their confidence, persuasion is avoided, lest their influence should seem a sort of violence offered to the will. They have no punishment but death. They have no fines, for they have no way of exacting them from freemen."

Such an absence of overt disciplinary control might be though to lead to the development of unbridled, unruly individuals and to social chaos. Such does not appear to be the case. The Cherokee government was an orderly one. The continued kindness of generations of parents to their children in itself is a partial answer to the point. Furthermore, the peaceful and kindly disposition of the adult Indians among themselves discredits the belief that the children would be apt to grow up into socially noxious adults.

It would be a mistake, however, to assume that there were no social checks upon individual behavior. Education was achieved through legend, precept, example and sanctions. The responsibility for the training of the youth usually rested with the clan. Since the Cherokee clans were matrilineal, and since it was rather common for the male to abandon one mate for another, the father's role in the education of his children tended, on the whole, to be a somewhat negligible one. The mother, the maternal uncles, and the old men of the tribe were the child's important mentors.

The legends and accounts of commendable deeds performed within the lifetime of living members of the tribe, and in which the narrator may have had a part, were intended to incite the young braves to the performance of similar deeds ...

Exhortations to the young men to be brave and good, as were their forefathers, were also employed as part of the religious ceremonial when the Cherokee believed the Great Spirit to have been offended and they wished to appease him by good deeds. The traditional history of their wars would be repeated by the wise men and doctors, the great chiefs would talk of their courage and virtues, and the young men would be urged to follow in the noble footsteps of their predecessors. At the same time that the ceremonies sought desirable moral behavior they also served to hand down the unwritten traditions of the tribe.

To help their children achieve the virtues extolled by the tribe, the parents sought to have transmitted to them the characteristics of the creatures or plants which personified the particular virtues. Describing such practices among southern Indians generally, it has been noted that, for a warrior, the first rudiments consisted of a bedding of panther's skin, the panther being endowed to a greater degree than his fellow beasts with qualities of smell, strength, cunning and agility. Since the female was expected to be shy and timorous, she was to lie on the skin of a fawn or a buffalo calf.

The use of sanctions played an important part in what might be called the remedial side of character education. One of the most effective types of sanctions in regulating behavior is ridicule. Among the Cherokees ridicule proved a powerful instrument of social control, at least until the influences of white civilization began to make themselves felt. Such a procedure was employed in punishing a person guilty of a petty crime "to which western laws annex severe punishment, but theirs only an ironical way of jesting." The Cherokee punishment was to "commend the criminal before a large audience, for practicing the virtue opposite to the crime, that he is known to be guilty of. If it is for theft, they praise his honest principles; and they commend a warrior for behaving valiantly against the enemies when he acted cowardly; they introduce the minutest circumstances of the affair, with severe sarcasms which wound deeply." The "sweetened darts" of satire struck home "so good naturedly and skillfully, that the culprits would sooner die by torture than renew their shame by repeating the actions."

The more material type of education and training was achieved through example, repeated imitation and practice. Often the material and moral phases of the training were closely interrelated. The teaching of the young in the arts of warfare and of getting food, furthermore, were saturated throughout by a note of encouragement from the tutors.

At a very early age, Indian boys generally were given miniature bows and arrows as playthings. As they acquired strength, they were encouraged to shoot at birds, squirrels, and small game. Praise greeted the first evidence of success and a ceremony usually marked the occasion. As the boys grew older, they began to hunt larger game, and the first success again was celebrated. Elders in the tribe would now counsel the youth regarding the chase and his own future, and also regarding the reverence and obedience to be accorded the aged.

A description of the early training of a prominent Cherokee will aid in giving a clearer picture of indigenous Cherokee education. In order to continue to live the free hunter's life to which he was accustomed, the father of Major Ridge, weary of the hostile incursions of the whites, removed to the mountains along the Tennessee River where game abounded. There Major Ridge was taught "to steal with noiseless tread upon the grazing animal to deceive the timid doe by mimicking the cry of the fawn—or to entice the wary buck within the reach of his missile by decorating his own head with antlers. He was inured with patience, fatigue, self-denial, and exposure, and acquired the sagacity which enabled him to chase with success the wild cat, the bear, and the panther. He watched the haunts and studied the habits of wild animals, and became the expert in the arts which enabled the Indian hunter at all seasons to procure food from the stream or forest."

For the girls of an Indian tribe life was busier. As they grew up, they were gradually instructed in the manifold tasks which devolved upon the adult women. First the girls served as assistants in the housekeeping work, later learning the agricultural and other duties which were expected of them. And just as the boys learned the traditions of the tribe from the old men, so were girls taught the tribal customs by the old Cherokee women.[10]

Indian children were taught societal norms and expectations through the vehicle of play. As George Bird Grinnell observed among the Cheyenne, parents taught their children the qualities any society would wish to see in its citizens: courage, independence, perseverance, virtue, devotion, and sexual morals.

The Indian child was carefully trained, and from early childhood. Its training began before it walked, and continued through its child life. The training consisted almost wholly of advice and counsel, and the child was told to do, or warned to refrain from doing, certain things, not because they were right or wrong, but because the act or failure to act was for his advantage or disadvantage in after life. He was told that to pursue a certain course would benefit him, and for that reason was advised to follow it. His pride and ambition were appealed to, and worthy examples among living men in the tribe were pointed out for emulation.

The infant's education began at an early age, its mother teaching it to keep quiet, in order that it should not disturb the older men in the lodge. Crying babies were hushed, or, if they did not cease their noise, were taken out of the lodge and off into the brush, where screams would not disturb anyone. If older people were talking, and a tiny child entered the lodge and began to talk to its mother, she held up her finger warningly, and it ceased to talk, or else whispered its wants to her. Thus the first lesson that the child learned was one of self-control—self-effacement in the presence of its elders. It remembered this all through life.

This lesson learned, it was not taught much more until old enough, if a boy, to have given him a bow and arrows, or if a girl, to have a doll, made of deerskin, which she took about with her everywhere. Perhaps her mother or aunt made for her a tiny board or cradle for the doll, and on this she commonly carried it on her back, after the precise fashion in which the women carried their babies. She treated her doll as all children do theirs, dressing and undressing it, singing lullabies to it, lacing it on its board, and, as time passed, making it various required articles of feminine clothing. Often as a doll she had one of the tiny puppies so common in Indian camps, taking it when its eyes were scarcely open, and keeping it until the dog had grown too active and too much disposed to wander to be longer companionable.

Boys learned to ride almost as soon as they learned to walk. From earliest babyhood infants were familiar with horses and their motions, and children two or three years of age often rode in front of or behind their mothers, clinging to them or to the horses' manes. They thus gained confidence, learned balance, and became riders, just as they learned to walk—by practice. They did not fear a horse, nor dread a fall, for they began to ride old gentle pack-ponies, which never made unexpected motions; and by the time they were five or six years of age, the boys were riding young colts bareback. Soon after this they began to go into the hills to herd ponies. They early became expert in the use of the rope for catching horses.

Little girls, too, learned to ride at an early age, and while they did not have the practice that the boys had, they became good horsewomen, and in case of need could ride hard and far.

Little companies of small boys and girls often went off camping. The little girls packed the dogs, and moved a little way from the camp and there put up their little lodges—made and sewed for them by their mothers—arranging them in a circle just as did the old people in the big camp. In all that they did they imitated their elders. The little boys who accompanied them were the men of the mimic camp.

Sometimes two camps of children, one representing some hostile tribe, were established near each other. The boys of one camp would go on the war path against those of the other, and they fought like seasoned men, taking captives and counting coups. They tied bunches of buffalo hair to poles for scalps, and after the fight the successful party held dances of rejoicing. They carried lances made of willow branches, shields made of bent willow shoots with the leafy twigs hanging down like feathers, and little bows and arrows, the latter usually slender, straight weed-stalks, often with a prickly pear thorn for a point. ...

Soon after the little boy was able to run about easily, a small bow and some arrows were made for him by his father, uncle, or elder brother, and he was encouraged to use them. When he went out of the lodge to play, his mother said to him, "Now, be careful; do nothing bad; do not strike anyone; do not shoot anyone with your arrow." He was likely to remember these oft-repeated injunctions.

After that, much of his time was spent in practice with the bow. He strove constantly to shoot more accurately at a mark, to send the shaft farther and farther, and to drop his arrow nearer and nearer to a given spot. As he grew more accustomed to the use of the bow, he hunted sparrows and other small birds among the sagebrush and in the thickets along the streams, with other little fellows of his own age; and as his strength and skill increased, began to make excursions on the prairie for rabbits, grouse, and even turkeys. Little boys eight or ten years of age killed numbers of small birds with their arrows, and sometimes even killed them on the wing.

Though he keenly enjoyed the pursuit, the Cheyenne boy did not hunt merely for pleasure. To him it was serious work. He was encouraged to hunt by his parents and relatives, and was told that he must try hard to be a good hunter, so that hereafter he might be able to furnish food for the lodge, and might help to support his mother and sisters. When successful, he was praised; and if he brought in a little bird, it was cooked and eaten as a matter of course, quite as seriously as any other food was treated.

In their hunting, these tiny urchins displayed immense caution and patience, creeping stealthily about through the underbrush of the river bottom, or among the sagebrush on the prairie, striving to approach the woodpeckers climbing the trunk of a cottonwood tree, or the blackbirds swinging on the top of a bush, or the meadow larks stalking about in the grass. ...

While engaged in this hunting, the boys not only learned how to approach and secure game, but also unconsciously picked up a knowledge of many other things incidental to success in life. They came to understand the signs of the prairie, to know the habits of wild animals, learned how to observe, how to become trackers, where the different birds and animals were found, and how they acted under different conditions; and were training themselves to habits of endurance and patience.

When a boy was about twelve years of age, some old grandfather began to talk with him, and advise him as to how he should live. He was instructed in manly duties. He was told that when older people spoke to him, he must listen and must do as they told him. If anyone directed him to go after horses, he should start at once. He should do nothing bad in the camp, and should not quarrel with his fellows. He should get up early; should never let the sun find him in bed, but must be early out in the hills looking for the horses. These were his especial charge, and he must watch them, never lose them, and see that they had water always. He was told that when he grew older it was his duty to hunt and support his mother and sisters. A man must take good care of his arms and keep them in good order. He must never boast. To go about bragging of the brave things that he might intend to do was not manly. If he performed brave deeds, he himself should not speak of them; his comrades would do that. It was predicted that if he listened to the advice given him he would grow up to be a good man, and would amount to something. In this way their fathers, uncles, and grandfathers talked to the boys, and often wise old men harangued little groups who were playing about the camp.

A boy had usually reached his twelfth, thirteenth, or fourteenth year when he first went out to hunt buffalo. Before this he had been instructed in the theory of buffalo running, and had been told how and where to ride, and where to hit the buffalo if he was to be successful. If on his first chase a boy killed a calf, his father was greatly pleased, and, if a well-to-do man, he might present a good horse to some poor man, and in addition might give a feast and invite poor people to come and eat with him. Perhaps he might be still more generous, and at the end of the feast give to his guests presents of robes or blankets. As soon as the boy reached home and his success was known, the father called out from his lodge something like this: "My son has killed a little calf, and I give the best horse that I have to Blue Hawk." If he gave a feast, he explained again, saying: "My little boy has killed a calf. He is going to be a good man and a good hunter. We have had good luck." The man to whom the horse had been presented rode about the camp to show it to the people, and as he rode he sang a song, mentioning the name of the donor and telling why the horse had been given to him.

My friend, Shell—who died years ago, more than eighty years of age—told me that his instruction came chiefly from his father, who gave much advice to him and to the other boys of the family. He remembered especially the father's warning to his children to be truthful and honest, never to lie. His father was a chief, and almost every night there were many people in his lodge, talking about different things, and the children listened to the conversation of their elders, and learned much.

As Shell and his brothers grew older, his father used to teach them all good things, but especially that when they went to war they must be brave. That is why the Cheyennes used to fight so hard. They were taught it from childhood.

His father used to tell him never to associate with women, and, above all, never to run off with one. He would say: "Whenever you find a woman you love, give horses and marry her. Then you will be married in the right way. Whenever a man runs off with a woman, both are talked about, and this is bad for both."

Older men gave much advice to their grandsons, sons, and nephews, and tried constantly to warn them against mistakes and to make life easier for them. A well brought-up man was likely to advise his grown son that occasionally, when he killed a good fat buffalo, he should seek out some old man who possessed spiritual power and offer him the meat, in order to secure his friendliness and the benefit of his prayers.

The training of the little girls was looked after even more carefully than that of the boys. Their mothers, aunts, and grandmothers constantly gave them good advice. They recommended them especially to stay at home, not to run about the camp, and this was so frequently impressed on them that it became a matter of course for them to remain near the lodge, or to go away from it only in company. Both mothers and fathers talked to their daughters, and quite as much to their sons, but in a different way. The mother said: "Daughter, when you grow up to be a young woman, if you see anyone whom you like, you must not be foolish and run off with him. You must marry decently. If you do so, you will become a good woman, and will be a help to your brothers and to your cousins." They warned girls not to be foolish, and the advice was repeated over and over again.

As a girl grew larger she was sent for water, and when still older she took a rope and went for wood, carrying it on her back. The old women early began to teach the girls how to cut moccasins, and how to apply quills and to make beadwork. As they grew older they learned how to cook, and to dress hides, but girls were not put regularly to dressing hides until they were old enough to marry.

Children seldom or never quarreled or fought among themselves, and though, as they grew older, continually engaging in contests of strength, such as wrestling and kicking matches, and games somewhat like football, they rarely lost their temper.

The Cheyenne boys were naturally good-natured and pleasant, and the importance of living on good terms with their fellows having been drilled into them from earliest childhood, they accepted defeat and success with equal cheerfulness. Among a group of white children there would be much more bickering.

A boy's education by advice and admonition usually ended with his first journey to war. When he had made that, he was supposed to have reached years of discretion and to have acquired by practical experience enough discretion to decide for himself what he ought to do, or to consult with older men and ask their advice. The first war journey was often long and hard and without any results, the boy returning to the village with nothing to show for his trip, but with a store of practical knowledge which would be useful to him all his life long.[11]

2

COLONIAL AND
EARLY AMERICAN EDUCATION

DURING THE AGE of European discovery four nations—England, France, Spain, and the Netherlands—embarked on the North American continent. The complex structure of traditional Indian education was greatly threatened by the European arrival. Indian institutions, if recognized by the Europeans, were regarded as inferior; blinded by their own sense of superiority, these Europeans, and later Americans, attempted to change the fundamental cultural orientation of the Indians. The Europeans believed that the Indians would eagerly abandon their own cultural and societal values to embrace those of the Europeans.

Concepts such as individualism, competition, and time—all of which were foreign to most Indian communities—were thrust upon the Indian students along with the Europeans' manners and styles of clothing and hair dress. Educational methods, such as the use of the written word, daily classroom routine, and indoor study, soon became a burden to many Indian students, who were used to oral tradition and experiential learning. Moreover, the Europeans attempted to change the Indians' spiritual orientation; almost all educational endeavors focused on religious instruction.

Among the colonial powers, the British had the greatest success in recruiting and training Indian students. France, Spain, and the Netherlands were less successful, perhaps because they were less interested in educating the Indians than in acculturating, converting, and exploiting them. The following selection by Task Force Five of the American Indian Policy Review Commission presents an overview of the early colonists' attempts to educate American Indians who were either willing students or coerced into accepting the "blessings" of European civilization.

Formal education for the Indian of North America has its roots in the missionary efforts of the European powers. During the period of exploration and colonization, zeal to spread Christianity was at a high. Many religious orders received support from their governments to assist them in their conversion work, not only because it was believed to be the will of God, but perhaps more significantly, because it facilitated their economic and political goals. The objective from the outset seems to have been to coerce the Indian to accommodate the presence of the white man. Thus, the educational practices of the colonial powers were more often rigidly pragmatic and less frequently adaptable to Indian ways.

The Spanish and French programs reflect a strong Catholic influence since their missionary efforts were largely performed by the Franciscans and the Jesuits. The Spanish influence can be seen mostly in the Southwest, and it was here that the Franciscans labored most extensively. They came to the continent to convert the Natives and so established communities centered around missions which taught the Indians religion and the agricultural way of life. There was less emphasis on learning strictly academic subjects than on acquiring skills conducive to becoming a farmer, and they attempted to integrate Indian language and customs, as these facilitated the teaching-learning process. The Spanish had a lasting influence on the Indians of the Southwest particularly because they provided the tools and domesticated animals, as well as the instruction needed to establish self-sustaining communities.

The French program was carried out mainly in the Great Lakes region, the Mississippi valley, and along the St. Lawrence River. Since the French interest in the continent was basically in the fur trade, their approach to the Indians was quite different from the Spanish. Instead of looking to change Indians, they wanted to secure their cooperation in order to enlist them as allies against the English and to assist them in trapping and hunting. The French were not adverse to assimilating into and with the Indian tribes and so were much more successful in gaining the friendship and cooperation of the Indians. The Jesuits conducted much of the missionary work and were most influential in keeping peace between the Indians and the French. They emphasized religious training more than formal academic instruction, even though one of the objectives of Louis XIV had been to educate the children of the Indians in the French manner. One very important reason for this was that continual fighting between the British and French in the New World often interrupted any continuous educational endeavor. Nevertheless, the French were very successful in dealing with the Indians—perhaps because their economic goals (i.e., hunting and trading) were more affirmative of the Indian way, and they did not try so much to change the Indian as other colonial powers did. Thus, they were able to solidify their Christianizing efforts and gain many Indian allies against the British.

The Dutch, until their conquest by the English, basically maintained strict economic dealings with the natives, ignoring conversion efforts and avoiding integration with the Indians. Trade and land acquisition were the major advantages they sought, and they pursued a policy of negotiating with the Indians in a most conciliatory manner in order to avoid conflicts.

The English program has perhaps been the most influential on the development of federal policy since it was the English colonies which eventually became the original thirteen states. Many of the religious groups which started missionary work among the Indians within and near the English settlements were the same groups which later utilized the federal support of the Civilization Fund to continue and expand their efforts: The Presbyterians, Moravians, Quakers, Puritans and Anglicans. Since religious groups were generally supported by the political structure within their colony and since education held a high priority to many of the English colonists, education was often a cooperative endeavor of both church and state. Instruction was often given in the industrial arts in order to teach the Indian youths the habits of civilized life. But, also, in consonance with the prevailing course of studies of the upper classes in England, more academic and philosophical subjects were taught, especially at the private schools and institutions of higher learning. Education took place at any location where concerned individuals or groups could persuade Indian youths to attend, including colonial homes and abroad, in boarding and day schools, in institutions of higher learning, and in a few Indian communities organized in Massachusetts, New Jersey and Pennsylvania.

Several humanitarian individuals also independently took up the call to civilize and convert the Natives, and these interested persons, both religiously affiliated and not, contributed their time and energy to teach the Indians. Many of these early efforts were assisted by the British Crown as well as by English lords and ladies who were independently wealthy, it being fashionable at the time to contribute to the cause of Christianizing the savages.

The earliest formal attempt by any of the British colonies to promote higher education for the Indians was started in the Virginia Colony by a directive of King James I to establish "some churches and schools for ye education of ye children of these Barbarians in Virginia." The Virginia Company attempted to further this objective by establishing a fund to support Indian youths to be boarded in the homes of colonists and taught the rudiments of civilized life. The Company had also set aside a piece of land at Henrico on which to erect an Indian College, which was to be supported by contributions from philanthropic individuals and groups in England. Another tract of land was selected for an Indian school near Charles City, to be supported by the East India Company. These attempts, however, never prospered because of the Indian uprising in 1622 and the revocation of the Virginia charter in 1624. From that time, until the founding of the College of William and Mary in 1691, there were no formal efforts to educate the Indian in Virginia, but several individuals were sent to England to be educated, with the hope that they would return to convert and civilize their brethren.[1]

In New England the Puritans made significant efforts to educate Indians. Among them John Eliot, the Algonquin-speaking preacher, stands out. Eliot and his contemporaries left a multifaceted legacy: Eliot's "praying towns" represent the first use of reserved lands for Indians, while efforts to provide for higher education of Indians were important in the founding of Dartmouth College and Harvard College. Again, from Task Force Five:

John Eliot was the most successful and dedicated of the Puritan missionaries, primarily because he was able to gain followers by learning the Algonquin dialect. With his interpreter Cockenoe, a Pequot Indian, his speech improved until he was able to preach in Algonquin throughout the various Indian settlements. It was largely to assist his efforts that the Society for the Propagation of the Gospel in New England was organized in 1647.

Reverend Eliot's persuasions were extremely successful. Many of his native followers agreed to cut their hair and, after four visits to the town of Nonantum, the entire village agreed to submit their children to a Puritan education. In time, the Indian converts requested their own English-style schools, government, clothes, and tools.

By 1651, the first "Indian Praying Town" was established at Natick by John Eliot. Since all the Indians in these so-called praying towns were of similar persuasion, the attempts to educate and Christianize them were relatively successful. The general Court of the Colony recognized the wisdom in the formation of the "towns" and authorized the purchase of land for that purpose. This was the first use of the "reserved" land system. Eventually, fourteen such towns were established; after many diligent fund-raising campaigns in London, enough monies were raised to begin plans for the Indian school at Harvard Yard, and the creation of an Indian library.

In 1664, John Eliot published a complete version of the Bible in Algonquin. Work progressed among the fourteen praying villages, and preparatory and grammar schools were also established. The progress was arrested suddenly with King Philip's War in 1691, a war which led to the demise of most of the Indians in the New England area.

The founding of Harvard College in 1636 was the first attempt by the New England colonies to provide for the higher education of Indian youths. Henry Dunster, the first president of the College, was a leader in work among the New England Indians, and he succeeded in establishing an Indian College at Harvard. He secured funds from the Society for the Propagation of the Gospel in New England which enabled him to erect a building to house Indian students. Despite the grand designs of Dunster and others who wished to see Harvard become an Indian Oxford, the overall effect was that the Indian students gradually lost interest or died, and the concerns of the administrators turned to the education of English youth.[2]

While the colonists attempted to acculturate the Indians, no attempts were made to assimilate them. Indeed, in the eighteenth century the main thrust of education seemed to be to destroy the Indian so as to save the person within. Even when educators acted out of humanitarian motives, the results were generally disastrous. The educational activities in colonial Virginia effectively isolated the Indians from the white population. Christianized Indians, or those American Indians who were educated in the colonial schools, were relegated to the frontier to serve as a buffer between the settlers and the tribes beyond the frontier. Laws in the colony prevented Indians from holding any office, testifying in court, or hunting on patented lands. In an effort to restrict the privileges that came with being white, any child born of Indian blood was termed a mulatto and considered a second-class citizen. Conversion to Christianity did not alter his or her status.

A most inhumane practice in Virginia was the taking of Indian children as hostages and educating them in the colonial schools for the purpose of coercing peace and friendship with the tribes along the frontier. Many of the children in the boarding facilities perished from the changed environment, diet, and manner of living; disease was always prevalent. Ironically, educated Indians found little employment, except in the only professions open to them—servant or maid work—and thus many reverted back to former habits and customs. Alice Fletcher, writing in 1888, describes these conditions:

> In Virginia, in 1713, the plan of removing friendly Indians upon land set apart for them upon the frontier, where they might act as a guard, was put in operation, it having been previously agreed to by treaty. As inducements to settle on the reservation the education of their children was promised. The school was opened under the care of Mr. Charles Griffen, his salary of 50 pounds being paid out of Governor Spotswood's pocket. By 1718, the opposition to the Indian trading company became sufficiently powerful to secure its legal dissolution, and the school was broken up to the distress of the Indians.

> As early as 1711 the governor of Virginia had demanded hostages, not only of the tributary Indians, but of the border tribes. The children, two from the great men of each town, were to be surety for the friendliness of their relatives. (The children were to be educated at the colonial colleges.) Those Indians giving their children to be educated were to have their tribute of skins remitted while they kept their children in school.

Governor Spotswood's interest in the welfare of the Indians seems to have been practical and sincere, but he labored at grave disadvantage, for public sentiment failed to second his plans and endeavors. He ventured not only his private purse, but his public reputation to secure to the natives some chance to become civilized and educated. ... He secured the little hostages; and the Nansemonds, the Nottoways, the Maherins, the Pamunkeys, and the Chickahominies, who sent their children, were well pleased with the treatment they received.

Mr. Hugh Jones, professor of mathematics in the college, states in his *Present State of Virginia*, published in London in 1724, that "the young Indians, procured from the tributary of foreign nations with much difficulty, were formerly boarded and lodged in town, where abundance of them used to die, either through sickness, change of provision and way of life, or, as some will have it, often for want of proper necessities and due care taken with them. Those of them that have escaped well, and have been taught to read and write, have, for the most part, returned to their home. Some with and some without baptism, where they follow their own savage customs and heathenish rites. A few of them lived as servants with the English, or loitered and idled away their time in laziness and mischief. But it is a pity more care is not taken of them after they are dismissed from school. They have admirable capacities when their humors and tempers are perfectly understood."[3]

Thus, Indians and colonists lived side-by-side but separate.

The Indian tribes were isolated and forbidden by law to share in the life of the whites; they were relegated to hunting in order to gain the pelts demanded by the trader in exchange for goods. No missionaries or schools were in their midst to uphold and encourage any new mode of life; and as to the surroundings of these Indian tribes which had been pushed to the frontier to guard the colonists from the Indians further to the westward, Governor Spotswood writes as follows: "As to beginning a nearer friendship by intermarriage (as the custom of the French is) the inclinations of our people are not the same with those of that nation, for notwithstanding the long intercourse between ye Indian inhabitants of this Country and ye Indians and their living amongst one another for so many Years, I cannot find one Englishman that has an Indian wife, or an Indian married to a white woman."

Ostracized by law and race prejudice, and remanded to the company of men not of a reputable type, it would be well nigh a miracle if the Indian should blossom out into a life of Christian civilization, or that Indian students who had gained a little English and could repeat the creed should, on their return, isolate themselves from their kindred and attempt to carry out principles but vaguely comprehended, and which, if carried out, would condemn the white population even more severely than the Indians themselves.[4]

The situation was quite different in Pennsylvania. Unlike the Virginians, the Pennsylvania colonists and missionaries formed strong bonds with the indigenous peoples. Moravian settlements such as Gnadenhutten provide the most prominent example of peaceful coexistence. Again, from Fletcher:

> Pennsylvania became the theater of one of the most remarkable examples of missionary labor in our country, not only on account of its success, but from its tragic fate; proving again, in records written in human blood, that failure lies with us, not with the Indians.

> When the Christian Indians of Shekomeko reached Pennsylvania ... they were permanently located [in] Gnadenhutten. Mills and shops were erected at a little distance from the town, and schools were provided for the children. In 1749 the Indian congregation contained several hundred persons.

> The French and Indian war terminated the mission at Gnadenhutten. Its situation upon the Indian frontier exposed it to the misfortunes of war, and the principles of its religion forbade the bearing of arms. The English and the French were alike suspicious of these peaceful settlements; and while the former were threatening their extinction the allies of the latter accomplished their destruction. Tens of the Christian Indians were massacred in November of 1755; on the next New Year's Day the entire village, together with the mill across the river was laid in ashes.[5]

Other Moravian settlements were massacred or destroyed during Pontiac's War and the American Revolution. In the interval between the wars, however, the settlements prospered.

> The inhabitants had become for the most part husbandmen, and possessed large fields and gardens, suitably fenced, excellent orchards, and herds of cattle, horses, and hogs. Their prosperity was endangered by the hostilities of the Revolutionary War. The fortunes of war were turning against the British, and their emissaries incited their Indian allies to renewed violence. The destruction of the Moravian settlements was determined, and in the autumn of 1781 the Christian Indians were removed by force to the desolate banks of the Sandusky River, in northern Ohio. Never did the Christian Indians leave a country with more regret.[6]

As peaceful and prosperous as the Moravian settlements were, still their goal was to acculturate and Christianize.

> A hunter and warrior, the Indian was constrained to give up his wild habits and cruel ways; to quench all the instincts of his savage nature; to change most of the customs of his race; to acknowledge woman as his equal; to perform the

labor himself which for generations has been put upon her; to lay aside his plumes, paint, and traditional ornaments of every kind; to assume the dress which white men wore; to plow and plant and reap like any farmer; to rove no longer through the wilderness at pleasure, building lodges here and there, but to remain with his family in one town; and above all, submit to municipal enactments, which were of necessity so stringent that nothing could be more galling to the native pride of American aborigines.[7]

In New York, where the Iroquois Confederacy held the balance of power, missionary work took a new turn: Indians welcomed teachers and ministers, but the colonists persecuted them. The first efforts to bring colonial education to the Iroquois was in 1709, when several chiefs went to London and asked Queen Anne to send ministers and teachers to live among them.

Fletcher describes the initial efforts of the missionaries at organized education.

One missionary, Reverend Andrews, was sent with his attendants, Mr. Clausen and Mr. Oliver. He was particularly directed by the society to use all possible means to persuade the Indians to let their children learn English. The Indians sent many of their children at first, and Mr. Oliver began to teach them English. The parents objected, and the society was forced to comply with the Indian obstinacy and devise means for instructing the children in their own language. Hornbooks and primers were procured in great numbers for the children, and inkhorns, penknives, paper, and other little necessities were also provided. No correction was ventured for the parents were so fond of their children and valued learning so little they thought it not worth gaining at the least displeasing of their children. Food and presents were used as inducements to attend. The instruction of adult Indians was attempted, but without success. Portions of the Scriptures were translated into the Mohawk tongue and evidences of missionary success appeared in the lives of both men and women. (The mission) seems to have reached its highest prosperity in 1715, when there were twenty children quite regularly attending school, sixty or seventy ordinarily attending church and thirty-eight communicants.

In the year 1740 Christian Henry Rauch arrived in New York. There were in the city at the same time several Mohegan Indians from the Indian town of Shekomeko in Dutchess County. Rauch met the Indians and they professed to desire instruction and invited him to go with them to Shekomeko and become the teacher of their tribe. He gladly consented, but when the time fixed on for departure came he found that they had evaded him and left. Nothing daunted he started out and, inquiring his way, at last reached Shekomeko and began his work. He found the surrounding white settlers unfriendly. Many of them were engaged in trade with the Indians and found profit in the depraved habits and ignorance of their customers. It is said that some of them even tried to bribe the Indians to kill their teacher.

Other missionaries came from the Moravian communities in Pennsylvania to assist Rauch. The opposition now took the form of persecution on account of the religious belief of the missionaries which impelled them to refuse not only to bear arms as soldiers but also to take an oath. To these charges was added the very absurd one that they were French emissaries. They were visited and searched for arms and finally cited to appear before the governor and council at New York. After an examination they were released. Their work prospered [and] deputations came from other Indian villages beseeching that missionaries might be sent them. Four missionaries were sent, and two stations and three preaching places were established in Connecticut and Massachusetts.

In the midst of this prosperity came an act of the governor and council which ended the usefulness of the mission. It required that all suspected persons should take an oath of allegiance or emigrate or be imprisoned, and it further commanded the several Moravian and vagrant preachers among the Indians to desist from further teaching or preaching and to depart the province. On December 15, 1744, the church and school house were formally closed by the high sheriff of Dutchess County.[8]

From the 1760s through the American Revolution, Samuel Kirkland proved to be very successful among the Oneida and Seneca tribes. Having first developed a high school for the tribes, Kirkland established Hamilton Oneida Academy in 1793. It later became Hamilton College.

New England

The educational endeavors in New England beginning in the early eighteenth century made use of boarding schools, which removed Indian children from the influences of their home environments. Also commonly used was the forerunner of the nineteenth-century outing system, in which Indian children were distributed among white families for the purpose of "civilizing" them. This system was commonly used for Indian girls. Colonial educators in New England paid the greatest attention to Indian girls. A Dr. Colman of Boston wrote in 1743 that educating Indian girls "is a matter of necessity wherein we are not left at liberty either as men or as Christians; for there can be no propagation of religion among any people without an equal regard to both sexes, not only because females are alike precious souls, formed for God and religion as much as the males, but also because the care of the souls of children in families and more especially in those of low degree lies chiefly upon the mothers for the first seven or eight years."[9]

Fletcher describes some girls' experiences.

The plan put in practice for the girls was to place them in white families some distance from their homes. They soon became discontented and returned to their parents. A few years later they begged for a new trial and offered to support themselves by their own labor. What was accomplished is unknown, but we learn that two girls were sent to Northampton and placed in good families there. The Indian girls were not disinclined to attend the school at Stockbridge. A writer in the Boston *Post Boy,* September 3, 1739, says: "I have lately visited my friends in Stockbridge and was well pleased to find the Indians so improved. I saw several young women sewing, but I was in special gratified to find them improved in learning. Several of them have made good proficiency and can learn in their Bibles, and some can write a good hand."[10]

Girls and boys alike came under the wing of Dr. Eleazer Wheelock, founder of the Moors Charity School in Lebanon, Connecticut. Fletcher elaborates:

The germinal thought, which eventually produced the Moor's Indian Charity School, was bred by the insufficient support given to the pastor, Rev. Eleazer Wheelock, by the people of Lebanon, Conn. Mr. Wheelock acted upon the principle that if his flock furnished him but half a living they were entitled to but half of his services, and concluded that the Indians merited the other half.

The most feasible plan of educating the Indians seemed to Mr. Wheelock to be one in which educated natives should unite with foreigners in giving instruction, and in which girls should be trained in home employments. Among the reasons assigned in favor of this scheme were the deep-rooted prejudice against the English, occasioned by sharp and unjust bargains; the greater usefulness and less expense of native missionaries; their better understanding of Indian temper and customs; the respect and attention they would command; the friendship which would arise between the scholars of different tribes and extend through them to their families; the assistance they would be to English missionaries; the absence of difficulties in matters of language; and the usefulness of attempting English schools in many of the Indian regions.

In November of 1761 the General Court of the province of Massachusetts Bay voted Mr. Wheelock 72 pounds for the education, clothing, and boarding of six Iroquois children for one year. Not long after this Mr. Wheelock reported on his work for Indian youth the following: "Several of my scholars are considerably well accomplished for school-masters, and seven or eight will likely be well fitted for interpreters in a few years more. And four of this number are girls, whom I have hired women in this neighborhood to instruct in all the arts of good housewifery, they attending the school one day in a week to be instructed in writing, etc., till they shall be fit for an apprenticeship, to be taught to make men's and women's apparel, etc., in order to accompany these boys, when they shall have occasion for such assistance in the business of their mission."[11]

The literature shows some difference of opinion as to the demise of the Moors Charity School. According to Task Force Five, financial difficulties, differences with Indian scholars over how to best convert Indians to Christianity, and interdenominational quarrels forced Wheelock to close the school in 1769. According to Fletcher, the school, which never received a charter of its own, was moved to New Hampshire, where it became the basis of Dartmouth College. Fletcher writes:

A charter was never obtained for Moor's Indian Charity School, but when its location was changed to New Hampshire, John Wentworth, governor of that province, took the opportunity to create, for the benefit of his people, a higher institution of learning. He endowed the new corporation with all the powers of a university and named it Dartmouth College. It was designed that the Indian School should be connected with it as a subservient institution. Thus superior and inferior institutions were established at Hanover, NH, the latter exclusively for Indian youth, and the former primarily for their education. Its charter states that it was created for the education and instruction of youths of the Indian tribes in this land, in reading, writing, and all parts of learning which shall appear necessary and expedient for civilizing and Christianizing the children of pagans, as well as in all liberal arts and sciences, and also of English youths and any others.

The first published report of the school, after its removal to Hanover, was issued in 1771. Then there were twenty-four charity scholars, eighteen English, five Indian, and one of mixed blood. During the next year there were from five to nine Indian scholars, and quite a number of English charity scholars fitting themselves for missionary labors. In 1773 there were sixteen or seventeen Indian pupils.

Samson Occum was the earliest Indian pupil of Mr. Wheelock that became widely known. He was a Mohegan, born in 1723, converted to Christianity in 1740, and received into Mr. Wheelock's family in 1743. He had already commenced studying, and he continued under tuition until 1748. Then he became a teacher, and afterward a preacher among his own people.

Joseph Brant, a Mohawk, was in Mr. Wheelock's school for some time previous to 1761, being about nineteen years of age. His early advantages of education were limited, but of these he evidently made the best use. His return to the books, after the Revolutionary War was ended, the progressive improvement in the style of his letters and the fruits of his labors in the translations he produced, are circumstances proving his perseverance amidst the most harassing cares and perplexities of his after life, and that he had a natural taste for literature and was zealous in the acquisition of knowledge. His solicitude was great for the thorough education of his children, and he had himself not only projected writing a history of his own people, but had it in contemplation himself to acquire the knowledge of the Greek language, that he might be enabled to read the New Testament in the original, and thus make a more perfect translation of the Greek Scriptures in the Mohawk tongue.[12]

Funding for the college was hard to come by, particularly during the American Revolution. According to Fletcher, by 1773 "funds committed to the London trustees had been expended, and the school was in destitution. ... The school had no patronage in America, and no help could come from abroad." [13] The school was not without its benefactors, however. The Continental Congress in 1775 and 1776 appropriated five hundred dollars for the support of Indian students at Dartmouth "as they believed it to be a means of conciliating the friendship of the Canadian Indians, or, at least, of preventing hostilities from them in some measure."[14]

The Colonial Legacy

While most efforts to educate Indians during the first two centuries of European settlement and colonization amounted to little more than failed attempts at acculturation, the colonial educators left a lasting legacy. According to Task Force Five,

> Although many interesting concepts developed out of the Puritan era, relatively few natives were converted. The important thing to note is that out of a concerted effort by both clergy and government to raise funds for Indian education, over fifteen schools were established, many directed by Indian teachers.

> In these early educational activities, it is clear that several practices evolved which influenced the policies of the government of the United States. Individual missionaries, as both preachers and teachers, were subsidized by private and governmental monies, and carried both Christianity and civilization to Indian communities. Reading, writing, arithmetic and catechism were the heart of their efforts. As Indian leaders and people were converted, they were asked to give their children over to boarding schools so that the habits of civilization and Christianity could be instilled in them. These seeds planted in the colonies became a direct thrust of the new nation's educational policies.[15]

3

A DEBT DUE: TREATY NEGOTIATIONS AND VIOLATIONS

IN THE HISTORY of Indian affairs the period between 1778 and 1871 is known as the treaty-making period. During this time almost four hundred treaties between the U.S. government and various Indian nations were signed and ratified. More than 110 ratified—and numerous unratified—treaties included educational provisions ranging from "instruction in agriculture as long as the President may think proper"[1] in the 1825 Creek treaty, to "six thousand dollars, annually, forever,"[2] as in the 1825 Choctaw treaty.

The Indian treaties signed after the American Revolution indicate that the new nation did not regard its political hegemony as absolute. Treaties with the Delaware (1778) and Cherokee (1785) nations, for example, allowed those tribes to send delegates to the U. S. Congress.[3] Provisions in the trade and intercourse acts required the use of passports for any non-Indian entering Indian country.[4] Although such rights and regulations were rarely granted or adhered to, they do indicate that the United States viewed the Indian nations as sovereign.

Treaty Provisions Relating to Education

When the Continental Congress enacted the Northwest Ordinance in 1787, it pledged to provide an education for the Indian people. The act stated: "Religion, morality, and knowledge, being necessary to good government and the happiness of mankind, schools, and the means of education shall forever be encouraged. The utmost good faith shall always be observed towards the Indians."[5]

The first treaty to actually contain an educational clause was the 1794 treaty with the Oneida, Tuscarora, and Stockbridge. This treaty promised to provide several persons to instruct the Indians in the arts of the miller and sawyer.[6] Not until 1803 did another treaty contain an educational provision. This provision, in a treaty with the Kaskaskia, provided one hundred dollars annually for seven years for the support of a Roman Catholic Priest to teach Kaskaskia children the "rudiments of literature."[7]

Treaties throughout the nineteenth century called for educational services. In the 1867–1868 Peace Commission treaties, signed with the tribes of the Great Plains and the Rocky Mountains, escalator clauses granted most of the tribes a school and teacher "for every thirty students" that could be induced or compelled to attend school.[8] These provisions, however, were never carried out. As Superintendent of Indian Education John H. Oberly noted in 1885, the federal government failed to give effect to most treaty provisions relating to education.[9] A year earlier, Secretary of the Interior Lucius Q. C. Lamar estimated that an appropriation of over four million dollars would have been necessary to fulfill the educational provisions of just eight treaties. The secretary noted in his 1884 report:

> This money is now due. A large part of the money so agreed to be paid was in consideration of land ceded to the Government by the Indians. It is not a gratuity, but a debt due the Indians, incurred by the Government on its own motion and not at the request of the Indians. It is true that the debt is due to dependent and weak people who have but little disposition to complain of the neglect of the Government to fulfill its obligation, and are wanting in ability to compel the performance thereof; yet their very weakness and lack of disposition to complain ought to stimulate the Government to sacredly perform all the provisions of treaties providing for the education and advancement of these people. Not only a direct regard for our plighted faith demands this, but our interest also demands it.[10]

Treaty provisions relating to education reflect two important concepts: Indian tribes have legal rights to educational services provided by the U.S. government, and the federal government has a legal responsibility to fulfill those rights. In 1871, after the House of Representatives attached a rider to the Indian Appropriation Act of 1871, Congress ended the treaty-making process. The act provided, however, that all existing treaty rights would remain valid and in force.[11]

For most tribes, the treaties' provisions, including those for funding, were administered through religious and mission organizations until the 1870s when the federal government took a direct role in educating Indian children. However, several tribes controlled their own schools and thus their own treaty funds. Most notable among these tribes are the Choctaws and Cherokees, who combined had nearly two hundred schools when the Indian Territory was dissolved in the early 1900s.

One of the problems the tribes faced in administering their treaty provisions, other than not receiving all of the resources they were promised, was that most schools were usually located outside of the reservations; the

Indians preferred to have the schools located near their villages and settlements. It was the Indian Bureau's belief, however, that the Indian should be
taken to "civilization" rather than taking "civilization" to the Indian.

Treaty Negotiations

In the following selection, Vine Deloria, Jr., provides a sampling of
treaty provisions relating to education as well as written treaty negotiations.
Taken together they amplify what the treaty said in light of what the Indians
believed the treaty to mean and what the commissioners actually stated.
Writing in 1975, Deloria used these comparisons to build a legal framework
for Indians' expectations of government assistance in the education.

> Since educational rights are a definitive part of treaty negotiations and, as an
> integral part of treaties, must have some effect in law, their legal status must
> be that of a continuing right.
>
> Educational treaty case law does not indicate much development until the
> present era when suits began to reflect efforts to get the courts to interpret
> the procedures under which educational services must be given. In a real
> sense then we are at the beginning of an era in which educational services
> will possibly become the subject of an expanding area of litigation.
>
> With case law developing in a regular and consistent manner, regarding the
> understanding of Indians concerning the treaty provisions, we must take a
> futuristic look at the various educational provisions of the treaties. One thing
> seems relatively certain: although the treaty articles may have had definite time
> limits in which the services were to be performed, one cannot date the time for
> performing the services from the date of ratification of the treaty.
>
> In many instances the government did not begin to perform its function as
> educator until long after the treaty was ratified and thus the definite term of
> years stated in the educational articles cannot be said to have lapsed without
> further investigation into the nature and extent of the services rendered. In
> other instances there was no mention to the Indians at the time of signing
> the treaty that they would have a limited number of years to receive the
> services, particularly in the field of education. They assumed, as often did the
> United States Commissioners, that the definite time period mentioned was
> simply a way of indicating that the services would continue until the tribe was
> adequately educated.
>
> We must therefore examine, insofar as it is possible, the recorded statements
> of both Indians and federal officials concerning the meaning of the
> educational provisions to determine the understandings which were shared
> at the time concerning education. The first problem that arises is simply that

of the number and extent of the records which have survived. Not all treaty negotiations were recorded. In many instances the commissioners wrote letters back to the Commissioner of Indian Affairs, their immediate military commander, the governor of the territory, or sometimes even the President, relating the substance of the discussions and mentioning, sometimes in the most casual manner, the promises made to the Indians.

Since we do not have accurate records for many of the treaties, we will examine the treaties for which some material relating to oral promises remains. We can only assume, but with good reason, that the other promises were similar in nature and content even though they were not recorded.

In order to make the format of our discussion easy to follow, we will develop samples of the treaty articles and recorded statements by treaty, indicating first the complete text of the article concerning education and then placing the recorded statements of explanation below it to illuminate the understanding of both the Indians and the treaty commissioners concerning its meaning. ...

RATIFIED TREATY WITH THE CHIPPEWAS
September 24, 1819
Article 8

The United States engage to provide and support a blacksmith for the Indians, at Saginaw, so long as the President of the United States may think proper, and to furnish the Chippewa Indians with such farming utensils and cattle, and to employ such persons to aid them in their agriculture, as the President may deem expedient.

Governor Lewis Cass, who negotiated the treaty, wrote a long letter of explanation to John C. Calhoun, then Secretary of War, outlining the difficulties he had in negotiating the treaty and reporting the promises he had made to the Chippewas. Portions of his letter are illuminating.

> That portion of the Chippewa Indians, which owned this land, have not made the necessary advances in civilization to appreciate the importance of education for their youth. It was therefore hopeless to expect from them any reservations for this object, or to offer it as an inducement for a cession of their country. Some considerations more obvious in its effects, and more congenial to their habits was necessary to ensure a successful termination to the negotiation.

> Viewing the subject in this manner, I finally concluded to admit a stipulation, conformably to their wishes, for an annuity of One Thousand dollars, but to secure the

payment of whatever additional sum the Government of the United States might think they ought to receive, in such a manner as would be most useful to them.

A stipulation therefore was inserted, that the United States should provide and support a Blacksmith for them, and should furnish them with cattle, farming utensils and persons to aid them in agriculture.

The amount which shall be expended for these objects by the United States, the term during which this expense shall continue, and the mode in which it shall be applied are left discretionary with the President.

Cass, later in his letter, changes his story somewhat about the Indians appreciating the importance of education, for he notes:

It is due to the Indians and to myself to say, that the sum, which it was expected by us, would be expended for the objects which I have mentioned, is from fifteen hundred to two thousand five hundred dollars annually. But they distinctly understand that the amount of this expenditure is entirely discretionary with the President. Of course the Government can now apply such a sum to these objects, as the value of the cession, and the wants and population of the Indians may justify.

In the meantime we may teach them those useful arts which are connected with agriculture, and which will prepare them by gradual progress for the reception of such institutions, as may be fitted for their character, customs & situation.

The measurement, according to Cass' understanding, of the Indians' rights to services, depends on the relationship of two facts,—the value of the lands ceded and the wants of the Indians. And he relates that the Indians are content to let the President exercise discretionary powers in relating these factors for them.

RATIFIED TREATY WITH THE CHOCTAWS
October 18, 1820
Article 7

Out of the lands ceded by the Choctaw nation to the United States, the Commissioners aforesaid, in behalf of said States, further covenant and agree, that fifty-four sections of one mile square shall be laid out in good land, by the President of the United States, and sold, for the purpose of raising a fund, to be applied to the support of the Choctaw schools, on both sides of the Mississippi River. Three-fourths of said fund shall be appropriated for the benefit of the schools here and the remaining fourth for the establishment of one or more beyond the Mississippi; the whole to be placed in the hands of the President of the United States, and to be applied by him, expressly and exclusively, to this valuable object.

Article 8

To remove any discontent which may have arisen in the Choctaw Nation, in consequence of six thousand dollars of their annuity having been appropriated annually, for sixteen years, by some of the chiefs, for the support of their schools, the Commissioners of the United States oblige themselves, on the part of said States, to set apart an additional tract of good land, for raising a fund equal to that given by the said chiefs, so that the whole of the annuity may remain in the nation, and be divided amongst them. And in order that exact justice may be done to the poor and distressed of said nation, it shall be the duty of the agent to see that the wants of every deaf, dumb, blind, and distressed Indian shall be first supplied out of said annuity, and the balance equally distributed amongst every individual of said nation.

Treaty Commissioners Andrew Jackson and Thomas Kinds wrote to Secretary of War John C. Calhoun concerning the nature of the educational provisions of the treaty:

> When the treaty reaches you, we believe it will be found as advantageous in its provisions, as under existing circumstances, we had a right to expect. We have amply provided for them schools, on both sides of the Mississippi. This was an object truly desirable to the nation, and only appreciated by the Commissioners. Without providing for them, we were satisfied that we could not obtain the signature of the treaty, securing an exchange as therein proposed. We enclose with the treaty a plan of Missionary W. Cyrus Kingsbury, for establishing schools in the Choctaw nation, on both sides of the Mississippi River to which we beg leave to call your attention, and hope it will be adopted, as far as the funds will permit, when raised.
>
> We must here remark, that we found some dissatisfaction in the nation, in consequence of their principal chiefs having made a donation of part of the annuity for the

support of these schools. For the purpose of producing harmony amongst them, by which alone our success could be secured, we proposed the article raising an equal fund and one thousand dollars more, as an annuity for sixteen years. This produced all the good effects which were anticipated.

RATIFIED TREATY WITH THE CHOCTAWS
January 20, 1825
Article 2

In consideration of the cession aforesaid, the United States do hereby agree to pay the said Choctaw Nation the sum of six thousand dollars, annually, forever; it being agreed that the said sum of six thousand dollars shall be annually applied, for the term of twenty years, under the direction of the President of the United States, to the support of schools in said nation, and extending to it the benefits of instruction in the mechanic and ordinary arts of life; when, at the expiration of twenty years, it is agreed that the said annuity may be vested in stocks, or otherwise disposed of, or continued, at the option of the Choctaw Nation.

By 1825 the Choctaws had produced a number of leaders familiar with the English language and capable of presenting demands to the United States in their own terms. The Choctaw delegation wrote to John C. Calhoun proposing terms for educational provisions in January 1825:

The terms which we proposed are the following:

1. Six thousand dollars a year, *perpetual annuity*—that annuity to be sold or continued by the Choctaws, at their option, any time after twenty years.

2. The annuity of six thousand dollars for sixteen years, promised in the treaty of 1820, to commence the present year.

3. The extinguishment (as suggested by you) of all claims which you may have against individuals of the Choctaw Nation for debt due to the Trading House, in consideration that we relinquish our claim to have a Trading house established west of the Mississippi.

4. An equitable settlement of the Pensacola claims, and of all other just claims which may be presented.

The foregoing are the principal conditions. There are others which we could wish granted but upon which we would not insist with pertinacity. For instance, we would rather take money and apply the interest to the purposes of education, than the fifty-four sections of land, provided to be set apart under the treaty of 1820.

This letter marked the final proposition sent by the tribe to the United States prior to the signing of the treaty of 1825. A long period of negotiation had led up to the agreement on the education article and the letter of November 22nd of the previous year to Calhoun, which had initiated the discussion of terms, gave the thinking of the Choctaws on education.

We made a direct proposition for the proposed cession west of the Mississippi. After the views we gave in the beginning of this letter, you will not be surprised that we think our terms reasonable. We ask, first, that thirty thousand dollars worth of goods be distributed as presents to our nation - $15,000 the first year & $15,000 the second. Second, that nine thousand dollars a year, for twenty years, be appropriated for the support of mechanical institutions among the Choctaws. Third, that the same sum be appropriated annually for twenty years, for the education of Choctaw children in colleges or institutions, out of the nation. Fourth, that three thousand dollars a year for twenty years, be appropriated for the education of Choctaws beyond the Mississippi, when they shall have settled there, and an agent appointed to live among them. These annuities to be applied, for the purposes expressed, under the direction of the President.

The price we ask may be more than has been usually given for lands lying so remote. But it is not more than what we think to be their just value. We wish our children educated. We wish to derive lasting, if not transient, benefits from the sale of our lands. The proceeds of those sales we are desirous should be applied for the instruction of our young countrymen. It is for this important object that we may seem to you unreasonable in our proposition. We feel our ignorance, and we begin to see the benefits of education. We are, therefore, anxious that our rising generation should acquire a knowledge of literature and the arts, and learn to tread in those paths which have conducted your people, by regular generations, to their present summit of wealth & greatness.

RATIFIED TREATY WITH THE OSAGE
June 2, 1825
Article 6

And also the fifty-four tracts, of a mile square each, to be laid off under the direction of the President of the United States, and sold, for the purpose of raising a fund to be applied to the support of schools, for the education of the Osage children, in such manner as the President may deem most advisable to the attainment of that end.

Article 10

It is furthermore agreed on, by and between the parties, to these presents, that there shall be reserved two sections of land, to include the Harmony Missionary establishment, and their mill, on the Marias des Cygne; and one section, to include the Missionary establishment, above the Lick on the West side of Grand river, to be disposed of as the President of the United States shall direct, for the benefit of said Missions, and to establish them at the principal villages of the Great and Little Osage Nations, within the limits of the country reserved to them by this Treaty, and to be kept up at said villages, so long as said Missions shall be usefully employed in teaching, civilizing, and improving the said Indians.

Governor William Clark negotiated the treaty on behalf of the United States and he wrote a letter to James Barbour, then Secretary of War, explaining the movement of the missionary establishments to the new Osage country:

> The missionary establishments in this state and in the Arkansas Territory for the benefit of the Osage Indians, are to be sold out, and established at the principal villages occupied by these Indians; It belongs to the President under the Treaty to give the necessary orders & to direct the mode of sale. Those missionaries may have objections to this removal, but their establishments were built upon individual and public contributions for the special benefit of the Indians, & to answer the purpose of their institution they must be located amongst Indians. ...

Governor Clark had negotiated treaties with the Kansas Indians as well; the Kansas treaty had almost identical provisions to the sixth article with the Osage. Writing to Barbour concerning both treaties, Clark noted:

> In the treaties concluded with the Kansas and Osages, the annuities are limited to twenty years, in the course of

which time the humane experiment now making by Government to teach them to submit themselves by the arts of Civilized life, will have had a fair trial & if it succeeds, they will need no further aid from the Federal Government. The two annuities amount to $10,500 per annum, the payment of which & of every other expense attendant upon the negotiation & the execution of these treaties, can be made from the sale of one-fifth of the lands ceded by them within the limits of this State, leaving nearly one hundred millions of acres west of the Missouri and Arkansas to be exchanged with tribes in the different States which may be willing to remove to the West.

RATIFIED TREATY WITH THE MENOMINEES
February 8, 1835
Article 5

In the treaty of Butte des Morts, concluded in August 1827, an article is contained, appropriating one thousand five hundred dollars annually, for the support of schools in the Menominee country. And the representatives of the Menominee nation, who are parties hereto, require, and it is agreed to, that said appropriation shall be increased five hundred dollars, and continued for ten years from this date, to be placed in the hands of the Secretary of War, in trust for the exclusive use and benefit of the Menominee tribe of Indians, and to be applied by him to the education of the children of the Menominee Indians, in such manner as he may deem most advisable.

In the council held at Green Bay on July 18, 1831, to discuss the interpretation of the treaty and the benefits which the Menominee would derive from it, their agent, Samuel C. Stambaugh, explained to the tribe what the educational articles meant:

Brothers, your good friend and brother Rev. Mr. Cadle, who now sits beside me, told you truly, when he spoke to you the other day, and said that your Great Father was anxious to see your children educated like the children of the good white men; and you have heard from what I have read to you that a large sum of money is to be given to you for that purpose. How proud the Menominees will be when their children can read and write; can calculate the prices of what they wear, of the furs they have to sell, and the powder and ball they have to buy. You will then be able to protect yourselves from being cheated and abused by bad traders who may get into your country, or

> by faithless agents who unfortunately are sometimes sent
> to live among Indian tribes.

When Stambaugh had finished his speech, Josette Carrin, the principal chief of the Menominees, rose and answered him:

> Father, we have heard what you know about educating
> our children. It is good, the Menominees wish to have
> their children laugh like the Americans.

RATIFIED TREATY WITH THE CREEKS AND SEMINOLES
January 4, 1845
Article 4

The Creeks being greatly dissatisfied with the manner in which their boundaries were adjusted by the treaty of 1833, which they say they did not understand until after its execution, and it appearing that in said treaty no addition was made to their country for the use of the Seminoles, but that, on the contrary, they were deprived, without adequate compensation, of a considerable extent of valuable territory; And, moreover, the Seminoles, since the Creeks first agreed to receive them, having been engaged in a protracted and bloody contest, which has naturally engendered feelings and habits calculated to make them troublesome neighbors, The United States in consideration of these circumstances, agree that an additional annuity of three thousand dollars for the purposes of education shall be allowed for the term of twenty years; that the annuity of three thousand dollars provided in the treaty of 1832 for like purposes shall be continued until the determination of the additional annuity above mentioned. It is further agreed that all the education funds of the Creeks, including the annuities above named, the annual allowance of one thousand dollars, provided in the treaty of 1833, and also all balances of appropriations for educational annuities that may be due from the United States, shall be expended under the direction of the President of the United States, for the purpose of education aforesaid.

It is apparent from the tone of the article above that the United States treaty Commissioners had a difficult time convincing the Creeks to accept the terms of the treaty. William Armstrong, P.M. Buttes, and James Logan were the designated commissioners and they sent a report to T. Hartly Crawford, then Commissioner of Indian Affairs, dated the same day as the treaty, explaining why they had gone beyond the terms listed in their instructions from the Commissioner to promise the Creeks and Seminoles additional benefits:

> To effect these desirable ends, it became necessary in
> addition to the inducements named in the instructions to
> promise the Seminoles that their annuity of $3,000 under
> the Treaty of Payne's Landing should be increased to
> $5,000 by the payment of $2,000 a year in goods. Also, to
> agree that an educational annuity of $3,000 for purposes
> of education should be allowed the Creeks, and that the
> annuity of $3,000 already granted them for the same
> purpose should be extended for thirteen years.

> These allowances were made to the Creeks in conse-
> quence of a claim to be compensated for admitting the
> Seminoles into their country.

The Commissioners concluded later in their report:

> And notwithstanding the inducements mentioned, even
> this concession would not have been made had not the
> Creeks consented that the moneys to be paid them should
> be devoted exclusively to the instruction of their children.

RATIFIED TREATY WITH THE POTTAWATOMIES, CHIPPEWAS, AND OTTAWAS
June 5 and 17, 1846
Article 8

> It is also agreed that, after the expiration of two years from the
> ratification of this treaty, the school-fund of the Pottawatomies shall
> be expended entirely in their own country, unless their people, in
> council, should at any time, express a desire to have any part of the
> same expended in a different manner.

We have a fairly complete record of the councils that led to the acceptance
of this treaty by the combined tribes. Negotiations began the November
prior to the signing of the treaty and continued intermittently until the
summer when the treaty was finally signed. Unlike other treaty proceedings,
the Pottawatomies were able to respond to the commissioners' proposals in
writing and make counterproposals and the record is unusually clear.

On November 10, 1845, Commissioners George Gibson and T. P. Andrews
told the assembled Indians:

> If the Pottawatomie Chiefs are wise they will make their
> people happy. Their lands are only held temporarily.
> This they know. They were reminded of it by Majors Davis
> and Dougherty in 1839 and by Mssrs. McCoy and
> Coquillard in 1840. We can't build their mills, their

blacksmith shops or their school houses or other improvements. If we did they would all be lost to them when they removed to a new country.

On Wednesday, November 12th, the chiefs responded to the commissioners' arguments with a written statement:

> We have asked for schools in our country as we were promised at Chicago, but they have been denied. Our children have been taken away, and when we desired them to be sent home, our Great Father's ears were closed. He did not hear us. Our hearts were sorrowful then. We desired to see our children and we desired to have our school monies expended in our own country. We did not know that the education of the boys in Kentucky was to be paid for out of our monies, or we would not have said yes when our Father at St. Louis asked for them.
>
> If our money for these purposes, and for schools, has grown larger, we are glad to hear it: for our Great Father can then give us what we want of it, in our own country.

The following Monday, November 17th, the commissioners, acting on instructions from the President, responded:

> This is not the time for fulfilling some of your treaty stipulations: Those which relate to mills, school systems, &c., are of a permanent character and cannot be carried out at present.
>
> So soon as you shall be at a permanent home, from which there will be no danger of your removing again, you will receive their full benefit.

The commissioners argued that the chiefs misread the treaty, remarking that their "paper stated the school funds was intended to be expended only in their Country" whereas the words of the treaty are as follows: "to be applied in such manner as the President of the United States may direct."

The Indians were unhappy with the commissioners' interpretation of the treaty and at a meeting a week later the commissioners adapted their position, stating that the President "will also, at the expiration of two years (if you have all removed), have your school fund expended at your new home, and among your own people—and forever thereafter." The negotiations continued for the rest of November and December and were reopened in May of 1846.

Commissioner Andrews, at a meeting with the Indians on May 7, 1846, a month prior to signing the treaty, informed them that "you will there have your school fund laid out in your own country forever; after the first two years ... " Finally Andrews reported to the President:

> We showed them the treaty of Chicago; & that the large improvement fund & school fund was left at the discretion of your Great Father, & we told them,—what you know must be true,—that so long as your people lived apart, these funds could not be wisely or fairly laid out to your advantage.

The removal of Indians from the Chicago area, therefore, was premised upon the explicit promise that the United States would provide educational services to the Chippewas, Pottawatomies and Ottawas forever.

RATIFIED TREATY WITH THE ROGUE RIVER INDIANS
November 15, 1854
Article 2

> In consideration of the foregoing stipulations, it is agreed on the part of the United States to pay to the Rogue River tribe, as soon as practicable after the signing of this agreement, two thousand one hundred and fifty dollars, in the following articles: ... hereafter to be located on said reserve, that provisions shall be made for the erection of two smith-shops; ... and for one or more schools; the uses and benefits of all which shall be secured to said Rogue River tribe, equally with the tribes and bands treated with; all the improvements made, and schools, hospitals, and shops erected, to be conducted in accordance with such laws, rules and regulations as the Congress or the President of the United States may prescribe.

In 1854 treaties with the Oregon tribes were negotiated by Joel Palmer who was commissioned specifically to clear the Indian title from the Oregon lands. Palmer wrote to Commissioner of Indian Affairs, George Manypenny, in December 1854, about his negotiations with the Rogue River Indians:

> The tribe was at first quite adverse to permit other Indians a location among them. They alleged that the dissensions already existing among themselves would be increased by the residence of strange Indians on the Reserve. But the consideration that the existing treaty made no provision for schools, smith shops, a hospital &c., so essential to their comfort and wellbeing; and their annuities were too limited to offer a means for such purposes, induced them at length to agree to the provisions of the accompanying agreement.

The same type of inducements were used by Palmer with the Chasta, Scoton and Umpqua tribes ...

Thus it was that the major portion of Oregon was ceded specifically to get education services for the tribal members.

RATIFIED TREATY WITH THE NISQUALLY, PUYALLUP AND OTHER INDIANS
December 26, 1854
Article 10

The United States further agree to establish at the general agency for the district of Puget's Sound, within one year from the ratification thereof, and to support, for a period of twenty years, an agricultural and industrial school, to be free to children of the said tribes and bands, in common with those of the other tribes of said district, and to provide the said school with a suitable instructor or instructors, and also to provide smithy and carpenter's shop, and furnish them with the necessary tools, and employ a blacksmith, carpenter, and farmer, for the term of twenty years, to instruct the Indians in their respective occupations. And the United States further agree to employ a physician to reside at the said central agency, who shall furnish medicine and advice to their sick, and shall vaccinate them; the expenses of the said school, shops, employees, and medical attendance, to be defrayed by the United States, and not deducted from the annuities.

The treaty, one of six proposed by Governor Isaac Stevens, has been one of the most controversial documents in Indian history. A considerable credibility gap has always existed between the text of the treaty and what Stevens actually told the assembled Indians. In regard to education, Stevens told the Nisquallys:

> The Great Father has many White Children who come here, some to build mills; some to make farms; and some to fish — and the Great Father wishes you to have homes, pasture for your horses and fishing places. He wants you to learn to farm and your children to go to a good school; and he now wants me to make a bargain with you, in which you will sell your lands and in return be provided with all these things.

Later in his report on the treaty proceedings, Stevens noted:

> The question of a Central Agency, Farm and Agricultural School was very fully discussed and unanimously voted as necessary for the civilization of the Indians and as no

more than justice to them considering that they cede to
the United States so large an amount of valuable land.

Steven continued in his report to the Commissioner of Indian Affairs:

The provision for an agricultural and industrial school I
deem of great consequence to the Indians. These Indians
will make good artisans and were even desirous that a
provision should be inserted in the Treaty binding out
the youths of both sexes as apprentices. Such a provision,
it was believed, was more germane to the laws regulating
intercourse than to a Treaty, and was in consequence not
inserted.

In the treaty with the S'Klallam, Skokomish and other tribes of the upper
inland waters (January 26, 1855), Stevens told the Indians:

This paper is such as a man would give to his children and
I will tell you why. This paper gives you a home. Does not
a father give his children a home? This paper gives you a
school. Does not a father send his children to school? It
gives you mechanics and a Doctor to teach you and cure
you. Is not that fatherly?

RATIFIED TREATY WITH THE MISSISSIPPI, PILLAGER AND
LAKE WINIBIGOSHISH CHIPPEWAS
February 22, 1855
Article 4

The Mississippi bands have expressed a desire to be permitted to
employ their own farmers, mechanics and teachers; and it is therefore agreed that the amounts to which they are now entitled, under
former treaties, for purposes of education, for blacksmiths, and
assistants, shops, tools, iron and steel, and for the employment of
farmers and carpenters, shall be paid over to them as their annuities
are paid; Provided, however, that whenever, in the opinion of the
Commissioner of Indian Affairs, they fail to make proper provision
for the above-named purposes, he may retain said amounts, and
appropriate them according to his discretion, for their education
and improvement.

Behind this article is an interesting story. The Chippewas were very dis-
gruntled about the poor manner in which the Bureau of Indian Affairs had
fulfilled its responsibilities under the previous treaties. The following
exchange took place between Hole-in-the Day, the Chippewa chief, and the
Commissioner of Indian Affairs:

Commissioner: I do not want to employ blacksmiths, farmers, &c for you any longer than till it shall appear you are competent to get along and manage your own business. The clause is conditional. I am willing to compromise the manner, and strike out all but teachers. I do not mean by that missionary teachers. I refer only to such as are capable of giving instructions in education, &c.

Hole-in-the-Day: The teachers who have been sent among us have never done us any good. They seem to care about nothing but their salaries. (Hon. H. M. Rice said that was literally true. He did not know a single Indian who had been educated by them, notwithstanding the large sums expended out of their annuities.)

Hole-in-the-Day: Listen, Father, to me one minute, and I will make you understand what I mean. In all our treaties, there are provisions made for laborers, blacksmiths, teachers, &c. and we have expended a goodly amount for them. It has done us no good. It is very essential that the Indians shall be thrown on their own resources.

Commissioner: I am willing to do away with the employment of men to work by the Government, but I want something reserved for educational purposes. Don't you, Hole-in-the-Day, feel the want of education? Would you not, for instance, like to know how to read this paper?

Hole-in-the-Day: Father, it is twenty years since we began to receive annuities. Refer back, and you will find those stipulations for the employment of laborers, teachers, &c. They have done us no good. We have remained long enough in ignorance, depending upon others, and we now want to try something for ourselves. You will see that for twenty years that money was appropriated for education, but what good has it done us?

Commissioner: How can you educate your children (unless) some such provision is made for the purpose?

Hole-in-the-Day: Father, as to education, I am in favor of it as much as any one. I know its value, and feel its want; but, if I wish to educate my children, I can now take my own money, and employ my own teachers. I want to educate my children, Father, the reason why I have said so much is that I am anxious to explain my motives. I want a good

pile of money to start upon. A good start is an important
point. We are all fond of our children. We know and feel
the necessity of education: to effect this, we must have
means. A lot of us get together, and we say our children
ought to be educated. To effect this, all know we must
have a teacher. We employ such a one as we think will suit.
We will then have him under our control, because there
is no other influence to operate with him. There is a
schoolmaster in our country, but I want the privilege, if I
don't like him, to employ another.

Commissioner. I agree to your proposition in the main, but
I cannot consent that you shall have the right to apply all
your funds, without any reservation whatever for education. ... I have no objection to your hiring your own
teachers, but there must be a fund reserved applicable to
that purpose. Go home, my friends, and consider of it.

Hole-in-the-Day. Father, you must not understand us. We
have no objection to education. I told you we wanted to
have our children educated. We also want schoolhouses,
but, as to teachers, such as have had, we know too much
about them. We object to have teachers, whom we don't
like, forced upon us. They come, not to teach, but to get
money and have their ease.

Commissioner. We will try and have the evil referred to
corrected. Suppose, however, we set apart the fund, and
let the Indians employ their own teachers. How would
that do?

Hon. H. M. Rice. I think that is a good idea and will be
acceptable.

Hole-in-the-Day. Father, if you want to have us educated to
read, why don't you take some of your own money,
instead of ours, and sacrifice it in upholding the present
system?

RATIFIED TREATY WITH THE YAKIMAS
June 9, 1855
Article 5

The United States further agree to establish at suitable points within
said reservation, within one year after the ratification hereof, two
schools, erecting the necessary buildings, keeping them in repair,

and providing them with furniture, books, and stationary, one of which shall be an agricultural and industrial school, to be located at the agency, and to be free to the children of the said confederated tribes and bands of Indians, and to employ one superintendent of teaching and two teachers; to build two blacksmiths' shops, to one of which shall be attached a tin-shop, and to the other a gunsmiths' shop; one carpenter's shop, one wagon and plough maker's shop, and to keep the same in repair and furnished with the necessary tools; to employ one superintendent of farming and two farmers, two blacksmiths, one tinner, one gunsmith, one carpenter, one wagon and plough maker, for the instruction of the Indians in trades and to assist them in the same.

Both Isaac Stevens and Joel Palmer were in attendance at the signing of the Yakima treaty. Stevens explained the treaty to the Yakimas as follows:

On each tract we wish to have one or more schools; we want on each tract one or more blacksmiths; one or more carpenters; one or more farmers; we want you and your children to learn to make ploughs ... and everything you need in your houses. You will have your own teachers, your own farmers, blacksmiths, wheelwrights, and mechanics; besides this we want on each tract a saw mill and a grist mill. Besides all these things, these shops, these mills and these schools which I have mentioned, we must pay you for the land which you give to the Great Father; these schools and mills and shops are only a portion of the payment. We want besides to agree with you for a fair sum to be given for your lands, to be paid through a term of years as are your schools and your shops.

Stevens made another treaty the following month with the Flathead, Kootenai and Upper Pend d'Oreilles (July 16, 1855), and he made essentially the same promises to these tribes:

If you live on the reserve as I said yesterday, all your sick will be cared for; we can only give you one physician. All will have a chance to have their wheat ground—we can only give you one grist mill. All will have the same chance to have houses—we can give you only one saw mill. Your farms, your schools, and your shops will be better; you will be better clothed and better provided for in every way; because all of you will equally have the care of the agent.

The chiefs will each year tell the agent what tools, what clothing, what goods, they want for their people; what

children go to school and learn trades, which children
shall learn to be blacksmiths, which to be carpenters,
which wheelwrights, which farmers. ...

Ratified Treaty with the Mississippi, Pillager and
Lake Winibigoshish Chippewas
March 11, 1863
Article 9

To improve the morals and industrial habits of said Indians, it is
agreed that no agent, teacher, interpreter, traders, or their employees, shall be employed, appointed, licensed, or permitted to reside
within the reservations belonging to the Indians, parties to this
treaty, missionaries excepted, who shall not have a lawful wife
residing with them at their respective places of employment or trade
within the agency, no person of full or mixed blood, educated or
partially educated, whose fitness, morally or otherwise, is not conducive to the welfare of said Indians, shall receive any benefits from this
or any former treaties.

Article 13

Female members of the family of any Government employee residing on the reservation, who shall teach Indian girls domestic economy,
shall be allowed and paid a sum not exceeding ten dollars per month
while so engaged; Provided, That no more than one thousand
dollars shall be expended during any one year, and that the President of the United States may suspend or annul this article whenever
he may deem expedient to do so.

The continuing conflict between the Chippewas of Minnesota and the
Bureau of Indian Affairs still raged when this treaty was being negotiated.
The articles do not reflect the major concern of the Indians, having a teacher
on each reservation, and the point of discussion revolved about the cost of
the educational services that were due under the treaty and the actual cost
of fulfilling the demands of the Indians as they understood them.

> *Chippewa Chief Obegwad:* Father, I have got a few words to
> say to you. The sentiments expressed by the chiefs that
> have spoken are my sentiments. In regard to our school
> teachers, our Great Father has promised us, when we
> reserved these tracts of land, and we earnestly requested
> that they should be granted us now on our reservations,
> where our children might learn to read and write. I want
> our school masters to be located just where they are not—
> where our village is. This is our wish and it is the wish of

our people we have left behind, to have schools located in our reservations.

Commissioner Dole. I want to make a statement in relation to this clause that the Government has promised to have schools upon all these reservations. The Government promised them so much money for schools. That amount is $4,333.33 a year. Now when a chief arises here and says that the Government promised them a school upon their reservation he is mistaken. The Government promised them so much money to be divided among them to the best advantage. Now they live upon eight reservations. It would amount to only a little over $500.00 for each reservation a year, which would not keep a school at all. Your agent informs me that he thinks he could employ one teacher at each reservation for $500.00. But then there would be the necessary expenses of school books, and the school houses to build, in addition to this, and there is no funds for that purpose. I want to say to them however, that there is no disposition on the part of the Government to do anything in relation to their schools but that which will gratify them most, if it is possible to do so, without a waste of money. I will take their requests into consideration and see what we can do to establish more schools. I would very much prefer, however, that they would decide to have less reservations and make less schools necessary.

RATIFIED TREATY WITH THE NEZ PERCE
June 9, 1863
Article 5

First, ... Ten thousand dollars for the erection of the two schools, including boarding-houses and the necessary out-buildings; said schools to be conducted on the manual-labor system as far as practicable.

Fourth, And it is further agreed that the United States shall employ, in addition to those already mentioned in article 5 of the treaty of June 11, 1855, two matrons to take charge of the boarding schools, two assistant teachers, one farmer, one carpenter and two millers.

One of the difficulties in negotiating this particular treaty was the fact that the United States had not yet begun to fulfill its obligations under the previous treaty of 1855. The Nez Perce, therefore, were rightly suspicious of the promises of the United States. Indian Superintendent Hale, writing a month before the treaty council, outlined the track record of the federal government with the tribe:

> On taking charge of the Office I took pains to ascertain what had been promised to, and what had been done for the Nez Perce nation. I found there was not as much as you had the right to expect, not as much as the U. S. Government supposed. I ... was surprised to see so little improvements made, in view of the large appropriations, which I know have been made. Your head chiefs had no house built, and no farm fenced or ploughed. The money for this had been appropriated, but did not come into my hands. Your head chief, Lawyer, was entitled to receive pay. The money had been appropriated, but I found none had been paid him, except what Mr. Hutchins paid. He had paid all that he received. I found that you had no school house, altho a Teacher had been sent; that you had no hospital built, and your mills were not furnished. This was not the fault of Mr. Hutchins [as] he had done what he could to complete the mills, although he had received no money either for Mills, Hospital or School.

THE INDIAN PEACE COMMISSION TREATIES 1867–1868

The Indian Peace Commission, or the Sanborn Commission, went to the tribes of the southern plains, Rocky Mountains and northern plains during the years 1867 and 1868 and signed a number of peace treaties with the tribes. The treaties all had the same basic formula which provided specific educational benefits. The following article, taken from the Sioux treaty of April 29, 1868, is typical of the provisions of these treaties:

Article 7

In order to insure the civilization of the Indians entering into this treaty, the necessity of education is admitted, especially of such of them as are or may be settled on said agricultural reservations, and they therefore pledge themselves to compel their children, male and female, between the ages of six and sixteen years, to attend school; and it is hereby made the duty of the agent for said Indians to see that this stipulation is strictly complied with; and the United States agrees that for every thirty children between said ages who can be induced or compelled to attend school, a house shall be provided and a teacher competent to teach them the elementary branches of an English education shall be furnished, who will reside among said Indians, and faithfully discharge his or her duties as a teacher. The provisions of this article to continue for not less than twenty years.

The tribes were primarily concerned with protecting their lands and ensuring that they would be allowed to live in peace with no further intrusions by the white man on their hunting lands. They did not contemplate settling down at agencies until they had exhausted the game and many figured that they still had a generation before they would have to farm. Therefore they did not give the idea of schooling very serious attention.

During the meeting with the Kiowas and Comanches, Senator Henderson, a member of the Peace Commission, told the tribes assembled at Medicine Creek, Kansas: "We are authorized to build for the Indians school houses and Churches, and provide teachers to educate his children."

Santa, the Kiowa chief, replied: "I don't want any of these Medicine Houses (schools and churches) built in the country. I want the papooses brought up just exactly as I am. ..."

On the whole the response of most of the tribes was that they could consider everything when the time came that they were forced to settle down. Until that time they had no desire to come to the agencies and live like white men. But they placed no bar to any of their people who wished to take advantage of the service.

CONCLUSION

We can see from the variety of treaty provisions and the recorded promises and comments by both Indians and treaty commissioners that a broad variety of services was promised to the tribes during treaty councils. In some cases, notably the Nez Perce and the tribes signing the 1867–1868 treaties, the government failed for many years to fulfill its obligations. In the case of the Chippewas, the performance was unsatisfactory and perfunctory at best.

The continuous reliance upon the President of the United States, or the Great Father, by the Indians is symptomatic of the conditions of the times. The tribes could not readily believe the treaty commissioners because they had often been betrayed by them in previous negotiations. Their only hope lay in appealing to the moral stature of the President with the hopes that he would act wisely on their behalf. Allowing the President to determine the manner and length of services due them was a way of placing responsibility in one person rather than in seeking to get satisfaction from a large bureaucracy which seemed to change with every shift of the wind.

There seems little doubt that in signing and ratifying the treaties the United States assumed a variety of legal obligations to Indians, many of which have not yet been adequately fulfilled.[12]

4

MISSION EDUCATION
IN THE TREATY YEARS: 1778–1871

THE FEDERAL GOVERNMENT'S first approach to educating American Indians involved cooperative efforts with religious organizations; the objective was to assimilate the Indians into American society. As Secretary of War John C. Calhoun stated in 1820, the Indians "should be taken under our guardianship; and our opinion, and not theirs, ought to prevail in measures intended for their civilization and happiness."[1]

In 1819 the federal government established the Civilization Fund to supply financial support for religious organizations engaged in educating Indians. The act authorized the president to employ agricultural instructors and schoolteachers "for the purpose of providing against the further decline and final extinction of the Indian tribes ... and for introducing among them the habits and arts of civilization."[2]

Ten thousand dollars per year was appropriated for the Civilization Fund. Although the funds were administered by the Indian Office under specific rules and regulations, the actual operation of the Indian schools was left to the religious organizations. Funds were secured by submitting a formal request to the Indian Office describing how the organization planned to use the financial subsidy in "civilizing" Indian children.

Mission schools received additional financial support from other sources. If a mission organization was active among tribes with treaty relations with the United States, it would have the benefit of using farming and mechanical implements, domestic animals, and tradesmen sent by the government to fulfill the treaty obligations. In addition, tribal annuities and education funds often supported mission schools. Discretionary funds administered by the Indian Office through federal appropriations for laws such as the trade and intercourse acts were also applied to the mission schools. Other funds were provided by the mission organizations themselves through the collection of individual contributions.

Making Christians and Farmers

The main objective of both the government and the missionaries was to encourage the Indians to become settled, practicing farmers and to discard their native traditions. To this end, the schools taught reading, writing, and elementary arithmetic, in addition to religious instruction. Many mission schools offered training in manual labor. Thus, it was common to have Indian boys work on a school farm, while girls were responsible for the domestic economy of the schools. Most mission schools were self-sustaining, providing clothing, supplies, and boarding facilities.

The question arises, "Why did the mission schools fail?" Martha E. Layman, in an unpublished history of American Indian education, identifies

> three well defined and conflicting forces which were at work throughout the entire period of Indian mission education. Foremost among these opposing forces was the Indian mission, intent on remaking the Indian religiously, linguistically and culturally according to the white man's standard. Opposed to the mission objectives were many thousands of Indians, consecrated to their own religion, proud of their own culture and desirous of perpetuating it. The third force was that of the traders in the Indian country who saw in Indian education an obstacle to their exploitation of the natives. It is little to be wondered that the Indians who were accustomed to dealing with the white traders, whose only interest was profit, looked with suspicion upon the missionaries.[3]

The missionaries themselves must be assessed a portion of the blame, as competition for students sometimes gained precedence over educational goals. As a result, according to historian Wilcomb E. Washburn, the missionaries "missed the real Indian in seeking to coerce him into an alien cultural mold."[4]

Because the missionary educators failed to realize that the Indian was intensely religious and intent upon protecting his religion at all costs, the Indians usually looked on the missionaries with suspicion. The Indians accused the representatives of the church of not only robbing them of their native culture and customs, but also of conspiring with the government to take their land. Coupled with this suspicion was the superstition of the Indians, who saw in the presence of the missionaries an explanation for all of the misfortunes that befell the tribe.

Finally, and perhaps most significantly, the Indian Office failed to set standards for mission school education. The net result of almost one hundred years of effort and the expenditure of hundreds of thousands of dollars for Indian education was a small number of poorly attended mission schools, a suspicious and disillusioned Indian population, and a few hundred alumni who for the most part were considered outcasts by whites and Indians alike.

In the following selection Layman describes various missionary efforts in Indian education.

The United States government, through its Commissioner of Indian Affairs, provided some financial support for Indian schools and acted as a clearing house for matters affecting Indian education. At no time, however, did the government undertake the formation of a definitive policy of Indian education. With the exception of some very general requirements included in the Civilization Act and in some of the Indian treaties, the matters of curriculum and methods were left entirely to the mission boards and as a consequence there were as many different kinds of education as there were missionary organizations, many of which completely subordinated the educational part of their work to the religious.

Though the first missionaries to the Indians in this period were supported by local missionary societies, it was not long before the general missionary boards and state and denominational societies began to take over the work of selecting the missionaries and supporting the stations. With the passage of the Civilization Act and the allocation of federal funds to the missionary societies for the education of the Indians, the missionary movement received its greatest impetus. The Civilization Act might be said to have been both a result of increased interest in missions and an incentive to further missionary activity. From the time of the passage of the Civilization Act in 1819 to 1873, when federal support of mission schools was discontinued, the missionary was the prime civilizing element among the Indian tribes.

The most extensive missionary and educational work in the Northeast was that carried on among the Iroquois of New York. The mission which Samuel Kirkland had established during the colonial period was virtually discontinued during the Revolution while Kirkland was serving as a chaplain in the Continental Army and as agent for the Continental Congress in its negotiations with the Indians.

By 1784 Kirkland was again among the Indians as a missionary under the sponsorship of the Society in Scotland for Propagating the Gospel. The year of his return the United States government made the Treaty of Fort Stanwix by the terms of which the Six Nations were to relinquish a large part of the territory they claimed as their own. For a time it looked as though Kirkland's missionary work would be seriously affected as a result of this treaty, for the agreement was very unpopular with certain leaders of the Iroquois, chief among them Joseph Brant. Brant's attempt to foster general dissatisfaction was, however, unsuccessful and within a few months after the treaty was concluded the Indians became fairly quiet and contented. This gave Kirkland an opportunity to push his plans for Indian education. He established in the

Oneida villages small schools in which the children were taught arithmetic, reading, and writing, both in their own language and in English. These schools were only the beginning of an elaborate scheme for the education of the Indians, particularly of the Five [sic] Nations.

Kirkland's plan included, in addition to the smaller schools in which the younger children were to be taught, the establishment of an academy in the vicinity of Oneida. It was to be contiguous to some English settlement, and both Indian and white students would be admitted to it. The Indian boys were to be carefully selected from the different nations of the confederacy after they had acquired the ability to read and write the Indian and English languages. At the academy they were to be instructed in "the principles of human nature, in the history of civil society, so as to be able to discern the difference between a state of nature [and] a state of civilization and know what it is that makes one nation differ from another in wealth, power and happiness and in the principles of natural religion, the moral precepts, and the more plain and express doctrines of Christianity." In addition to the provision for regular academic education, Kirkland proposed the instruction of the boys in agriculture through the cultivation of a small tract of land near the school and eventually the erection of a workhouse in which the girls, after having learned reading and writing, might be taught spinning and weaving, "together with domestic economy." The proposed academy was supported by many intelligent and influential persons who had emigrated from new England and settled in the neighborhood of Oneida. The white settlers had faint hopes of any great benefit to the Indians from such an institution, but they did realize the advantage of the academy to their own families and the growing communities around them.

The school, however, proved to be of considerably more value to the white settlers than to the Indians. Ebenezer Caulkins, the teacher, wrote to Dr. Thacher of the Boston Board in June of 1794, that there had been only four Indians enrolled as pupils during the past winter. The Board of Correspondents of the Society in Scotland sent a committee to visit the missions among the Oneida in 1796. This committee reported the Hamilton-Oneida Academy as being in a hopeless financial state, with its building incomplete and the school suspended since 1794 for want of financial support. By 1799 the academy had been reopened, and Kirkland reported fifty students, only one of whom was an Indian. He stated that many Indians had applied for admission, but that the provision for their support, on which he had relied, had not been made. Occasionally small sums were granted to the academy, by the Corporation of Harvard College, the Society for the Propagation of the Gospel and after 1819 from the Civilization Fund, for the education of a few Indians at the school. For many years it endured a severe financial struggle, and though from time to time there were Indian students enrolled, their number was never large. There was considerable opposition to Kirkland's plan by certain persons in New York who were also interested in Indian education. In 1812 the academy was granted a new charter as Hamilton College.

In the decade following 1807, the New York Yearly Meeting of Friends became very active in Indian work, especially among the Oneida, Onondaga, Stockbridge, and Brotherton Indians.

... In New York the Liberal branch of Friends received the funds of the Indian committee and used them principally in behalf of that branch of the Seneca nation living at Cattaraugus, where a school was opened in 1833. The principal effort of the Friends in New York from 1838 to 1842 was the struggle to protect the Seneca Indians in their ownership of lands. After the reservations of Allegheny and Cattaraugus had been secured to the Seneca in 1842, the Friends devoted their efforts more particularly to education and civilization.

It was toward the close of the decade 1839-1849 that the women Friends, no doubt influenced by the movement for women's rights which was then sweeping the country, felt that some definite work should be done for the Indian women. Consequently, as the result of a council held in 1846, the Friends opened a Female Manual Labor School at Cattaraugus. There twenty-eight pupils were boarded in the mission family and taught to card and spin wool, knit stockings and sew. Four at a time, the Indian girls were taken into the family of the superintendent where they learned to wash and iron clothes, make bread, and do plain cooking.

Soon afterward the Friends felt that the Indians at Cattaraugus were able to work out in practice what the Quakers had labored so many years in teaching them. Therefore, in 1849, the farm lease was returned to the Indians, and the active work of the Liberal Friends for the Seneca Nation was closed.

That the Friends were able to win the confidence of the Indians to a greater extent than most of the other missionary groups was undoubtedly due to the restraint which they exercised in presenting their religious beliefs. They made it distinctly understood that their purpose was to educate, not to convert. At a council held in 1850, a Friend explained this purpose by saying to the assembled Indians: "With your religious concerns we have studiously avoided to interfere, not because we have deemed Religions an unimportant subject, but because we have not been called upon by our position or sent among you to teach it. It is not the extent of our theological instruction but our fidelity in the performance of manifest duty that is the measure of our acceptance in the Divine Sight."

In 1811 the New York Missionary Society sent the Reverend John Alexander as Missionary and Jabez Backus Hyde as teacher to the Seneca on Buffalo Creek. Though the chiefs refused to receive the missionary, some of them wished to have their children taught and accepted Hyde as the teacher.

Hyde was commissioned by the missionary society as a teacher only, yet he could not refrain from attempts to evangelize the Indians. Opposed as certain parties of the Seneca and Tuscarora were to interference with their religion, it is easy to understand why they impeded the missionary's education work.

At that time there were fifteen or sixteen children enrolled in the school. Arrangements were then made that as soon as a new building was ready for them, the children would be boarded in the mission family. A council was arranged for May 22 at which the missionary hoped to select the pupils to be received into the new boarding school. Late in the afternoon of the day set aside for the council the chiefs arrived without the children and gravely informed the missionary that they did not wish to have their children instructed in agriculture, that reading and writing were sufficient for the purposes of the Gospel, and that the children's parents could teach them agriculture if they wished.

Eventually the chiefs promised to send their children from home every day, but would not consent to their living in the mission family. This was, however, an Indian promise, not intended to be kept, for the entry in the missionary's journal for the day following the council reads: "May 23. Mr. Young ready to go into school, but no children came."

For several weeks the controversy continued. Finally the Indians were shown that unless agriculture was taught and the children made to work, the money from the government would be withdrawn, and the school would have to be closed. On July 1, fifteen children were sent to live at the mission. This number, within ten days, was increased to twenty-four. A week later, however, several boys deserted the school, and on September 24 all of the girls ran away.

Meanwhile, Red Jacket and the pagan group continued their opposition to the missionaries. Failing in their attempt to replace the missionary teacher with Jacob Jemison, one of their own young men who had been educated among the white people, they entered a formal complaint against the mission family, and under a New York law of 1821 forbidding the residence of white men on Indian lands, the district attorney was compelled to notify the missionaries to leave the reservation. Consequently, from March of 1824, to June of 1825, the work of the mission was discontinued. Shortly afterward, the United Foreign Missionary Society was merged in the American Board of Commissioners for Foreign Missions, and the Seneca, Cattaraugus, and Tuscarora missions were formally transferred to that control.

In October, 1800, the Connecticut Missionary Society sent the Reverend Joseph Badger as a missionary to the Wyandot and other Indians living on the Western Reserve and along the Sandusky and Maumee Rivers. For a number of years he engaged in religious work only, but in the year 1806 he received a formal appointment by the Western Missionary Society to establish an Indian mission on the Lower Sandusky. There the mission buildings were erected, and a school established. ... However, his mission found itself in the path of war parties along the northern border during the War of 1812. Badger's house was burned, and the mission was abandoned, but the missionary succeeded in keeping his Indians loyal to the Americans.

In 1817, the Reverend Isaac McCoy received an appointment from the Baptist General Convention as its first Indian missionary. McCoy located his first mission at Fort Wayne, Indiana, but finding the Indians prejudiced against the white men and opposed to the Christian religion, the missionary soon decided to move the station. The new station was called Carey in honor of one of the most distinguished of Baptist missionaries.

In 1823, William Keating gave perhaps the best account of the school which is available. He said: "The school consists of from forty to sixty children of which fifteen are females. The plan appears to be a very judicious one; to instruct them in the arts of civilized life, to teach them the benefits which they may derive from it without attempting to confuse their heads with ideas of religion, the value of which is in their present state impossible for them to appreciate." He described the curriculum of the school as including reading, writing and arithmetic for all pupils, farm work for the boys and house work for the girls. In addition, the girls were taught spinning, weaving and sewing and were just beginning to embroider. Keating said of the embroidering that it was "an occupation which may, by some, be considered as unsuitable to the situation which they are destined to hold in life, but which appears to us very judiciously used as a reward and stimulus."

In the upper peninsula of Michigan, Sault Ste. Marie and Mackinaw were the important mission locations. Though the Catholics for many years had a mission among the Chippewa at Sault Ste. Marie, no Protestant mission was established there until 1828 when the Baptist Board sent Reverend Abel Bingham to that station.

Bingham's description of his school sheds some light on the methods of teaching in the 1830's. He wrote, "I attached a large sheet containing the alphabet to the side of my room, formed the small scholars into classes and placed a monitor over them, whose business it was, through the day, to march those classes one after another to the card and teach them, the whole class speaking at once. In a few weeks we had them all nicely through their alphabet."

Bingham and his assistants had the usual opposition from liquor dealers. The Catholics also opposed his work. Nevertheless, the Baptist Mission at Sault Ste. Marie continued for many years. In 1835, a Methodist missionary was also sent to Sault Ste. Marie and conducted a school for Indian children.

In the South were the Five Civilized Tribes. This group of Indians, so called because of the high degree to which they accepted the culture and customs of their white neighbors, included the Cherokee, Chickasaw, Choctaw, Creek and Seminole tribes.

In 1803, Reverend Gideon Blackburn, a minister of the Presbyterian Church, established a mission station for the Cherokee in Blount County, Tennessee, which he called Highwassee. ... Like other teachers of Indian children, Blackburn was confronted with the problems of irregular attendance and lack of application on the part of his pupils. The former problem he ingeniously solved by getting the chiefs to agree that if any children left the school without permission or stayed away longer than ten days, they would forfeit the clothes which he had given them. In case of their refusal to give up the clothes, at the next distribution of the annuity Blackburn had the right to deduct from the annuity of the chiefs an amount equal to the value of the clothing. The latter problem he met by giving small presents to every child and a prize to the best student at the annual examinations.

The curriculum of the school included reading, writing, ciphering, "spelling off the books," and singing spiritual songs. The children rose very early, prayed and washed. The school then opened with the reading of Scripture, praise and public prayer, followed by lessons, after which the pupils had breakfast. Immediately following breakfast they were given an hour for recreation. School was resumed from nine until twelve. After the noon meal the children were again given a recreation period, then returned to the classroom where they remained until evening. In the summer between sun-down and dark and in the winter between dark and nine o' clock they had spelling lessons, which were followed by the singing of a hymn and prayer by the master. Thus, it is apparent that there was considerably more religion than education in this school.

Blackburn gives a vivid description of taking his twenty-five pupils and their master down the Highwassee River in a canoe in the year 1805 to attend a council of Indians at which commissioners of the United States and of the state of Tennessee were present. There the children marched before the council and, as proof of their progress, each scholar read such portion as was requested. The different classes then spelled a number of words without the book. Specimens of their writing and ciphering were shown and the exhibition closed with the children singing in a clear and distinct voice, a hymn or two committed to memory.

A period of several years elapsed following the establishment of the Presby-terian mission at Highwassee before any other missionary organization entered the field among the southern Indians. Then, in 1817, the American Board of Commissioners for Foreign Missions sent Reverend Cyrus Kingsbury as a missionary to the Cherokee, thereby beginning what was to become the most extensive mission work carried on by any missionary organization in the United States.

The plan of the American Board in beginning its work among the Cherokee was "to establish schools in the different parts of the tribe under the missionary direction and superintendence for the instruction of the rising generation in common school learning, in the useful arts of life and in Christianity, so as gradually to make the whole tribe English in their language, civilized in their habits and Christian in their religion."

The plan of the Board was to organize the school at Brainerd, and others to be established thereafter, according to the Lancastrian system, which used monitors, selected from the older and more advanced pupils, who taught the younger ones. The curriculum consisted almost wholly of instruction in reading, writing, arithmetic and morals or religion. The principle purpose of instruction was the imparting of information and development of the memory.

According to practice of the day, rewards were given to the best students, but the system was a more ingenious one that could be found in most of the Indian schools. The teachers prepared cards bearing the initial letters of the words "punctual attendance," "behavior" and "diligence." These cards were assigned values of one-half cent, one cent, and one and one-half cents. They were given to the children in recognition of the virtues which they represented and were used as money which the children could use to purchase knives, books and anything else which the Indian pupils might need. The tickets served another purpose as well—that of punishment—for if a child damaged his slate, lost his pencil, or exhibited any other kind of negligence, he was fined in tickets.

It was the purpose of the American Board of Commissioners for Foreign Missions to make Brainerd the center of operations for reaching the entire Cherokee Nation. Beginning in 1819, new stations in the Cherokee country were established, each of which housed a school modeled on the one at Brainerd and supported, in part, by the civilization fund. By 1825 the Cherokee schools under the control of the American Board reported an enrollment of forty-two, which by 1830 had increased to 194.

The various missionary organizations did not limit their activities among the southern Indians to the Cherokee tribe. Within four years of the establishment of Brainerd, the American Board of Commissioners for Foreign Missions had missions and schools among both the Choctaw and Chickasaw tribes. As soon as Cyrus Kingsbury had the mission at Brainerd started, he left Tennessee with an assistant named Williams and selected a site for a new station on Yula Bush Creek in the Choctaw Country.

From the beginning, the Choctaw were eager for education and generous in their support of the schools. That they were willing to pay out of their own funds for the education of their children was no doubt due largely to the influence of Kingsbury. In reporting the progress of the Indians, Kingsbury wrote: "It has been our endeavor to impress on the minds of this nation the advantages of instruction and the propriety of their contributing towards the education of their own children. We are decidedly of the opinion that, in every point of view, it is important that they should learn to help themselves.

Notwithstanding the hardships caused by fever, floods, whiskey and lack of food, the Choctaw continued to send their children to the mission schools. The missionaries of the American Board always took an active interest in the political affairs of the Indians they served. When the slavery agitation arose, the missionaries among the Choctaw, led by the Reverend Cyrus Kingsbury, supported slavery, while those among the Cherokee, led by the Reverend Samuel A. Worcester, opposed it. By 1855 the missionaries among the Choctaw, as a result of the controversy over slavery, expressed a desire to separate themselves from the American Board. Four years later, because of its own volition, the Board severed connections with the Choctaw missions, and the Presbyterian Board of Foreign Missions stepped into the breach.

The most extensive western experiments in Indian education, exclusive of Indian Territory (Oklahoma), were in the present middle-western states of Minnesota, North and South Dakota, Iowa, Nebraska and Kansas and in the northwestern states of Washington, Oregon, and Montana. The Great Plains, from the present Kansas and Nebraska to California, were for the most void of missions during the treaty period. Along the California coast and in the Southwest the Catholic missions of the Spanish period continued.

The earliest school of which there is record amoung the Minnesota Chippewa was an outgrowth of the work started at La Pointe, Wisconsin. In 1833, at the insistence of William Aitkin, who at that time was in charge of the Fond du Lac department of the American Fur Company, Frederick Ayer, the teacher at La Pointe, moved to Sandy Lake and opened a school for fifteen to twenty pupils in which very elementary instruction was given. The mission report of that year states that "not only the very young pupils but youth and even adults, among untutored Indians, are so unaccustomed to all purely intellectual efforts that they acquire knowledge very slowly when communicated in the ordinary manner, and feel little interest in it, even though it is presented in the simplest language and accompanied with the most familiar illustrations; while their attention is at once riveted by the exhibition of pictures, maps, articles of common school apparatus, simultaneous recitations, and other objects which appeal to the senses."

From the beginning, the principle difficulties of the missionaries to the Chippewa appear to have been the unsettled mode of Indian life, the opposition of the Indians who clung to their old religious beliefs and the influence of the Roman Catholic Church in the region.

In 1832, by the Treaty of Rock River, the Winnebago agreed to move from their Wisconsin home to the Iowa Reservation.

Soon after the ratification of the treaty, Father Samuel Mazachelli applied to Governor George B. Porter of Michigan Territory, petitioning that the education of the Winnebago children be entrusted to the Catholic Church. His application came too late, however, for the Reverend Daniel Lowry of the Cumberland Presbyterian Church had already been appointed as the government teacher. This misunderstanding began a long and bitter struggle between the Catholics and Protestants over the education of the Winnebago. Mazachelli's fight was seconded by the American Fur Company whose agents were adverse to any education and self-support of the Indians. Moreover, the Winnebago agent at that time was bitterly opposed to the influences of the American Fur Company among the Indians and favored Lowry's educational plan.

Joseph Rolette, Jr., son of an American Fur Company operator, told the Indians that Lowry had come to make their children slaves. Even after the school was completed, Lowry had much difficulty in getting enough Indian children to fill it. ...

The efforts of the American Fur Company and the Catholics, however, were not successful in securing the closing of Lowry's school. In 1840 the school was moved from the Yellow River to the Turkey River, also in Iowa. When the Winnebago were removed to Minnesota in 1848 Lowry followed them and kept their school and mission open until they moved to South Dakota in 1863. The Catholic Church did not establish a mission among the Winnebago until 1845.

The first mission to the Shawnee was established by the Missouri Conference of the Methodist Episcopal Church in 1830. The mission owned 2,240 acres of good land, received the Delaware Indian school fund of $4,000 a year for ten years, and the Shawnee school fund of $5,000 a year. With the addition of a large amount of money from the treasury of the Missionary Board, work was begun on the buildings in 1839. Two large brick buildings were erected and, by fall, the school was opened in its new location.

During the first year there were seventy-two pupils in attendance from the Shawnee, Delaware, Chippewa, Gros Ventres, Peoria, Pottawatomie, Kansas, Kickapoo, Munsee and Osage tribes. Not only Indian boys and girls attended the manual labor school, but also the sons and daughters of the neighboring white settlers and the children of Johnson's slaves were numbered among the school's pupils. The enrollment grew to 137 by 1845 and from time to time additional teachers were added to aid the original faculty of four.

In 1845, when the Methodist Episcopal Church was divided over slavery, the Shawnee Indian Mission fell to the Methodist Episcopal Church South. The school continued to grow and in 1848 a classical department, called the Western Academy, was added to it. But the history of the mission, like that of so many others, was to be greatly influenced by the white man's insatiable greed for land. In 1854 the Indians agreed to a treaty whereby they took part of their land in severalty and sold the rest to the government. Three sections of land were deeded to the Methodist Episcopal Church South for the mission, and $10,000 in ten annual payments was to be supplied for the education, board and clothing of a certain number of Indian children for a period of ten years.

The treaty of 1854 also marked the closing of the manual labor part of the school. From that time on the enrollment steadily decreased. When the struggle over "Bleeding Kansas" was at its height, the Shawnee Mission was the center of the milieu. In one of the mission buildings the first territorial legislature of Kansas was held and Thomas Johnson became the president of the territorial council. His last report of the mission school was made in 1862, and sometime between then and 1864 the school was closed. Thus came to an end one of the best of the early mission schools. During the Civil War the old brick buildings of the mission were used as barracks for the soldiers. In 1865, Thomas Johnson, the missionary who for almost a quarter of a century had labored with the Shawnee, was killed by bushwhackers.

The Delaware Tribe was served by two missions, one established by the Methodists and the other by the Baptist. The Methodist mission was established in 1832 by the Reverend William Johnson and Thomas B. Markham. Though a school was established at once, it was unsuccessful and in 1844 an agreement was made with the Shawnee Manual Labor School whereby the Delaware were to devote all of their school fund for ten years to the education of their children at that institution. The tribe, however, was indifferent to education and consequently, attendance at the Shawnee school was irregular.

Hardly had the Methodist mission to the Delaware begun when Baptists established a Delaware mission on the site of the present Edwardsville, Kansas. The Baptists, like the Methodist, had disciplinary difficulty with the children. The Indian pupils did not want to speak English, were adverse to work and especially resented the process of neck and ear scrubbing and delousing. Fearing that corporal punishment would alienate the parents, the mission teachers devised some unique and ridiculous methods of curbing their unruly charges. One of the teachers wrote: "To keep the little ones from mischievously annoying one another we often pinned their aprons over their heads, or tied their hands behind them, even blindfolded them on occasion. If the tongue became unruly, a chip was put between the teeth. Around the yard were numerous stumps, two or three feet high, where the quarrelsome boys were sent to stand, living statues adorning the grounds for a while."

In the far west, in 1836, the American Board of Commissioners for Foreign Missions sent Dr. Marcus Whitman and the Reverend Samuel Parker beyond the Rocky Mountains to determine a site for an Indian mission. After consulting with traders and Indians, they decided that the mission should be established somewhere on the Pacific slope.

Following the Oregon Trail, Dr. Whitman and his party, returning from the east, reached the Hudson's Bay Company post at Walla Walla in September of 1836. Having surveyed the field, the missionary decided to establish two missions, one among the Cayuse not far from Fort Walla Walla, and one on the Clearwater River near the Nez Perce. The women were left at Vancouver while the men proceeded up the Columbia River to begin the erection of the necessary buildings and to start their work among the Indians.

The missionaries began their Indian school at once. Dr. Whitman reported in the spring of 1838 that he had fifteen or twenty children "many of whom had made good proficiency in learning to read the English language." He was, however, handicapped by the lack of books, for the only ones he possessed had been furnished to him by the Methodists at the Willamette mission.

The year 1842, however, marked a change in the mission as quarrels among the missionaries had been going on for some time. This situation, together with the changed attitude on the part of the Indians, brought an order from the American Board that all the missions among the Cayuse and Nez Perce should be closed. The missionaries, however, decided that they would request the Board to postpone final decision until it became acquainted with the new developments in Oregon; thus, they appointed Dr. Whitman to carry this message to Boston. Having received satisfaction from the Board that the Oregon missions might continue as they were, Whitman started back to Oregon in May, this time accompanying a large emigrant train.

The emigrants reached Oregon in early fall, and Dr. Whitman rejoined his station. He found the Cayuse even more opposed to his mission than they had been before he left for the east. Though advised by the representatives of the Hudson's Bay Company that he was in grave danger among the Indians, Dr. Whitman proceeded to make preparations for the building of a church and other buildings and to arrange with the Methodists for taking over the Dalles station. These plans were never to be realized, for on November 29, 1847, occurred the Whitman massacre in which Dr. and Mrs. Whitman and eight members of the mission family lost their lives.

At the time, the massacre was blamed on the influence of the Catholic Church and the American Fur Company representatives, but it has now been established that the tragedy would have occurred even if the Catholics and traders had not been present in the Oregon country. The catastrophe was the result of a combination of causes among which was the ever increasing encroachments of the white people, the slander of ignorant half-breeds and the deaths of many Indians from an epidemic of measles and dysentery which was then sweeping the Oregon Country.

Along the California coast and in the Southwest the Catholic Franciscans continued to educate the Indians. Though Philip de Neve, who was appointed Spanish governor of California in 1777, was hostile to missions and attempted to remove the Indians from their control in all matters except the purely religious, he met such opposition that his plans were never fully carried out. Consequently, the California missions reached the apex of their developments between 1782 and 1810.

With the outbreak of the Hispanic-American wars for independence, Spanish support for the missions was cut off. In 1813 a Spanish law was passed which provided for the secularization of the missions. This was applied to California in 1821. After Mexico secured her independence from Spain in 1822, the dispute over secularization of the missions continued, until 1834 when the California missions were finally removed from the control of the church. As a result, the mission funds and herds were confiscated, mission property was carried away by vandals and the mission Indians were scattered.[5]

THE RELIGIOUS SCHOOL CONTROVERSY

In 1869, in a first-of-its-kind experiment, the Indian agencies in Kansas and Nebraska were placed under the control of the Society of Friends, or Quakers. Beginning in 1870, at President Ulysses S. Grant's urging, all vacated Indian agencies were filled by appointment upon the recommendation of the various religious denominations. Each of the denomination-controlled agencies assumed responsibility for the intellectual and moral education of the Indians under their influence.[1]

Agent–Missionary Feud

Foremost among the reasons for giving religious groups control of the Indian agencies was to secure peace and harmony between Indian agents and missionaries. There had been frequent complaints of Indian agents interfering with the work of missionaries whose religious views often differed from their agent's. This problem was especially acute where Protestant agents dealt with Catholic missionaries. A secondary purpose for giving religious groups control of the agencies was to remove the agencies from the domain of politics.

Religious control of the Indian agencies was far from successful, as most agents failed to appreciate the Indian cultural perspectives and needs. Perhaps more severe was the interdenominational rivalry that developed among many of the religious organizations. The conflict that existed between the Protestants and Catholics, for example, proved to be nothing short of vitriolic, as illustrated in a letter written in 1874 by the Reverend Isaac Baird, Superintendent of the Odanah Indian Mission at Bad River, Wisconsin, to the Commissioner of Indian Affairs.

> If only we could be allowed to labor here undisturbed by others it would
> be a pleasant, cheerful field of labor. Up to the time of the coming of the

Roman Catholic priest among us, a month or two ago, ours was a comparatively united and happy band; but since his arrival they have been split into factions, dissensions have been rife, and the whole band more or less agitated. Fortunately my own people have had comparatively little to do with these dissensions. Still it is a grief to me to witness them. The question continually arises in my mind, why could not the priest have gone elsewhere? There are but a mere handful of his followers here, while there are five or six other reserves in this agency, every one of which is without a missionary, and two or three of these reserves have a largely Catholic population. Now if this man is seeking honestly the glory of God and the good of men, why could he not go to one of these other reserves, where he might have a united people, and where he would have the whole field to himself? This would seem to be the proper course. It seems to me, however, that such interference as we are having here just now on the part of men calling themselves religious teachers ought not to be allowed on an Indian reserve.[2]

By 1882, because of political and religious conflicts, most of the Indian agencies were back under military control.

As discussed in Chapter 4, Indian education prior to 1870 was almost exclusively in the hands of religious organizations. Contract schools, funded by treaty monies and usually controlled by religious groups, expanded in number and cost until by 1892 they consumed more than one-fourth of the federal Indian school budget. (The total school budget in 1892 was $2,291,650, of which $611,570 went to religious bodies.) A good overview of the contemporary state of sectarian schools is given in an 1892 report of the General Assembly of the Presbyterian Church.

... [T]here are at present two kinds of schools among the Indians— Government schools and contract schools. The Government schools, as their name imports, are founded, supported, and controlled exclusively by the Government. There are three classes: industrial training schools, boarding schools, and day schools. The industrial schools, additional to the ordinary branches of an English education, teach their pupils some trade, handicraft, or industrial art by which they are fitted for the avocations of civilized life. Nineteen of these are now in full and successful operation. The largest, with capacity for the accommodation of 1,000 pupils, is located in Carlisle, Pa.; the others with capacities ranging from 75 to 600 are located chiefly in the far West. They contain altogether some 5,000 Indian youth.

Scattered at irregular intervals over the reservations are large numbers of boarding and day schools, whose names sufficiently indicate their general character. They embrace altogether some 9,000 pupils, 6,000 in the boarding and 3,000 in the day schools. For more thorough supervision, the entire Indian country is divided into four districts. Over each is a superintendent, whose duty is to visit and ascertain the exact condition of any school in his district and report the facts fully to the Indian bureau for their information and guidance.

It is the policy of the Government to give a thorough English education, and to instruct in the duties and responsibilities of American citizenship, thus doing for the children of the Indians precisely what the common schools are doing for the children of foreigners who are crowding to our shores—assimilating and Americanizing them. Unsectarian from the beginning, they have recently been made nonpartisan by the introduction of the civil-service rules. Since their first establishment, as they have been continually perfecting themselves from the lessons of an ever-enlarging experience, they have been steadily growing in the confidence of the Government and Congress. No better evidence of this can be found than the constantly increasing appropriations for their support from year to year. In 1877 the appropriations for Indian schools was $20,000; in 1892 it is $2,291,650.

The Government schools, in the judgment of your committee, have now reached a position as to numbers, equipment, and methods of instruction and discipline, and general efficiency, where the whole work of common-school education among the Indians may be safely and wisely intrusted to them. Additional to these Government schools, and often side-by-side with them, are the contract schools. They are called so because the Government entered into a contract with certain religious societies for their joint support and control. They were founded originally by the different churches as mission schools, and were of course sectarian. The Government schools at first encountered the most strenuous opposition, could receive only the most meager appropriation, and, with the means provided, could accomplish almost nothing. Finding the mission schools at hand, often in the very locality they wished to occupy, instead of founding new schools, they resolved to subsidize the mission school, and so the experiment of contract schools was entered upon. By the terms of the contract school the Government was to appropriate a certain amount of the public money, and was to be admitted to a certain measure of control, on condition that the sectarian schools should cease to be sectarian so far forth as to avoid the appearance of sectarianism. The plan was essentially a vicious one, and could never have been designed to be permanent. Under its operation friction was inevitable, and an ever-increasing antagonism, defeating the chief end of both parties, was sure to arise. Whatever seeming necessities may have existed for its adoption at first, and whatever temporary advantages may have been received by it in the experimental stages of Indian education, the time has now fully come, in the judgment of your committee, for a complete severance between Government and sectarian schools.[3]

The Protestant–Catholic Feud

At this time the Protestant denominations began to withdraw from the contract school system for reasons they ascribed to separation of church and state. They urged all religious denominations to do the same. The Catholics—who by this time far outstripped individual Protestant denominations in the number of mission schools they administered and the amount of federal Indian funds they received—refused. They saw in the Protestants' move a conspiracy to evict the Bureau of Catholic Indian Missions from contract education. The bureau charged that Protestant objections to sectarian education stemmed from disgruntlement over Catholic success in the area. Furthermore, because Protestant denominations taken together formed the dominant religious group in the nation, the Catholic bureau believed that the Protestants would be able to exert religious influence over secular Indian schools.

On the administrative front, the Bureau of Catholic Indian Missions questioned the assertion made by the Protestant-dominated Indian Rights Association that funds used in educating Indians were federal funds; the Catholic bureau viewed education funds as treaty and trust funds belonging to the Indians.

The money under discussion was no small amount. In 1890, the Bureau of Catholic Indian Missions received appropriations totaling $356,957. The gap between Catholic and individual Protestant denominations was large; in the same year the Presbyterians, who were second to the Catholics in funding, received only $47,650. Three other denominations—Congregational, Episcopal, and Friends—received about the half the amount appropriated to the Presbyterians, and a number of groups received amounts under $10,000. Writing in 1892, Joseph T. Smith, chairman of the General Assembly of the Presbyterian Church, explained the disproportionate funding:

> This enormous disproportion can not be attributed to any undue favoritism on the part of Congress or to any superiority in the Catholic over the Protestant schools. It arises from the fact that the Catholic Church is administratively one and can bring its united influence to bear for its own advancement. There is a Catholic Indian bureau established in Washington which concentrates in itself the whole power of the papal hierarchy and wields the entire strength of the papal church. With a united papacy there is at the same time a divided Protestantism. Its unity is no less real than that of the papacy, but it has no common organ, no federal head, no council or bureau to represent it. In the absence of such, each particular denomination acts apart and in seeming rivalry with all the rest, each seeking to advance its own special interests. Of course, the divided weakness of Protestantism is overborne by the united strength of Romanism.

When the Presbyterian or the Methodist ask for an appropriation for his school, he asks only for a small section of Protestantism separated from, if not in actual antagonism with, all other sections. Were there a Protestant bureau in Washington or anywhere else, speaking in the name of all and representing the real unity of Protestant Christians, the present state of things could never have arisen, and having arisen, could not be maintained for an hour.[4]

In subsequent years, funding fell off. In 1895 the Catholic share grew to $359,215 and the Lutherans doubled their appropriation to $15,120, but funding for other groups was reduced or eliminated altogether. The following year even more denominations dropped out of the program, including the Lutherans. By 1897 only the Catholic church continued to receive federal Indian funds, and those in diminishing amounts.[5]

The selections that follow, taken from the annual reports of the Board of Indian Commissioners, candidly present the positions of the Protestant and Catholic churches in this feud. Perhaps more important than the opposing viewpoints is the manner in which the Indians were only obliquely mentioned. Historian Francis Paul Prucha observed that "one cannot help escape the conclusion that in the battles described here the Indians were on the outside, the ones in whose name the religious groups fought but with little direct part in the events." Prucha argued that the Indians were "but pawns in the hands of the managers of the campaigns."[6] The sectarian education conflict thus centered on the differing Protestant and Catholic societal views (since both believed the Indians had to be Christianized) rather than on the educational rights of the Indian communities.

ANTISECTARIAN CONTRACT SCHOOL ARGUMENTS
by Reverend James M. King (1892 Board of Commissioners)

In representing The National League for the Protection of American Institutions before this conference, I desire it to be clearly understood that we have nothing to say in opposition to the contract schools which are not under denominational control. It is against the partnership between the National Government and the churches that we contend, are a dangerous step in the direction of the union of church and state. ...

The Commissioner of Indian Affairs in his report for 1892 says: "There has been during the past year a great deal of public discussion regarding the matter of contract schools, and there is a very general consensus of opinion among the great masses of the people that the work of education for the Indians should be carried on either by the Government, through its own agencies, or by individuals and churches, at their own expense. The appropriation of public funds for sectarian uses is almost universally condemned; and, while there has been no radical change in the policy of the Government regarding this matter, there has been a very practical change in the attitude of the churches."

Since I last addressed this conference remarkable progress has been made in the divorce proceedings between the churches and the Government.

Be it said to its credit, the Baptist Church has never taken any funds from the National Treasury for sectarian Indian education.

The General Conference of the Methodist Episcopal Church, in May 1892, took the following action:

"Whereas the appropriation of public funds for sectarian purposes by the national Government is not only wrong in principle, but in violation of both the letter and spirit of the Constitution of the United States: Therefore,

"Resolved, That this General Conference of the Methodist Episcopal Church requests the missionary societies working under its sanction or control to decline either to petition for or to receive from the national Government any moneys for educational work among the Indians."[7]

King goes on to quote similar resolutions and actions by Presbyterian, Episcopal, and Congregational churches, as well as the American Missionary Association and Quakers. The Unitarian, Lutheran, and Mennonite churches never received large sums from the government, and King predicted that they would soon refuse all funds. His comments resume:

The National League made the same appeal to withdraw from the receipt of national funds for Indian education to the Bureau of Catholic Indian Missions that it made to the missionary boards of the other religious denominations. The only response received was from Bishop Marty, president of the bureau.

The bishop contended that "the money given to them (the Indians) is not raised by taxation. It is not public money, but private property of the Indian tribes and families, belonging to them as payment for ceded lands." The records of the Indian Department prove the bishop to be entirely in error in this matter. He asserts that "the Indian schools are not benefiting the denomination, but the Indians alone." He argues for the religious training of the youth, with which we all agree, and closes with the admirable assurance that "the church will endeavor to provide for her own, no matter what the state may do."

The question is raised, if all the churches but one withdraw, will not the remaining one get all of the money and more of the schools? My response is, first, if that should prove to be the result, it affords no reason for the violation by religious bodies of a sacred principle involving American institutions. Secondly, if only one church seeks and secures funds for its own sectarian uses from the national Treasury, while all the other churches withdraw and protest, the question comes to be one of the definite union of church and state; and this the American people would not long endure.

Let us no farther make an attempt at the solution of the question of Indian education which embarrasses the solution of broader questions. Let us not make him the prey of denominational bickerings. Give him the American public school, or its equivalent, and then let religious denominations prove their faith by their works, and try to Christianize him. When the churches know that they can no longer depend upon the Government for money to prosecute their mission work among the Indians, and the work is put upon their consciences, they will take care of it and push more successfully than they do now. This will be the inevitable result.

This question forces sectarianism into politics, and makes cowards of law makers. All over this country at the present time the power of ecclesiasticism is asserting itself in local, state, and national political issues. It is a present and pressing peril.

Rev. J. A. Stephan, of the Bureau of Catholic Indian Missions, makes a vigorous and unscrupulous attack, in a pamphlet of 32 pages, upon the Government schools, for one reason because they have the Protestant Bible and gospel hymns in them. He also attacks the President of the Republic, the Secretary of the Interior, and the Commissioner of Indian Affairs; and this pamphlet, we understand, is sent to every Roman Catholic priest in the Republic. This is the essence of partisan politics.

In this Columbia year it becomes us to remember that our civilization is not Latin, because God did not permit North America to be settled and controlled by that civilization. The Huguenot, the Hollander, and the Puritan created our civilization. Let us not put a premium by national grants on a rejected civilization in the education of a race who were here when Columbus came.

The assumption that Indians can not be taught in the Bible and in the fundamentals of the Christian religion without Government aid to the sects is a fallacy. Let the churches push their work and pay their own bills. Why keep on treating the Indians differently in religious and educational matters from our treatment of other races, and then expect the same results? We don't parcel out other races to the sects.

If the churches do a Christian work among the Indians that is entirely dependent upon appropriations from the Government, it is not of a sufficiently vigorous character to do much uplifting. The Indians know they are wards and in a sense pensioners and if the proposed christianization depends upon Government money bounty, the same as their rations, the effect must it have upon the more thoughtful among them? Christian benevolence and Christian character are both robbed of their power.

Let us face some facts.

While some of these sectarian contract schools are doing excellent work in preparing Indian children for intelligent and loyal citizenship, many are not. I know the facts, and it is my duty to state that much Roman Catholic teaching among the Indians does not prepare them for intelligent and loyal citizenship. The solution of the Indian problem consists in educating them for citizenship, as we educate other races.

This conference, if its action is to be effectual, must recognize principle, and not be controlled by policy. ...

Let the churches wash their hands of all responsibility in the matter of the division of the national school funds for Indian education on sectarian lines, and the patriotic citizenship will defend and perfect the public schools in the states.[8]

Speaking on behalf of the Presbyterian Church, Reverend Dr. William Roberts asked the following questions of the Board of Indian Commissioners in 1894:

1. Is it the intention of the Government to put into its own treasury the funds which the Christian churches decline to accept? If so, Presbyterians believe that great injustice will be done to the Indians. Even if every dollar of this saved money is afterwards given to the tribes for food, farming implements, and home comforts, it will not be half so valuable as education would be to them in early life. The guardian in such a case would not be doing, in our judgment, the best possible thing for his ward.

2. Or is it the intention of the Government to ask Congress for the same amount of appropriation and give the whole of it to those churches which are willing to accept it? That will be deemed an outrage, for the whole or nearly the whole of it in that case would go to the Roman Catholic Church. That is the only body at present which introduces into the schools sectarian doctrines and forms of worship, which has furnished any ground for the charge of the union of church and state. Such a course will inevitably bring upon the Government the anathemas of all the Protestant denominations in our land. The synods and the general assemblies of the church I have the honor to represent will certainly continue to issue their protests against it until such a practice ceases.

3. Or is it, on the other hand, the purpose of the Government to ask for the same amount of appropriations from Congress and spend it all in the multiplication and betterment of its own schools? If this be the plan, I am sure the Presbyterian Church will aid the Government by all means in her power. She will use her utmost endeavor to supply the religious element which it can not supply for the civilization and Christianization of the Indians.[9]

Unlike the Protestant churches, the Catholic Church (Bureau of Catholic Indian Missions) believed that treaty and trust monies belonged to the Indians and therefore were not public monies subject to the sectarian limitations. The Indians were then, according to this view, free to use their money for sectarian education. Furthermore, the Catholic Church saw a Protestant plot to evict the church from the field of Indian education—and consequently secure for the Protestant denominations an unchallenged right to teach Indian children dominant Protestant values through the public, nonsectarian school system.

PROSECTARIAN VIEWPOINT OF THE CATHOLIC CHURCH
The Bureau of Catholic Indian Missions
Washington, D.C., December 14, 1893

The Bureau of Catholic Indian Missions, for the current fiscal year, conducts the following schools under contract with the United States Government: thirty-nine boarding schools, with 3,265 pupils, and thirteen day schools, with 292 pupils. The total compensation for the above service amounts to $369,535.

In addition to the foregoing the Bureau of Catholic Indian Missions supports five other Indian schools at its own expense. About $50,000 for support of teachers and scholars is expended by the Catholics themselves ...

I think the idea that any important element of American society really desires the withdrawal of all religious influence from the Indians may be dismissed without discussion. The indications are strong that the most vehement of those who demand secularization of Indian education are to be found among the narrow class of sectaries, and that their insistence upon the secular theory of education is not ingenuous, but is only a cloak for ulterior designs of a practically sectarian character.

Speaking without regard to church or creed, I believe it to be the universal judgment of all competent persons who have been brought in contact with the Indian problem, that its solution in respect to Indian civilization is impossible upon a strictly non-religious basis. To civilize the Indian, to awaken and vivify his moral nature, he must be brought to an understanding of the existence, the power, the omnipresence, omniscience, and the perfect justice and goodness of the Supreme Being ...

This view of the matter being accepted, it appears to me idle to accord any weight to the demands for nonsectarian education, because, if we are to give the Indians, and the Indian children especially, any Christian teaching whatever, that teaching will be, and in the very nature of things must be, sectarian ... If any Christian teaching at all be allowed, is not that sectarian as between Christians and Jews, Buddists and Atheists? Equally, much might be taught that would be nonsectarian as between the views of the leading Protestant denominations, but which would be sectarian as to Catholics. It may be set down as axiom that whatever religious instruction our Indians are to receive will be sectarian, no matter what policy or system may be adopted; nothing else is possible ...

It matters not whether the Indian school be Government, contract, denominational, or secular, the conscientious teacher in it will teach the truths of Christianity, and necessarily will teach them in accordance with the light he has received through the teachings of his particular creed and religious organization. No religious denomination, no individual adherent of one, when placed in charge of an Indian school, will be confined to the teaching of only the natural branches of learning. On the contrary, the most extreme claimants for secularization now would be found incorporating all the elements of their peculiar religious systems in the Indian schools when once they had control, and the sectarian phenomena of "rivals," Young Men's Christian associations, Christian Endeavor societies, King's Daughters, and so on, would be introduced in the "nonsectarian" schools as they have been hitherto. God forbid that I should find fault with any honest effort to Christianize the Indians.

What I do object to is that the effort now being made to secularize, to "nonsectarize" the Indian schools, is a dishonest, hypocritical one, whose sole aim and purpose it is to drive the Catholic Church out of the Indian educational and missionary field, in which it has gained glorious laurels, and to substitute for its influence and teachings the influence and teachings of other religious bodies.

... It is not only the duty but the pride of those who represent the various churches in Indian school contracts to ... maintain high standards of moral and secular training in order to reflect credit upon the religious body represented ...

The denominational contract schools are not only good but economical. While the Government pays on most of the contracts from $108 to $125, and in only a few cases $150 per capita per annum, and this strictly for only those children who actually attend the schools, the Government schools, as the record shows, cost at least $300 (and often over) per capita per annum, in addition to salaries of teachers which form a fixed charge, whether the attendance of pupils be 1 or 100. It is a fact, which the records of the Indian office will demonstrate, that the Government schools have all proven relatively expensive, and some of them otherwise objectionable.

I am sorry that I have to call attention to a cry raised of late by certain religious anarchists who call upon the country to behold how much public money the Catholic Church is drawing from the National Treasury for the support of sectarian Indian schools! ... These professed enemies of religious Indian education are careful to conceal the fact that the money is not public money, but is Indian money, the little all of a tangible nature that the poor red men have left of all their once vast possessions. The duty on the part of the Government to use it for the benefits of the Indians in the most economical manner possible, and the further and no less plain and important duty to use it with reasonable reference to the wishes of the Indians themselves, are never mentioned by these "nonsectarian" adversaries. It does not come out of the National Treasury, and it does not go to the church ... The buildings, other improvements, facilities, salaries of teachers, matrons, etc., have been freely contributed by this much-abused church or its members, and, as stated before, the charity of Catholics for such purposes has already reached the important sum of $1,500,000 and over.

If the amount paid for the support and education of Indian children in Catholic institutions appears large in comparison with amounts paid for the same service under other denominational effort, it is only because the Catholic community has used its charity, zeal, and organization in response to the invitation and avowed policy of the Government to a more liberal extent than have others. If one individual boards, feeds, and clothes 150 persons at the rate of $3 per week, while another does the same for only 25 persons, is the first obnoxious to public policy because his allowance amounts to $450, while that of the second is only $75? The argument of our enemies is a ridiculous one.

In God's name, are there not thousands of Indian youth whose wild untutored souls are crying aloud for the enlightenment of the Gospel, and human knowledge as well ... ?

From this, or any other good work, the Catholic Church does not desire to shut out adherents of any Christian communion. The Catholic Church only objects and regrets that it is not love for the Indian that underlies the "nonsectarian" clamor, but pharisaical hatred of itself.[10]

Whose Money Is It?

Congress acquiesced to the demands of the Protestant churches in 1895 by limiting federal spending for sectarian education among the Indians. Between 1896 and 1900 federal appropriations for sectarian Indian education were reduced on the average of 20 percent per year.

Beginning in fiscal year 1901 no federal appropriations were made for sectarian education.

The Bureau of Catholic Indian Missions, believing that educational funds were tribal monies, continued to push for federal funding of its schools. However, Indian Commissioner William Jones supported the "Browning Ruling." Issued by Commissioner Daniel Browning in 1896, the ruling required all Indian superintendents to fill government day schools before allowing Indian children to attend mission schools. For the most part the Browning ruling affected Catholic schools because there were few Protestant mission schools still in existence. In 1901, Jones changed his stance, tentatively allowing Indian children to attend mission schools as long as such attendance did not prove "detrimental to the Indian children."[11]

Largely for political reasons, President Theodore Roosevelt responded favorably to the Bureau of Catholic Indian Missions' requests for funds. By 1904 eight contracts were signed with the Catholic bureau and one with the Lutheran Board of Indian Missions, totaling nearly $100,000. The contracts had barely been consummated, however, when the Indian Rights Association renewed its opposition.

From the start the association contemplated a court challenge to the Catholic contracts, seeking to establish a clear separation of church and state. However, for fear of a possible setback in the federal courts (and lack of financial support from the Protestant churches to wage a court battle), the Indian Rights Association pressured Congress to amend the Indian Appropriation Act of 1906 to prohibit the use of any federally appropriated monies for sectarian education. The amendment was unsuccessfully argued in Congress and failed to be enacted.

In an attempt to clarify the confusion over sectarian funding, Roosevelt wrote in 1906:

> There are two kinds of Indian funds involved in this matter. One is the trust fund, which requires no appropriation by the Congress, and which clearly is to be administered as the Indians themselves request. As regards this fund, you will treat it on the assumption that the Indians have the right to say how it shall be used, so far as choosing the schools to which their children are to go is concerned; and each Indian in a tribe is to be credited with his pro rata share of the funds, which you will apply for him to the Government school where that is the school used, or to the church school where that is the school used, instead of segregating any portion of the fund for the support of the Government school and prorating the balance.
>
> The other fund consists of moneys appropriated by Congress in pursuance of treaty stipulations. As to these moneys it is uncertain whether or not the prohibition by Congress of their application for contract schools applies; that is, whether or not we have the power legally to use these moneys, as we

clearly have the power to use the trust funds. It appears that certain of the contract schools are now being run in the belief that my letter quoted above (which noted that "the practice of making contracts with certain mission schools will be continued by the Department unless Congress should decree to the contrary, or, of course, unless the courts should decide that the decision of the Department of Justice is erroneous.") authorized the use of treaty funds. It would be a great hardship, in the absence of any clearly defined law on the subject, to cut them off at this time arbitrarily; and inasmuch as there is a serious question involved, I direct that until the close of the fiscal year these schools be paid for their services out of the moneys appropriated by Congress in pursuance of treaty obligations, on the same basis as the schools paid out of trust funds—always exercising the precaution to see that any petition by the Indians is genuine, and that the money appropriated for any given school represents only the pro rata proportion to which the Indians making the petition are entitled. But no new contracts are to be entered into for such payments from these funds after the close of the present fiscal year, unless there is authorization by Congress or some determination by the courts.[12]

Educational contracts for fiscal year 1906 were withheld pending an attorney general's opinion requested by President Roosevelt. In 1906 the attorney general opined that mission education funds were trust and treaty monies belonging to the Indian tribes, not the federal government. Thus, even though the funds were on deposit in the federal treasury, they belonged to the tribes; the federal fiduciary responsibility required the executive branch to maintain such funds to be expended for the Indians.[13] Soon after the attorney general's opinion, the Indian Rights Association instituted an injunction suit in the federal courts.

In May of 1908, the U.S. Supreme Court heard the case of *Reuben Quick Bear v. Leupp* on appeal from the Court of Appeals for the District of Columbia. The court held that funding for sectarian education was legal, because treaty and trust fund monies belonged to the Indian tribes and thus were not public monies appropriated by Congress. Chief Justice Fuller delivered the opinion of the court:

We concur in the decree of the Court of Appeals of the District and the reasoning by which its conclusion is supported, as set forth in the opinion of Wright J., speaking for the court.

The validity of the contract for $27,000 is attacked on the ground that all contracts for sectarian education among the Indians are forbidden by certain provisos contained in the Indian Appropriation Acts of 1895, 1896, 1897, 1898 and 1899. But if those provisos relate only to the appropriations made by the Government out of the public moneys of the United States raised by taxation from persons of all creeds and faiths, or none at all, and appropriated gratuitously for the purpose of education among the Indians themselves, then the contract must be sustained. The difference between one class of appropriations and the other has long been recognized in the annual appropriation acts. The gratuitous appropriation of public moneys for the purpose of Indian education has always been made under the heading "Support of Schools," whilst the appropriation of the "Treaty Fund" has always been under the heading "Fulfilling Treaty Stipulations and Support of Indian Tribes," and that from the "Trust Fund" is not in the Indian Appropriation Acts at all. One class of appropriations relates to public moneys belonging to the Government; the other to moneys which belong to the Indians and which is administered for them by the Government ...

In the appropriation act of 1896 ... appears the express, "and it is hereby declared to be the settled policy of the Government to hereafter make no appropriation whatever for education in any sectarian school." This limitation, if it can be given effect as such, manifestly applies to the use of public moneys gratuitously appropriated for such purpose, and not to moneys belonging to the Indians themselves ...

As has been shown, in 1868 the United States made a treaty with the Sioux Indians, under which the Indians made large cessions of land and other rights. In consideration of this the United States agreed that for every thirty children a house should be provided and a teacher competent to teach the elementary branches of our English education should be furnished for twenty years. In 1877, in consideration of further land cessions, the United States agreed to furnish all necessary aid to assist the Indians in the work of civilization and furnish them schools and instruction in mechanical and agricultural arts, as provided by the Treaty of 1868. In 1889 Congress extended the obligation of the treaty for twenty years, subject to such modifications as Congress should deem most effective, to secure the Indians equivalent benefits of such education. Thereafter, in every annual Indian appropriation act, there was an appropriation to carry out the terms of this treaty, under the heading "Fulfilling Treaty Stipulations with and Support of Indian Tribes."

These appropriations rested on different grounds from the gratuitous appropriations of public moneys under the heading "Support of Schools." The two subjects were separately treated in each act, and, naturally, as they are essentially different in character. One is the gratuitous appropriation of public moneys for the purpose of Indian education, but the "Treaty Fund" is not public money in this sense. It is the Indians' money, or at least is dealt with by the Government as if it belonged to them, as morally it does. It differs from the "Trust Fund" in this: The "Trust Fund" has been set aside for the Indians and the income expended for their benefit, which expenditure required no annual appropriation. The whole amount due the Indians for certain land cessions was appropriated in one lump sum by the act of 1889. This "Trust

Fund" is held for the Indians and not distributed per capita, being held as property in common. The money is distributed in accordance with the discretion of the Secretary of the Interior, but really belongs to the Indians. The President declared it to be the moral right of the Indians to have the "Trust Fund" applied to the education of the Indians in the schools of their choice, and the same view was entertained by the Supreme Court of the District of Columbia and the Court of Appeals of the District. But the "Treaty Fund" has exactly the same characteristics. They are moneys belonging really to the Indians. They are the price of land ceded by the Indians to the Government. The only difference is that in the "Treaty Fund" the debt to the Indians created and secured by the treaty is paid by annual appropriations. They are not gratuitous appropriations of public moneys, but the payment, as we repeat, of a treaty debt in installments. We perceive no justification for applying the proviso or declaration of policy to the payment of treaty obligations, the two things being distinct and different in nature and having no relation to each other, except that both are technically appropriations.

Some reference is made to the Constitution ... on the ground that the actions of the United States were to always be undenominational, and that, therefore, the Government can never act in a sectarian capacity, either in the use of its own funds or in that of the funds of others, in respect of which it is a trustee; hence that even the Sioux trust fund cannot be applied for education in Catholic schools, even though the owners of the fund so desire it. But we cannot concede the proposition that Indians cannot be allowed to use their own money to educate their children in the schools of their own choice because the Government is necessarily undenominational, as it cannot make any law respecting an establishment of religion or prohibiting the free exercise thereof. The Court of Appeals well said:

> "The 'Treaty' and 'Trust' moneys are the only moneys that the Indians can lay claim to as matter of right; the only sums on which they are entitled to rely as theirs for education; and while these moneys are not delivered to them in hand, yet the money must not only be provided, but be expended, for their benefit and in part for their education; it seems inconceivable that Congress should have intended to prohibit them from receiving religious education at their own cost if they so desired it; such an intent would be one 'to prohibit the free exercise of religion' amongst the Indians, and such would be the effect of the construction for which the complainants contend."

The cestuis que trust cannot be deprived of their rights by the trustee in the exercise of power implied.[14]

6

TRIBALLY CONTROLLED
EDUCATION: 1819–1915

THE EXPERIENCE OF the Five Civilized Tribes (Cherokee, Creek, Choctaw, Chickasaw, and Seminole) is unique in the history of Indian education. The Five Tribes, particularly the Cherokee and the Choctaw, recognized the value of the "white man's" education and sought funding for education in their treaties with the United States. Among the Five Tribes (to a lesser degree among the Seminole) there were three distinct phases of educational management. In the early years, as was discussed in chapters 4 and 5, the federal government used treaty funds to support mission schools. In this way the federal government sought to discourage the "perpetuation of the indigenous cultures." [1] The 1791 Treaty of Holston, for example, provided funds that were to be used to assist the Cherokee youth to attain "a greater degree of civilization." [2] Similar provisions were in the 1790 treaty with the Creek Nation.

Over the course of the next eight decades, numerous treaty provisions provided educational funds for the Five Tribes. In the 1825 Choctaw Treaty, for example, the United States pledged "six thousand dollars, annually, forever" for the support of Choctaw education. [3] In later years educational funding became contingent upon the tribes' removal to the West. Following passage of the Indian Removal Act in 1830 and the westward migration of the Five Tribes, the second phase of educational management began: tribal management. In this phase the Five Tribes applied treaty funds to a national system of self-directed education. Except for disbursing funds to private or mission schools from the Civilization Act, the federal government exercised little control over the educational pursuits of the Five Tribes in the Indian Territory. For example, the 1855 Treaty with the Choctaw and Chickasaw provided "a permanent annuity of six thousand dollars for education." [4] Article seven of the 1856 Treaty with the Creek Nation provided the following:

It being the desire of the Creek people to employ their own teachers, mechanics, and farmers, all of the funds secured to the nation for educational, mechanical, and agricultural purposes, shall as the same become annually due, be paid over by the United States to the treasurer of the Creek Nation.[5]

The 1866 Cherokee treaty called for 35 percent of the proceeds from all Cherokee funds to be applied for the support of Cherokee schools.[6] As these treaty examples illustrate, prior to the dissolution of their governments, the Five Tribes applied tribal funds to their education themselves. Of the Five Tribes, the Choctaw and Cherokee established the most unique system and operated the most extensive network of tribally controlled schools, with over two hundred schools and academies between them.

The tribally controlled educational system operated very successfully, providing an education that satisfied most of the needs of the tribes. Where the tribes were unable to provide for the higher educational needs of their members, tribal funds were used to send students to the some of the most prestigious of American institutions of higher learning.

The third phase of educational management commenced after the enactment of the Curtis Act in 1898 when the federal government dissolved the tribal governments. The tribal governments were patterned after the Constitution of the United States and operated under a legislative, executive and judicial branch system. They acted independently of the United States in the operation and management of their own schools systems. At this point educational institutions fell under the auspices of the Secretary of the Interior and later under the Oklahoma school system.

The documented result of the loss of tribal control over the education of their youth was nothing short of phenomenal: among the Cherokee a 90 percent literacy rate became a 40 percent illiteracy rate within several decades of federal and state control. The primary cause for such educational atrophy, according to scholar Alfred Wahrhaftig, was the "almost complete alienation of the Cherokee community from the white-controlled public school systems."[7]

The Rise and Fall of Tribal Schools

The development of the remarkable tribally controlled educational systems operating in the Indian Territory is described by Helen M. Scheirbeck in *They Ran Their Own Schools: Education in the Five Civilized Tribes, 1819–1915*.

After their removal to Indian Territory, in the 1830's, the Five Civilized Tribes renewed their interest in developing school systems. The importance they gave to education is reflected in the level of financial commitment to school funds that were made in the various treaties with the United States Government. In the treaties and in the constitutions and laws that the tribes adopted, lands were reserved on which to build neighborhood schools and mission and other boarding schools, including academies or high schools, and institutions of higher learning. Treaties provided much of the money for school funds, often from the sale of lands that the tribe had ceded to the United States.

Tribal constitutions and laws set up organizational structures to carry forward their educational programs. Whether the structure was headed by a Superintendent of Schools or by a School Board, exact requirements were spelled out concerning the school program, the staff, the operating expenses, the student admission policy and enrollment. The staff at the neighborhood level was required to report to the Principal Chief or to the National Council. School officials, such as superintendents and local trustees, were held accountable for what happened in their districts. Along with other reports, the teaching and administrative staffs of the schools were required to indicate which students had been in attendance and which had been absent.

The educational efforts of these schools were quite successful because of tribal involvement in education at all levels of authority; the assessing and reporting activities in the schools themselves also made for successful education endeavors. Although authority was delegated to a superintendent or board, both the tribal executive and the tribal legislature held the authority for final confirmation of hiring and final approval of requisitions for money. This authority, plus the reports they received relating to current conditions, number of students and expenditures, gave them a fairly accurate basis for assessing what had been achieved and what was needed for the coming year.

The Choctaws seem to have taken the lead in establishing an educational system, and theirs was used as a pattern by the Creeks, Chickasaws, and Seminoles. By 1835 there was a real movement to establish and operate their own schools in their own communities in the West.

The Commissioner of Indian Affairs reported in 1833, that the Choctaws wished to use their removal money for education. Twelve schools were to be built in the West, and the teachers were to be "stable married men." Both females and males were to attend the schools. Reading, writing, arithmetic, and English grammar were to be taught; courses such as husbandry for the boys and spinning for the girls were also taught. In addition, three other schools of a higher level were to be established.

By 1837 the Cherokees had four schools and one printing office located in Indian Territory. According to the Superintendent of the Western Territory, the Cherokees "generally showed a great deal of improvement, and would soon equal whites but for alcohol." The Choctaws were also showing rapid progress during this time. Two of their public school teachers were Natives. Choctaw Academy was sending home well-educated men and the hope was to fill most of the schools with native teachers. There was a strong desire to use native teachers in the schools of all the Five Civilized Tribes.

One of the earliest educators among the Creeks and Seminoles was Dr. R. M. Loughridge. He founded numerous schools in the early settlement of Indian Territory, and remained to rebuild schools after the Civil War. Lilah Denton Lindsey, a Creek student, reminiscing about a conversation she had with Dr. Loughridge, remembers him talking about his work this way:

> The Tullahassee Mission was a large three story brick building. The Board sent out teachers and I was appointed Superintendent. The first day of March, 1850, found us ready to commence the school. Out-buildings were erected such as stables, corn-cribs, fences, etc., cattle, horses, wagons and teams had been purchased, furniture for the building and provision of all kinds, books, paper, etc., had been provided, and the school was opened with thirty pupils. Our full number of eighty was not received until fall because it was deemed best to begin with a few and get them under training before the whole number of raw recruits should arrive. Later, experience proved the wisdom of the course.

> The exercises were conducted on the manual plan and the usual time of six hours daily was spent in study. The pupils were employed about two hours daily in some useful exercises, the boys working on the farm, in the garden, or chopping firewood, and the girls in household duties, assisting in sewing, cooking, washing, and the care of the dining-room. The children were provided with three good meals a day and abundant time given for sleep and recreation. Religious exercises were regularly kept up, preaching on Sabbath and prayers morning and evening through the week. Daily, at the supper table, in connection with singing and prayer, every pupil was expected to recite a verse of scripture.

Three types of schools existed, to some degree, among all the Five Civilized Tribes. They were the tribal neighborhood schools, the tribal boarding schools, conducted under contracts with various religious denominations, and the male and female academies or seminaries operated under contract with religious denominations or private individuals. In a sense, all of them were tribal schools. Those operated through the contracting power of the tribes were financed in large measure with interest on treaty funds, added to what private organizations or individuals raised for the schools.

Many written statements of the tribes, the Federal Government, and private organizations recognized the need for educating and civilizing the children of these tribes. However, the various missionaries and federal officials saw a need to convince themselves that Indians could be educated just like the whites. Therefore, many of the schools which operated under contract with the tribes almost became showplaces for what the students could do, especially at commencement time. The end of the school year was not only a time for review and examination, but it was also a great social occasion. Public officials from the tribe, parents, and distinguished visitors all came to hear and participate in this affair. Later, after the examination, a great feast was spread and everyone had time to renew acquaintances and enjoy seeing old friends.

By 1859, the schools among the Five Civilized Tribes reached their maximum level of enrollment and development of facilities. The tribal governments had made a strong organizational and financial commitment to educational activities. Each of the tribes had its own newspaper and printing press, so that the native language as well as English could be used in the printed work. The Cherokees, through the work of George Guess (Sequoyah), had succeeded in developing their own alphabet. This permitted them to excel in the development of specialized primers, books, and newspapers.

With the Civil War came a great division of political loyalties within each of the tribes. During the war years, their country was overrun, and the schools and churches were closed.

In 1866, as soon as new peace treaties were signed with the United States, each of the Five Civilized Tribes began reestablishing its educational system. Most of the schools had either been burned or used for military installations during the war. Thus, a great deal of money was needed for restoring them to a usable state. In the treaties of 1866, the United States Government, in return for concessions, reinstated the financial clauses of the old treaties and agreed to renew payments on all annuities. These enabled the Five Civilized Tribes to begin rebuilding their schools.

The Chickasaw Tribe is an excellent example of the post-Civil War development of tribal schools—the growth of several types of tribal schools; the attitude of public officials and tribal leaders towards the educational endeavors of the tribe; the effectiveness of the system in terms of preparing Indian children for life in their communities; and later, the undermining of the tribal school system as a result of the movement toward Oklahoma statehood.

Neighborhood schools were central to the life of the Chickasaw:

> As the country or village school in the States was the heart
> of the rural life of the community, so these schools
> represent the true nature of the Chickasaw Indian; most
> of these schools were built in the full-blood communities
> with native teachers and trustees. Much Chickasaw was
> spoken in the schools although classes were conducted in
> English. The school houses were erected and equipped
> by the community, or by some individual within the
> community, often being built from the lumber at hand;
> the cost was covered, at least in a number of cases,
> through appropriations by the National Legislature.

The great concern of the Chickasaw legislature to provide a meaningful, well-organized, and properly managed school system is evident by their desire to make educational opportunities available to all the people in the Nation:

> The Chickasaws were very eager to supply teachers, at
> least for the neighborhood schools, from the Nation
> itself; this desire accounts for the act stating that 'hereaf-
> ter all citizens who may wish to teach school in this nation,
> shall not be required to undergo an examination as to his
> or her qualifications as teacher before being permitted to
> teach said school.' This same act provided for a general-
> ized salary of $450 to be paid each teacher of a neighbor-
> hood school; lengthened the term into a ten month
> session; and stated that no teacher should be allowed to
> take charge of more than thirty scholars. A real step
> forward was taken when the legislature made provision
> for a uniform system of adopted texts to be used through-
> out the Nation. The act reads: 'That the standard of
> school books for the several schools shall be of uniform
> character, and shall be of the Southern series of school
> books, and no other books shall be used or taught in any
> of the schools of this Nation.'

Higher education was stressed both within and outside the boundaries of the five tribes' country. One well-known effort was started by Dr. Almon Bacone, a former teacher at the Cherokee Male Seminary. In 1881 he started the Baptist Academy at Tahlequah with three pupils, and by 1884 the field report on this school indicates the enrollment showed seventy-five students.

By September 1885, he was ready to expand his effort. A portion of land had been obtained from the Creek Council, funds had been raised, and a new building had been dedicated. The Baptist Academy was then re-named the Indian University.

Following Dr. Almon Bacone's death, the school's name was changed to Bacone College and the student body was opened to all the Five Civilized Tribes and eventually to all Indian groups throughout the United States.

That the schools of the Five Civilized Tribes attempted to prepare their students for meaningful citizenship in the tribe is apparent in a talk given on the occasion of a public examination at one of the Chickasaw schools in 1876—certainly they reflect the true spirit of commencement:

> Jesse Bell gave a talk admonishing the children that in a few years they would be called upon by their people to serve as governors, senators, representatives, supreme court judges, and that they would have to protect their tribal rights under treaties with the Federal Government, and to compete with educated, sagacious and unscrupulous white men. That they should remember that the appropriations made by their Legislature to educate them was interest on purchase money paid to the tribe by the Federal Government for old homes in Mississippi.

Tribal Laws and Their Provisions for Education

THE CHOCTAW NATION

The General Provisions of the 1842 Choctaw Constitution stated that $18,000 of the interest from the funds obtained under the treaty of 1830 were to be used for educational purposes in the nation. Section 20 made further provision for education by authorizing the General Council to "create by law such Regulations, Commissioners, Superintendents or other such officers as the case may require for the promotion and advancement of all the schools in the Nation."

The Choctaw Nation began printing its laws as early as 1834. From these printed records it appears that the first piece of legislation concerning education was passed in 1842. An Act respecting Public Schools established six academies or boarding schools: Spencer Academy, Fort Coffee Academy, Koonsha Female Seminary, Ianubbee Female Seminary, Chuwahla Female Seminary, and Wheelock Female Seminary. It appropriated money for the support of these institutions and placed them under the direction of different missionary societies, which were to contribute additionally to their support. It also required that training be given in practical skills as well as in strictly academic courses, and that one tenth of the students in the academics be Choctaw orphan children.

The funds used for support of the schools were partially those granted by various treaty stipulations as well as allowances drawn from the funds of the Nation.

An Act to amend the various acts in relation to education and for other purposes was passed in 1853 and provided for a revised system of public instruction in the Choctaw Nation. This legislation established a Board of Trustees to oversee the operations of the national schools and academies. The Board was to be composed of one member from each District and a Superintendent of Education for the Nation who would be its ex-officio President. All were to be elected by the General Council for a term of four years.

The Superintendent had general supervision over educational matters, including:

> the system of education, the kind of class books, the progress of the pupils, the cost of tuition, board, and expenses, the amount and nature of the revenue received by the teacher or superintendent appropriated by the Council, Missionary Board, or received from the labor of the student, or from any other source, together with such information touching the character, qualification and fitness of the various persons employed in, or in connection with the school.

He was required to visit all schools and academies at least once a year, to correspond with each of the District Trustees and individual school superintendents, and to report to the National Council on conditions at the schools.

The Board of Trustees mediated between the Superintendent of Education and the superintendents of the schools and academies. Its function was to settle any question or disputes that might arise within or between any of the school communities, to make recommendations for changes or improvements, and generally to see that the system operated smoothly. The Board was authorized to contract with missionary boards or individuals who wished to establish educational institutions in the nation. In addition it appointed scholars to attend the academies and high schools.

Many bills were enacted which governed the use of funds obtained under the 1830 Treaty of Dancing Rabbit Creek which had been specifically set aside for education of Choctaw youths in the United States. The first of these bills, in 1841, authorized boys to be educated at Ohio University, Jefferson College in Pennsylvania, Asbury University at Green Castle, Indiana, and another institution to be named. In 1853, a law was passed which authorized the Choctaw Superintendent and Trustees to take control of this fund, subject to the consent of the President of the United States. In 1888 an amendment to the existing law concerning the State Scholars was passed and provided that the number be increased to allow fifteen boys and twelve girls to attend schools in the United States.

In 1866 the Choctaw General Council extended the neighborhood schools throughout the Choctaw Nation. Schools were to be started "where there are Choctaw children of proper age to attend the school." The neighborhood schools of the nation were to enroll a minimum of 10 Choctaw children. The teacher received $2 per month per pupil who attended at least fifteen days and 10 cents per day per pupil for less than fifteen days of attendance. Class was conducted for six hours every day, except Saturday and Sunday. Parents who refused to send their children were fined 10 cents for each day of absence.

THE CHICKASAW NATION

The earliest attempts of the Chickasaw Nation to organize their own government and to adopt a written constitution were made in 1846, 1848, and 1851. These efforts at independence were tempered by the fact that, according to existing treaties with the United States, the Chickasaw Nation was still a part of the Choctaw Nation. The Treaty of 1855 officially separated the Chickasaws from the Choctaws, and established definite boundaries for each nation.

The first Act establishing a system of public schools in the Chickasaw Nation was passed in July of 1867, the year the constitution was adopted; but it was quickly repealed and superseded by one approved the following October. This law provided that three neighborhood schools be established in each county of the Nation, provided there were at least 15 pupils; an Act of 1870 reduced this number to 10. Tuition was $30 per student per year with the teacher agreeing to provide books and supplies in addition to the usual services. Teachers were also required to report to the School Superintendent at the end of each quarter on the attendance and progress of their students.

According to section 3 of the 1867 law, any county could establish a school if it could furnish 10 students, and provided that the parents made application to the School Superintendent for a teacher. It was then the duty of the Legislature to make the necessary appropriations for building and maintaining the school. Section 4 permitted white children to attend these neighborhood schools, as long as the school did not already have more than 30 Indian students. White students were charged the same tuition and board as Chickasaw children. Any student or teacher who was a citizen of the Nation and who lived more than two and a half miles from the school was entitled to receive, from national funds, $7 per month for board.

The 1867 Public Education bill dealt largely with the education of Chickasaw children at schools in the United States. Superseding a quota of 100 set earlier that year, the act allowed sixty students (30 boys and 30 girls) between the ages of 13 and 25 to attend school in the States, at public expense, for a period of three years. These students were to be appointed by the School Superintendent upon the recommendation of a school committee in each county, which would select the top scholars in the district. Preference was given to orphans in the selection process when they were equal to others in the district in academic achievement. It was the duty of the School Superintendent to transport the children to their respective schools and to contract with the principal of the school for the education and necessary services while they were in attendance there.

In 1867, the Bloomfield Seminary for girls and the Chickasaw Manual Labor Academy for boys were established for Chickasaw children of high school age (i.e., between 9 and 18 years of age), The Waupanucka Institute for male and female Chickasaw children between the ages of 8 and 14 who were living in the Choctaw Nation, was also established. After completing four years at Waupanucka, the students were to transfer to one of the high schools to finish their studies. All of these institutions operated on a contract basis, the contracting parties agreeing to provide "tuition, good board, bedding, washing, mending clothes, medicine and medical attention" as well as all necessary supplies and books for their students. For each scholar at Bloomfield and Chickasaw Manual Labor academies the contracting parties received $194 for a ten-month scholastic year. At Waupanucka the rate was $175 per student per academic year.

In 1898, the Chickasaw Governor approved an Act which provided for the education of mutes of the nation who were of school age. This Act appropriated $200 a year for each such child to attend school in the United States or elsewhere, provided he applied for and was granted a certificate to do so from the School Superintendent.

THE CHEROKEE NATION

The first Cherokee Constitution appears to have been written in 1839 at a national convention of both the eastern and western members of the tribe.

Article VI of the Cherokee Constitution emphasizes the importance and necessity of education as a crucial part of the Cherokee life. It reads:

> Religion, morality, and knowledge being necessary to
> good government, the preservation of liberty and the
> happiness of mankind, schools and the means of educa-
> tion shall forever be encouraged in this nation.

Among the laws of 1839 was a general act concerning schools. Existing institutions and others to be established were to come under the supervision and control of the National Council. Any new missionary schools were to obtain permission and were to operate under the general regulations of the National Council. A committee of three was appointed by the National Committee, upon the recommendation of the Principal Chief, to develop laws which would support a system of general education for the Cherokees.

It was the duty of this committee to visit all the schools, review their programs and pupils, and report their findings to the Principal Chief who in turn would submit them to the National Council.

The Superintendent was further authorized to appoint a three-man Board of Directors for each school. These boards would locate and supervise the building of schools in their districts, employ the teachers and examine them for competency, and dismiss them from office with the concurrence of the Superintendent. The boards also had the power to approve the books and the courses taught in the schools, as well as to approve the yearly school calendar and the vacation times. Once in every three months they visited the schools under their care. Education was made possible for orphan children by placing them with families near the school and providing them with clothing. A maximum of two hundred dollars yearly was to be paid by the tribe for such expenses.

Great emphasis was given to the establishment of male and female seminaries for education beyond the grade schools. To develop this level of the educational system a five-man Board of Directors was nominated by the Principal Chief to be approved by the National Committee. The Principal Chief served as an ex-officio member of the Board. Teachers were hired and fired by the Board, which also fixed their salaries and organized the school calendar. In addition to having authority for setting the policy and establishing programs, the Board of Directors was responsible for procuring the books, stationery, school apparatus, furniture, tools, etc., and for putting the Seminaries in operation. The Principal Chief was authorized to pay all bills related to the operation of the schools.

Prior to being admitted to the Seminary, students were required to show competency in reading and spelling the English language, arithmetic, grammar, and geography. Students were entitled to four years of instruction without payment of tuition and board as long as they behaved and performed well in class. The Board of Directors set the number to be admitted to the Seminary, at which time they came under the supervision and control of the tribal government and the teachers. Near the end of the school year each student was given a thorough examination at which both the teachers and the Board of Directors could participate.

The Cherokee Constitution was extensively amended in 1866. At this time a number of educational laws were substantially revised.

The Cherokee goal for education was stated as follows:

> For the purpose of maturing and adopting the best possible system of education for the youth of the Nation, and for the purpose of devising the best means of placing a

liberal education within the reach, as nearly as possible, of all the children of the Nation, and enabling those who speak only the Cherokee language, to acquire more readily a practical knowledge and use of the English language, there shall be permanently established a Board of Education, with such powers as shall be confirmed by law.

Under the 1866 amendment the Board was required to report to the Principal Chief and the National Council on the conditions of the schools, the number of students and the program. Furthermore, the board maintained "complete supervision and control of the orphan Asylum, the male and female Seminaries, and of the educational interests of the Nation at large." The School Board also served as an examining group to certify, grade, and set the salary for teachers. A school census was to be taken of all students, including orphans, by the commissioners on the Board of Education. They also took charge of the school calendar, textbooks, and other instructional aids and school equipment.

The new Constitution and accompanying laws empowered the Board of Education to have overall responsibility for reorganizing and setting up an educational system responsive to Cherokee needs. Both the Executive and Legislative bodies required the board to report and recommend changes to them annually.

THE CREEK NATION

The Creek (Muskogee) Nation's Constitution authorized three separate branches of government—the Executive, Legislative, and Judicial, quite similar in functions and terms of office to the United States Government.

In 1880, the interest from the Creek trust fund was assigned for the use of the 28 neighborhood schools in the Creek Nation. Seven of these schools were for the children of the freedmen of the Creek Nation, with the remaining twenty-one serving the Indian children of the tribe. These schools were under the supervision of the Superintendent of Public Instruction, whose responsibilities included appointing teachers as well as three trustees from the local neighborhood for each of these schools. The trustees were to oversee both the work of the teachers and the conduct of the students. They also acted as truant officers to make sure the students attended school or, if needed, to expel students for disorderly conduct.

One duty of the Superintendent of Public Schools was to preside over the National Teachers' Institute—an annual meeting of all the teachers of the neighborhood schools. This was also a time of examination and certification for teachers who were interested in teaching in the Creek schools. A second responsibility of the Superintendent was to serve as a member of a Board of Examiners, which included three other Creek citizens. All were to be present during the sessions of the Teachers' Institute at the Creek capitol to examine the prospective teachers. The teachers received "certificates of competency," valid for one year if they proved themselves in the following areas:

a) higher arithmetic
b) English grammar and composition
c) U.S. history
d) geography and penmanship
e) the practical knowledge of the duties of teachers

The Creek Government was very exacting in its contract relationships with both the neighborhood and mission schools. The Principal Chief appointed the Boards of Trustees, composed of five local members each. These Boards, in turn, were delegated the power to contract with the religious denominations for the various schools. These contracts then had to be approved by the National Council. The Supervisor over the mission contract schools was directly under the Superintendent of Public Instruction. Each of the mission school superintendents was required to furnish an annual report on number of pupils, the schools each pupil attended, the students absent and the reasons for such absence. Basic requirements for admittance were: a minimum age level, a basic knowledge of mathematics, and the ability to read the English language.

The Council even decided the types of textbooks to be used in neighborhood schools. In 1881 they sent out a list of approved books which included the following:

> *Harvey's Primer*
> *Harvey's Revised Grammars*
> *Roy's New Arithmetic*
> *Eclectic Geographics*
> *Eclectic History*
> *Eclectic Copy Books*

This was also an important year for higher education among the Creeks. The National Council gave permission to the American Baptist Home Mission Society to work through a Board of Trustees to:

> found, establish, and maintain, within the limits of the Creek Nation, an Indian University that shall be to the Indian Territory, as nearly as practicable, all that State Universities are to the several states in which they are located, and shall be open to the reception of students from the citizens of the Creek Nation and other Indian Tribes or Nations.

The appointed Board of Trustees was composed of missionaries, chiefs of several Indian tribes, the Creek Superintendent of Public Instruction and the Principal Chief. This Board of Trustees was to decide on the location of the school and exercised control over the buildings and property of the school. Additional duties delegated by the Council to the Board were the selection of programs of study, staffing faculty and administration positions, and authorizing the award of degrees. Land was authorized for the school and the first Indian University, later to be called Bacone College, was established in Indian Territory.

According to the revised Creek laws of 1893, a three-member Board of Education was appointed by the Principal Chief and confirmed by the National Council. The Board was given "complete control and supervision of all the schools and educational interests of the Nation at large, subject to such restriction and direction as may be imposed by law." Specifically, the board was given authority to adopt rules and regulations for the schools established and maintained by the Nation. Reports were to be made of all board actions, and funds for the support of the schools could be requisitioned by the board from the National Treasurer. In addition, the Board was to set up the necessary rules for admitting students, examining and hiring the teachers and superintendents, and setting up and approving the curriculum and textbooks of the schools. The Board of Education was required to visit each Boarding, Manual Labor and High School at least twice each scholastic year and each member of the Board was to visit the Primary and Neighborhood Schools in his district twice a year. Careful examinations into the operation and management of each school was to be made and reported.

THE SEMINOLE NATION
There are no known tribal laws of the Seminole Nation that refer specifically to their schools.

In the laws of 1903, the office of the Treasurer was authorized to "disburse such National Funds in accordance with the acts of Council." He was also to pay the "accounts of the schools of the Nation." These rules also stated that the treasurer was to "pay all the National Warrants signed by the chiefs of the Nation."

The Seminole Nation operated two academies (Emahakai and Mekusukey) and eight district schools. These schools, prior to 1898 were financed by the interest, at 5 percent per annum, on $50,000, which was part of the payment by the United States to the Seminole Nation for the western lands ceded by the 1866 treaty.

Dissolution of the Tribal Schools

It is difficult to imagine the state of affairs which faced the Five Civilized Tribes with the passage of the Dawes Act of 1887 and the creation of the

Dawes Commission in 1893. These events formalized a trend which had been developing since the post-Civil War days, that is, the gradual dissolution of tribal life in the Indian Territory and preparation for eventual statehood of the Oklahoma Territory. Before that time, the Indian people of the Indian Territory had experienced some sense of stability and peace in their lives. For the most part their tribal governments were operating smoothly and they were able to manage the affairs in their territory very well.

Angie Debo describes the pre-Civil War era of the Five Civilized Tribes as such:

> In their western refuge they were undisturbed by white intruders. ... They had an active commerce with the outside world, carried on mainly by their own citizens, usually mixed bloods. Graduates of their boarding schools often went to the States for further education, returning to become leaders of their people.

With the confusion and disorganization generated by the Civil War and its aftermath, the way of life in the Indian Territory was permanently and profoundly changed. Despite the treaties of 1866 with their promises of protection, the Indian Territory had already lost its protective isolation. When railroads were constructed through Indian Territory, its abundant resources caused a large immigration of white people, which resulted in towns being built upon the common property of the tribes. The tribes did collect revenue by taxing all non-Indians on their lands for the privilege of engaging in their various occupations or businesses. While each tribe owned all the land within the borders, it could dispose of it only with the consent of the United States Government.

The presence of non-citizens and intruders, the arrival of a large number of "freedmen," and the passage of railroads through the territory caused a situation which was difficult for the tribal governments to deal with. At first the Federal Government made an effort to maintain order and protect the rights of the tribes, but as the situation became steadily worse and the non-Indian population grew the federal government succumbed to what seemed to be an irreversible trend; by 1880 they had given up assisting the tribes. Without the full cooperation of the Federal Government the tribes were almost helpless in trying to enforce their laws against intruders and resolving problems of criminal jurisdiction over non-Indians in their territory. Thus, tribal authority was gradually undermined and tribal life was headed for dissolution.

The Dawes Act of 1887 was designed specifically to end communal ownership of Indian land and promote private ownership by allotting sections of land to individual members of tribes. Although this law did not apply to the

Five Civilized Tribes, it was clear to them what the Federal Government's policy was; undoubtedly the five tribes saw it as a threat to their tribal life.

Shortly after the passage of the Dawes Act, in 1889, the Federal Government secured a tract of land in the western portion of the Indian Territory from the Creeks. This land was opened for homesteading that same year, causing a land rush of enormous proportions. In 1890 a territorial government was established in Oklahoma and, in 1893, Congress passed the legislation which created the Commission to the Five Civilized Tribes, commonly referred to as the Dawes Commission. Although this Commission was only authorized to negotiate with the Five Civilized Tribes, this Act began the actual process which culminated in the dissolution of tribal life among the Five Civilized Tribes.

Prior to the Allotment Period, the Five Civilized Tribes exercised control over the education of their children. Tribal schools were operated within the tribal structure and under the auspices of tribal officials. The independence and autonomy of the tribes, which allowed them the freedom of operating their own school systems, stems in part from their having responsibility for the management of their tribal funds and disbursement of tribal revenues. This allowed them to make decisions about what kind of educational system would be supported by their funds and how it would operate.

The Curtis Act of June 28, 1898, however, made radical changes in the affairs of the Five Civilized Tribes, which had previously been autonomous, self-governing and independent of the United States Government. The Curtis Act embodied general provisions applicable to all tribes and gave the United States supervision over the tribal schools. The act provided for the per capita distribution of the tribal lands; abolition of the tribal courts; continuance of modified tribal governments for eight years; and assumption by the federal government of supervisory control over the tribal schools.

The Secretary of the Interior was authorized to assume supervisory control over tribal schools through the Superintendent of Schools for Indian Territory, whose duty was to supervise Indian education generally. The Superintendent had four assistant supervisors, one for each tribe excluding the Seminoles; the assistants kept him informed on the state of educational affairs and conditions in the tribal schools.

Initially these United States supervisors had little direct control over educational matters since the tribal authorities maintained control over funds which supported the schools. But the supervisors gradually assumed more active influence. Under the Curtis Act, the Indian agent was authorized to disburse all money held and collected by officials of the United States for the benefit of the tribes, and to do so under rules and regulations promulgated by the Secretary of the Interior rather than the tribes.

Control of the tribal schools during this period was essentially in the hands of the people who were in charge of the disbursement of funds needed for the maintenance of these schools. Since the Curtis Act directed the federal government to assume control of the finances of the Five Civilized Tribes, this established an avenue for Federal monitoring of expenditures of tribal funds. It made no difference whether the interest on tribal funds or royalties were used for support of the schools since the procedure was similar—all warrants for such expenses were to be approved by the United States supervisor. The demise of tribal governments and the increased influence of the Federal Government seem to have jointly contributed to this shift in control.

By the terms of the 1898 agreement with the Choctaws and Chickasaws, the United States assumed supervisory control over the schools in these nations. In October of 1899, the Choctaw national council questioned the right of the Secretary to assume control of its schools under this provision of the 1898 agreement and directed their education officials to conduct schools according to their own laws. Tribal and federal officials renegotiated the issue and reached another agreement in 1901 which placed the schools under joint control of a tribal representative and a government supervisor whose actions would be subject to the approval and instructions of the Department of the Interior, through the Superintendent of Schools for Indian Territory.

The Chickasaw Nation similarly resisted government control in educational affairs, denying any right in this matter to the Secretary of the Interior until 1901. As long as tribal funds, not royalties, were used for maintenance of schools, the United States government did not interfere. But with the agreement of 1901, school expenses were to be paid from royalty funds, held and collected by the U. S. Government, under regulations of the Department of the Interior. In addition, a Board of Examiners consisting of three members, one of which would be appointed by the Secretary, was established to control Chickasaw schools.

Prior to an agreement with the Creek Nation on May 25, 1901, tribal officials maintained complete control over their schools, while federal officials had only a supervisory role in the process. However, this 1901 agreement established joint control over Creek schools by the United States supervisor and the tribal superintendent of education, subject to the rules and regulations of the Secretary of the Interior.

The schools of the Cherokee nation were put under joint federal-tribal management by an agreement of July 1, 1902, and they were maintained under rules and regulations prescribed by the Secretary of the Interior.

The Seminole Nation, by an agreement of December 16, 1897, accepted allotment of their lands but otherwise maintained complete control over their own affairs. Their tribal governments were continued and acts of their national council were not subject to federal approval. Since they had exclusive control over their educational affairs, there was no official federal supervisor for their schools.

The Act of Congress, on April 26, 1906, for the final disposition of the affairs of the Five Civilized Tribes markedly changed the situation in the Seminole nation. Section 10 of the Act authorized the Secretary of the Interior to assume control of the schools of all the Five Tribes, to conduct them under rules and regulations prescribed by him, and to direct disbursements of tribal funds through an officer appointed by him. This Act led Seminole officials to question the authority of the Secretary of the Interior to assume control over their schools and over the use and expenditure of tribal funds and distribution of annuities. An opinion of the Comptroller of the Treasury, on October 19, 1906, held that this specific authority of the Secretary of the Interior was established under Section 10 of the Act of April 26, 1906. The Seminole government again objected in 1907, but the Attorney General reached the same conclusion in an opinion dated August 19, 1907.

In this way the Federal Government gradually assumed control over tribal schools and acquired responsibility for Indian education in the territory which was soon to become part of the State of Oklahoma.

While the superintendent of schools for Indian Territory was specifically charged with Indian education, he was constantly aware of the problems of education for non-Indian people in the Indian Territory. Some public schools were established in the large towns to accommodate the increasing number of white children in the Territory. A few denominational schools enrolled white children and a few scattered private schools educated a small number as well. Tribal schools, however, were by far the most widespread and organized; these schools were conducted almost exclusively for Indian citizens. There were, however, a few non-Indians who paid tuition and were allowed to attend these schools. The changing conditions of the Indian Territory and the increasing number of white children without schools created a problem that could not be ignored. The Superintendent of Schools repeatedly requested Congressional aid to relieve this situation. Finally, in 1904 the Congress passed an act to ameliorate the situation.

> For the maintenance, strengthening, and enlarging of the tribal schools of the Cherokee, Creek, Choctaw, Chickasaw and Seminole nations, and making provision for the attendance of children of non-citizens therein, and the establishment of new schools under the control of tribal school boards and the Department of the Interior, the sum of one hundred thousand dollars, or so much thereof as may be necessary, to be placed in the

hands of the Secretary of Interior, and disbursed by him
under such rules and regulations as he may prescribe.

The act established a fund which was to be used mainly for paying the salaries
of teachers and establishing a system of schools for Indian and white
students. Such schools were to be under the joint control of the United
States superintendent of schools and tribal school authorities.

The period beginning with the passage of the Dawes Act (1887), through the
work of the Commission to the Five Civilized Tribes and the passage of the
Curtis Act (1898), until the admission of Oklahoma to the Union (1907), was
a time of transition for the Indians in Indian Territory. Despite attempts to
maintain their unique status, their way of life shifted from tribal to federal-
tribal control to state-tribal control. There is little doubt that there was a need
to meet the educational needs of the great number of school-age children
throughout Oklahoma. Since the existing tribal schools were operating
efficiently, they provided the surest vehicle for realizing this purpose. The
appropriation which supplemented tribal funds also served as a transitional
mechanism for the tribal school system until a stable system of taxation, which
would eventually provide the basis for a public school system to serve all
children in the state, could be established. The rationale behind the push to
consolidate educational efforts and establish a single school system serving
both Indian and white children was succinctly stated in a Congressional report.

The Indian must lose his identity by absorption, and such
absorption will be rapid and positive; and he must soon
cease to be recognized as a separate and distinct race.[8]

The Consequences of Federal and State Control

In 1969 the Kennedy Report, *Indian Education: A National Tragedy—
A National Challenge,* prepared by a special Senate Subcommittee on
Indian Education, documented the demise of the Cherokee educational
system subsequent to federal supervision.

One of the most remarkable examples of adaptation and accomplishment
by any Indian tribe in the United States is that of the Cherokee. Their record
provides evidence of the kind of results which ensue when Indians truly have
the power of self-determination:

• a constitution which provided for courts, representation, jury trials and the right to vote for all those over 18
years;

• a system of taxation which supported such services as
education and road construction;

• an educational system which produced a Cherokee population 90 percent literate in its native language and used bilingual materials to such an extent that Oklahoma Cherokees had a higher English literacy level than the white populations of either Texas or Arkansas;

• a system of higher education which, together with the Choctaw Nation, had more than 200 schools and academies, and sent numerous graduates to eastern colleges; and

• publication of a widely read bilingual newspaper.

But that was in the 1800's, before the Federal Government took control of Cherokee affairs. The record of the Cherokee today is proof of the tragic results of 60 years of white control over their affairs:

• 90 percent of the Cherokee families living in Adair County, Okla. are on welfare;

• 99 percent of the Choctaw Indian population in McCurtain County, Okla. live below the poverty line;

• the median number of school years completed by the adult Cherokee population is only 5.5;

• 40 percent of adult Cherokees are functionally illiterate;

• Cherokee dropout rates in public schools are as high as 75 percent;

• the level of Cherokee education is well below the average for the State of Oklahoma, and below the average for rural and non-whites in the States.

The disparity between these two sets of facts provides dramatic testimony to what might have been accomplished if the policy of the Federal Government had been one of Indian self-determination. It also points up the disastrous effects of imposed white control.

The Cherokee education system itself was just as exemplary as its governmental system. Using funds primarily received from the Federal Government as the result of ceding large tracts of land, a school system described by one authority as "the finest school system west of the Mississippi River" soon developed. Treaty money was used by Sequoyah to develop the Cherokee alphabet, as well as to purchase a printing press. In a period of several years the Cherokee had established remarkable achievement and literary levels, as indicated by statistics cited above. But in 1903 the Federal Government appointed a superintendent to take control of Cherokee education, and when Oklahoma became a State in 1906 and the whole system was abolished, Cherokee educational performance was to begin its decline.

Authorities who have analyzed the decline concur on one point: The Cherokees are alienated from the white man's school. Anthropologist Willard Walker simply stated that "the Cherokees have viewed the school as a white man's institution over which parents have no control." Dr. Jack Forbes of the Far West Regional Laboratory for Research and Development said that the Federal and State schools operated for the Cherokee have had negative impact because of little, if any, parent-community involvement. Several researchers have also commented upon the lack of bilingual materials in the schools, and the ensuing feeling by Cherokees that reading English is associated with coercive instruction.

Alfred L. Wahrhaftig makes the point that the Indian child communicates in Cherokee and considers it his "socializing" language. English is simply an "instrumental" language one learns in school, a place which the Cherokee student sees no value in attending anyway.

In the 1890's Cherokees knew there was a forum for their opinions on how their children should be educated, and they used that forum. Wahrhaftig's study showed Cherokee parents haven't lost interest in their children's education, just their faith in a white-controlled system's ability to listen to them and respond. "Cherokees finally have become totally alienated from the school system," he reported. "The tribe has surrendered to the school bureaucracy, but tribal opinion is unchanged."[9]

GOVERNMENT INDIAN SCHOOLS

DURING THE LATTER part of the nineteenth century, the Bureau of Indian Affairs initiated an intense effort to assimilate American Indians into mainstream American society. Reservation day and boarding schools and off-reservation industrial schools all shared this objective. The premise was that if the Indians failed to be assimilated they were doomed to extinction. Beginning in the late 1870s, government officials adopted the view that off-reservation boarding schools offered the best opportunity for incorporating Indian children into the white-dominated society, simply because such schools kept Indian children away from their homes for protracted periods—in some cases years at a time. The educational theory held that the release of the Indian child from the "slavery of tribal life" would help to solve the Indian "problem" and the Indians would be assimilated as were immigrants. This theory subscribed to the belief of uniformity in all Indian schools; uniformity in dress, curriculum, and methodology. The promise given to the Indian children was a new culture which would allow them to compete as equals in American society; the promise held that the academic life of the child would be sufficient time to prepare the Indian students for this new challenge. Indeed, many philanthropists subscribed to the theory of Richard H. Pratt, who advocated the removal of Indian children as far as possible from their home environment at the earliest possible age.

The federal education system for Indians was viewed as the surest and quickest way to acculturate and assimilate Indian children. In theory, the children would become literate in English and would gain the skills needed to compete in the white-dominated society; the system would "give the Indian a white man's chance." In practice, that rarely happened; all too often the children were not prepared to make it in either the white world or the Indian world.

Indeed, despite its promise and intent, the government education system failed most of its students. Abuse, neglect, lack of genuine concern on the part of the government, and the Indian children's desire to retain their cultural heritage contributed to this failure. Disease also hampered the performance of the government schools. In 1897 Indian inspector William McConnell lamented the policy of filling the Indian schools at all costs, even when it meant admitting diseased and unhealthy children. In 1907 a health survey at Haskell Indian School found deplorable conditions.

> The people slept two, three, or more in single beds. Both pulmonary and glandular cases (of tuberculosis) were found occupying beds with supposedly healthy pupils. Common towels, common drinking cups, and no fresh air in the dormitories were the rule rather than the exception. No attention was paid to decayed teeth and tooth brushes were not regularly used or their use insisted upon.[1]

In 1913 the U.S. Public Health Service reported similar findings in its examination of Indian schools.[2] In 1923 the American Red Cross conducted a survey and concluded that students were more prone to contract tuberculosis at the Indian schools than if they had not attended such schools.[3]

The product of the government school system was a people not adequately prepared for their new life. In many instances, the skills taught were unproductive or obsolete or were not applicable on the reservations. Standard agricultural practices were of little use in the diverse agricultural settings of the West.

Not surprisingly, by 1910 many Americans believed American Indians to be a vanishing race. Land loss, social and cultural displacement, decaying tribal institutions and political disruptions, and poor health all lent credence to this belief. The tenacity of the children who clung to their culture is truly remarkable in light of the obstacles before them.

The Promise

In 1888 the Board of Indian Commissioners, which was responsible for recommending and evaluating Indian policy, encouraged the adoption of an educational policy that in effect called for the destruction of the "Indian" so as to save the individual. The board deemed twenty years a sufficient time to accomplish this goal and withdraw government support.

> If anything in the world is certain, it is that the red man's civilization will disappear before the white man's civilization, because, of the two, it is inferior. The Indian problem, in its fundamental aspect, is, then, Must the red man disappear with his civilization? Is it possible that in Christian times the Indians themselves have got to disappear with their inferior civilization?

I think we can say certainly that unless we can incorporate the red man into the white man's civilization, he will disappear. Therefore, the one question behind the land question, behind the education question and the law question, is, How can we fit the red man for our civilization?

There is needed an annual expenditure of $4,000,000. The call for such an amount need not frighten us. We have abundant means to meet it. Were the demand twice as large we ought not to hesitate. We ought not to make it a mere question of cost. It is a question of saving or destroying a race within our borders. And, even on economical grounds, it is cheaper to educate and train to self support than to feed and clothe and guard the Indian in perpetual pauperism. Ten years of thorough training of all Indian children in industrial schools will take a large portion of them off our hands, and in twenty years there would be but few Indians needing the care and support of the government.[4]

In 1885 John H. Oberly, superintendent of Indian education, outlined the purpose and machinery of the Indian school system.

It is an understood fact that in making large appropriations for Indian school purposes, the aim of the Government is the ultimate complete civilization of the Indian. When this shall have been accomplished the Indian will have ceased to be a beneficiary of the Government, and will have attained the ability to take care of himself. Hence national selfishness, as well as a broad philanthropy, calls for the earliest possible achievement of the end in view. But anxious and eager as the patriotic humanitarian way may be on this point, it is conceded on all sides that the permanent civilization of the Indian can only come ... by slow processes of education, which lead from lower to higher, and refine while they elevate. The Government has begun to act upon the belief that the Indian cannot be civilized until he has received an education that will enable him to catch at least a glimpse of the civilized world through books. But the Indian might have all the knowledge of the books, and he would remain a barbarian nevertheless, if he were not led out of his prejudices into the white man's ways, if he were not won from slothfulness into industrious habits, if he were not taught to work, and to believe that he, as well as the white man, is in justice bound by the law that if a man will not work neither shall he eat. Appreciating this fact, the Government has slowly organized a system of Indian schools for the purpose of teaching the Indian child to read and write, the Indian boy to till the soil, shove the plane, strike the anvil, and drive the peg, and the Indian girl to do the work of the good and skillful housewife.[5]

The Outing System

One of the dominant characteristics of the off-reservation boarding schools was a system of work and study called the "outing system."

Designed by retired Army officer Richard H. Pratt, the outing system was designed to place Indian children in white households where they would learn the virtues of living in white America; the school itself was operated in a meticulous fashion, with strict discipline. As part of this process, it was hoped, all Indian characteristics would presumably fall by the wayside; only too often, however, Indian children learned skills which were useless on the reservation.

The outing system served as the model for many Indian schools. The established schools were in well-populated districts as far from the tribes as possible. Captain Pratt outlined his philosophy in an address to the Board of Indian Commissioners in 1889. "My theme is 'a way out' or ... the 'outing system,'" he said.

> I say that if we take a dozen young Indians and place one in each American family, taking those so young they have not learned to talk, and train them up as children of those families, I defy you to find any Indian in them when they are grown. I believe if we took one of those Indians—a little papoose from his mother's back, always looking backward—into our families, face it the other way, and keep it under our care and training until grown, it would then be Anglo-Saxon in spirit and American in all its qualities. Color amounts to nothing. The fact that they are born Indians does not amount to anything.

> We have been told there are 35,000 or 40,000 children to look after. If we place these children in our American lines, we shall break up all the Indian there is in them in a very short time. We must get them into America and keep them in. By our acts we say, if the tribes can take hold of themselves by their own bootstraps, and lift themselves as tribes bodily into our civilization, we are ready to let them in as a body, but we will not let them in unless they come in this way. It is a very peculiar situation that in this country and at this time we have no individual Indians here and there in our communities— none that live with us. The idea is segregation and Indian reservations everywhere. At Carlisle I cannot work the Indians en masse. If I send them in numbers to Sunday school, at once a class of Indians is formed. If I send them out into the country into public schools, in numbers sufficient in any one school, forthwith there is segregated a class of Indians. To overcome this hindrance, which is our own act, we must by thorough distribution make it impossible to create a class of Indians. Forty thousand Indian children! I do not remember the number of our schools exactly; but as I do remember, there would be only about one Indian boy or girl to every five or six schools in the United States. Such distribution would not burden our public schools. The end is in this direction. We must work it out on this line some way, in order to succeed.

> The idea that we cannot teach the Indians our civilization and to join us in it and compete with us is nonsense. It is a little hard to bring ourselves to do

it in the right way—that is all. The old ones are not irredeemable, as is alleged. It is harder to bend the tree than the bush; but force enough will bend anything. Take an individual Indian—an old one, off by himself, away from the public Indian sentiment of his tribe. Immerse him in civilization, and he becomes willing in a very short time to cut off his hair and adopt civilized dress. He will quit painting himself, quit his other peculiar Indian ways, and strive to be one with those about him.

Considering the case of the Indian youth, we must of necessity take some preliminary care of them in Indian schools; but at the very earliest moment we ought to have them in our schools and dispense with purely Indian schools. Carlisle has over two hundred Indian youth out in families and in the public schools of Pennsylvania. We ought to save them as individuals, invite and urge them out of their savagery and into our civilization one by one, the whole of them. How long would it take to assimilate them if we went about it with all our forces? Not more than from three to five years. We have plenty of room. It would only make nine Indians to a county throughout the United States.[6]

Pratt was not the first white educator to attempt to divorce Indian children from their culture. A century earlier Eleazar Wheelock's students "were taken out of the reach of their Parents, and out of the way of Indian examples, and kept in School under good Government and constant Instruction." Despite this and other early trials, off-reservation industrial schools did not become firmly established until the decade subsequent to the Civil War, when Captain Pratt became one of the leading forces in the field of Indian education.

In the fall of 1879, Pratt opened Carlisle Indian School, which soon became the nation's center of Indian education. By the end of the first school year Pratt had placed sixteen Indian children among white American families. By 1890 Pratt's outing system had placed a total of 662 pupils.

Despite receiving high marks during the first years of operation, Pratt never attained his goal of absorbing all Indians into mainstream America. In assuming that Indians could be completely assimilated—as European immigrants were—Pratt underestimated the tenacity and desire of the Indians to retain their cultural heritage.

By the mid-1890s, Pratt's critics began questioning the value and effectiveness of the off-reservation school in "civilizing" the Indians. Also questioned was the concept of how well the Indian students adjusted to their new environment after leaving Carlisle. Pratt argued that most Indian students found a place in American society; the evidence, however, indicates that many of Pratt's students returned to their reservation communities. By the late 1890s the concept of off-reservation schools was supported by many "friends of the Indians." In 1904, after numerous intemperate remarks, Pratt was removed from his post at Carlisle.

In the following excerpt, taken from *Pratt: The Red Man's Moses*, Elaine Goodale Eastman examines the outing system and Pratt's application of the principle of association to the Indian "problem."

He admitted having said in 1884: "There are about 260,000 Indians in the United States, and there are 2,700 counties. I would divide them up in the proportion of about nine Indians to a county, and find them homes and work among our people ... It is folly to handle them at arm's length."

Pratt was apt at dramatizing his program, and it is obvious that the suggestion of nine Indians to a county was not intended to be taken literally. As a figure of speech, it was explicit enough.

This man pinned his faith to no formal institution, but rather to a principle as broad as human nature itself—the principle of association.

In 1888, he philosophized: "The great need of the Indian is the language, intelligence, industry and skill of the white man. Some say he can best acquire these by keeping away from the white man, but proof and common sense are all the other way. Those who claim to be friends to the Indians and yet seek to limit their range of opportunities for association with the whites ... are not less real enemies than those who destroy them with powder and sword.

"An Indian can do no better thing for himself than to spend years among the best whites, gaining their language, intelligence, and skill in the fullest and quickest way, and if he begets a desire to continue that association for life ... why forbid or limit his possibility, his rights as a man, or his liberty, under any pretense whatever?"

Said he prophetically: "We may have our contract schools, our church schools, and our government schools till Gabriel blows his horn, and we shall always have Indians and be struggling with the Indian problem. ..."

The plan had strong contemporary support. General Armstrong, at Hampton, used and endorsed it. George Bird Grinnell, best known for his excellent and sympathetic studies of the old Indian life, was certainly not a man to be prejudiced in favor of drastic treatment of Indians. After making a careful personal investigation of its workings, he wrote (in 1903): "It (the outing) seems capable of indefinite extension ... [and] may accomplish more for the Indian than anything that has ever been done for them ... Should be tried in the West, and if as successful as in the East, the whole problem will be simplified and hastened."

Pratt repeatedly affirmed that in three years he could prepare a boy or girl "straight from the camps" so as to be acceptable in our common schools and in the homes of our people. He believed it feasible for such a one to earn board and clothing from that point on, and so gradually work his way up to any position that he might be ambitious and competent to fill. This assumed a rather late start; and in fact most early pupils at Carlisle and Hampton were in their teens, some even in their twenties. The Captain continuously demonstrated his thesis by placing these young people in selected homes, mainly among prosperous farmers, and so forwarding considerable numbers into the public schools and higher educational institutions of Pennsylvania. ...

This system, Pratt believed, should be made to reach practically all Indian youths eligible for training. In his own words: "It enforced participation— the supreme Americanizer." He may have underestimated the difficulties of administration. No other non-reservation school was as favorably situated as Carlisle to press the plan, and abuses may have crept in later, in connection with industrialized agriculture in the far West. For that matter, Pratt seems to have distrusted the future of the great open spaces, and habitually reversed Horace Greeley's famous maxim.

"'Out' is the Carlisle watchword," wrote a correspondent of the *Outlook* at the schools's height of prestige and popular acclaim. "Out of the tribal bond, out of the Indian narrowness and clannishness into the broad life of the nation. The Carlisle 'outing' is by no means a summer holiday. It has become a fundamental part of the Carlisle training, a definite method— perhaps the method—of Americanizing Indians. The aim is not to produce an abnormal being, out of harmony with his environment, but a capable and acceptable citizen.

"Six hundred boys and girls are now placed in country homes every summer at reasonable wages, and 311 are out this present winter, for the most part working for their board and care while attending the nearest public school. For several years past, only about 4 per cent have failed to give satisfaction.

"Boys and girls are encouraged to volunteer for the outing. After they have been assigned to homes, with due consideration of the special needs of both parties, pupil and patron sign a statement of the rules which are to govern their relations. It is distinctly understood that the young people are not placed out as servants merely but as pupils, for whose proper care, teaching and oversight their employer is responsible. They are usually treated as members of the family.

"A monthly report is required for each pupil in the country, covering items of conduct, health, wages and expenditures. Twice a year each one is visited by an agent of the school, who looks closely into conditions and investigates every complaint. There is at Carlisle a separate office with three clerks, where the large correspondence is handled and a complete record kept of every outing.

"Nearly all these pupils-workers receive wages except while regularly attending school, which they must do for eighty consecutive days if out for the year. They are paid fully as much as others receive for similar service ... The formation of a habit of saving, so foreign to the tradition of the Indian, is especially emphasized. ..."

Not all young people were placed on farms, although the fixed policy of the Indian Office made this line of work almost mandatory throughout the service. Luther Standing Bear, for example, worked in the great Wanamaker store in Philadelphia. Dr. Grinnell, probably an unexcelled authority on the natural red man, sustained Pratt's belief that they vary in tastes and aptitudes "as much as white children do." He writes of seeing blanket Indians at work in a blacksmith shop, probably two generations ago, and of being told at that time, "Oh, Omahas are mighty handy with tools." Other close observers have found them, as a rule, better fitted for trades than agriculture, having unusual manual dexterity. A comparatively large proportion of graduates have preferred professional work or other intellectual pursuits.

The *Outlook* correspondent defended Carlisle's separation of Indian families.

"Parents and kindred are not forgotten. No more unjust charge can be laid at the door of the system than the oft-repeated accusation that it destroys the family. Pupils are required to write home every month and may write as much oftener as they choose. Nearly all lovingly inquire after absent brothers and sisters, invariably urging that they be sent to school. Many send money home—ten or twenty dollars at a time of their own hard earnings. What a lesson to poor and unthrifty parents!

"The number of good homes open to Indian pupils is greatly in excess of the supply. Applications are denied by the hundred, and they come from almost all parts of the United States, although it is the policy to place students only within easy reach of the school. They are welcomed into the public schools everywhere, and learn so much faster in competition and association with white children that, although attending less time than those who remain at Carlisle throughout the year, they easily keep up with their classes and are sometimes able to skip a grade.

"Why not have a National Bureau of Outing, whose function it shall be to select pupils from all reservation and other schools and place them for terms of one or more years in selected homes, where they shall be required to attend the public schools? The plan has virtually been approved by Congress and calls only for executive action. The pupils are self-supporting while out, so that the expense is much less than for any other system that is measurably satisfactory. ..."

In 1881, a clause was placed in the Indian appropriations bill by Senate amendment and annually repeated for many years following, endorsing the outing system throughout the Indian service. Pratt constantly urged its extension in letters to high officials, and specifically in his annual reports, from which we may quote:

>(1882) "The order and system so necessary in an institution retards rather than develops habits of self-reliance and forethought. Individuality is lost. The thousand petty emergencies of everyday responsibility they do not have to meet. Placed in families where they have individual responsibility, they receive training that no school can give. ..."

>(1891) "Our outing system brings our students into actual personal and commercial relations with the better class of industrial people of our race. ..."

>(1895) "Experience proves that the kind of education that will save the Indian to material usefulness and good citizenship is made up of four parts, in order of value as follows: First: A useable knowledge of the language of the country. Second: Skill in some American industry. Third: The courage of civilization. Fourth: A knowledge of books.

>"(The outing system) is replete with benefits, giving to the students facility in using the English language, a practical knowledge of business methods, and the ability for direct contact in the labor market with the competing race. I am glad to report that the Indian always holds his own, and is often the preferred laborer."

>(1897) "Our statistics show that we had sixty-eight different tribes and different languages in our school membership. I venture the assertion that in no other institution in existence are there so many different nationalities and languages as are gathered here, with the object of molding all into one people, speaking one tongue, and with aims and purposes in unison.

>"Through contact only will the prejudices of the Indians against whites, and the prejudices of the whites against the Indians be broken up. I have repeatedly urged within the last four years that Carlisle could most economically take care of fifteen hundred children by enlarging its outing. I have always advocated that schools for Indian youth be so located and conducted as to be the means of getting young Indians into our American life."

> (1901) "All Indians need in order to become English-speaking, useful, intelligent American citizens are the same opportunities and responsibilities accorded to our own people, and to all foreigners who emigrate to and locate among us. I have always seen, and now more than ever see, that it is impossible to give these opportunities with any force in their tribal aggregations, and their reservations. As I have no sympathy with any methods of tribalizing or catering to useless Indians, not even with schools when used for that purpose, I feel that I am becoming more and more extraneous to about all that is being done ... because I see that much failure is bound to come in the final reckoning. It will continue to be alleged, and alleged to be proven, that Indians cannot take on our education and civilization successfully—but in truth they have never really been invited into nor allowed any real opportunity to enter civilization's family."

In view of the considerable failure of governmental policies, freely admitted by the Bureau's responsible head, these last few lines deserve careful study, thirty-three years after Pratt penned them.

He was fond of contrasting the segregation and isolation deliberately forced upon the natives with what he termed the comparatively humane school of slavery, which by intimate association transformed exotic black men into useful, productive, English-speaking citizens. The once popular symbol of the melting pot supplied him with another striking analogy.

Immigrants of all nationalities, said Pratt, with customs and ideals far removed from our own, are welcomed and assimilated in immense numbers every year, while we continue to gag at a few hundred thousand indigenous red men of at least equal capacity.

The devastating effect of his program upon clan and tribe seems not to have seriously disturbed him. Certainly, we waste no regrets upon the lost tribal loyalties, the forgotten cultures, of millions of Afro-Americans. Our best wish for later immigrants is that the hyphen be dropped, as often happens with the first, and practically always with the second generation. Why make any exception to the general rule that strange tongues and alien traditions act as a practical handicap upon the rising generation of American citizens?

Even his enemies endorsed the outing. Said Indian commissioner Leupp: "I have had occasion to differ with him (Pratt) on so many points that it gives me all the more pleasure to add here my small tribute to his fame. His establishment of the outing system was an inspiration. (It is) one idea which will remain."

"The so-called outing system, originally established at the old Carlisle School, is still praised by graduates of that institution wherever one finds them," asserts those modern experts who conducted the Indian field and school survey of a few years ago. "Its possibilities ... have hardly ever been given a fair trial." General Pratt's plans were not only sound, but of great benefit to the race," wrote Warren K. Moorhead, archaeologist, and for many years a member of the Board of Indian Commissioners.

Charles F. Meserve, former superintendent of Haskell Institute from 1884 to 1891, writes in a private letter in 1934: "The funds used under the direction of the present commissioner would have accomplished infinitely more good if they had been spent in extending the outing system throughout the entire United States. To develop the highest type of citizenship should be the aim, and this means for each of us the right to live and work in the state of his choice."[7]

Performance

The federal school system for Indians was poorly administered, managed, and operated. Administrators often competed for students to fill their schools. In some areas, such as the vast Navajo reservation, force was used to bring the Indian children to the agency from where they were shipped off to fill boarding schools across the West.

The express purpose of the Indian schools was to teach the rudiments of reading and writing. Manual labor was required so that the schools could operate self-sufficiently. Because many of the Indian schools were remote, school superintendents often ruled with the power of a dictator. Such was the case at Genoa Indian School, in Genoa, Nebraska, where Samuel B. Davis was superintendent. Testimony by Julia C. Carroll and Ina M. Livermore, matrons at the school, exposed Davis' abusive rule, corrupt leadership, and attempts at personal gain.

Not all of the Indian schools were as poorly administered and operated as the Genoa School. Most schools were, however, guilty of poor diets, lack of proper educational material, neglected health conditions, overcrowded facilities, and unqualified personnel.

The selections that follow illustrate a few of the deficiencies of the government school system. The first, "Kid Catching on the Navajo Reservation," was presented by Dana Coolidge to the Senate subcommittee investigating the conditions of Indians in the United States. The second selection, based on the testimony of Julia C. Carroll and Ina M. Livermore, is taken from the Senate subcommittee hearings of 1929.

KID CATCHING ON THE NAVAJO RESERVATION

I am making a brief statement of my experience with what I consider the greatest shame of the Indian Service—the rounding up of Indian children to be sent away to government boarding schools. This business of "kid catching," as it is called, is rarely discussed with outsiders, either by the Indians or by the government employees, but during my numerous visits to the Navajo Reservation I have picked up a knowledge of its working.

In the fall the government stockmen, farmers, and other employees go out into the back country with trucks and bring in the children to school. Many apparently come willingly and gladly; but the wild Navajos, far back in the mountains, hide their children at the sound of a truck. So stockmen, Indian police, and other mounted men are sent ahead to round them up. The children are caught, often roped like cattle, and taken away from their parents, many times never to return. They are transferred from school to school, given white people's names, forbidden to speak their own tongue, and when sent to distant schools are not taken home for three years.

Those children who are fortunate enough to be kept in the reservation schools are allowed to go home every summer until they have passed the lower grades. Then they are sent far away—to Albuquerque, Phoenix, or Riverside—where they remain until from sixteen to eighteen years of age. During all this time they are under institutional care, such as with us is considered fit only for orphans, at a minimum of expense; and they return to their homes with a white man's education but unable to talk to their parents.

It is the claim of the Indian Service that this education is "necessary to fit the Navajos to meet the competition of the outside world," but most of them come back to herd sheep. A few work in the railroad towns as mechanics and laborers, the girls as cooks and servants, but the majority of the schoolboys who go into the outside world do so as common laborers.

Back in the hogans of their people the returned schoolboys are quite unfitted for their life. They can not even herd sheep. But generally the parents or some rich members of their clan will give them a start on shares and, marrying some returned schoolgirl, they will take up the life of an Indian. In exceptional cases they become truck drivers and traders or go into government service, but for the girls there is almost no opportunity except in domestic service in town. They start in all over again to learn to spin and weave and handle their sheep and goats.

It is a question, therefore, whether the benefits of this compulsory education justify the separation of little children from their mothers at the tender age of six or seven. If they run away from school on account of homesickness, they are transferred to Phoenix or some far distant place to be kept there three years, unreturned. In 1925, while visiting Henry Chee Dodge, then chief of the Navajo Council, I noticed a sad-faced little boy who sat alone, always looking down the road. He had been to the Tohatchee School, some sixty miles from his home, but becoming lonely for his mother had run away several times. For this he had been ordered transferred to Phoenix and had run away again. He had come to appeal to the chief of all the Navajos to save him from that long separation, but even the chief was powerless. He was compelled to surrender the boy to the school authorities and see him sent away.

While at Klag-e-toh trading post a Navajo girl ran away from the Burke School, about a hundred miles away, and came home. She was nearly sixteen years old, but had been hidden in different sheep camps by her mother and could not speak a word of English. When she was taken to school she wore all her necklaces and jewelry, which were heirlooms, but these were taken from her. Then she was punished and shut up in a closet for repeatedly speaking Navajo. She ran away at last, but the trader did his duty and reported her presence to school.

At this same post a government stockman was boasting of his kindness while out collecting school children. In all his experience, he said, he had never had a mother make serious objection when he explained to her through his interpreter how well her child would be treated and how necessary it was that he should go. But the previous week, while driving along the highway near Houck, he had seen a boy herding sheep and had turned out across the flat and caught him. The mother wept and protested and even used violence; so, having no interpreter to explain, the stockman had taken the boy by force.

This stockman had previously been describing the overcrowded conditions at Fort Defiance where, according to him, the children slept three in a bed like sardines. But when I suggested that, knowing the crowded conditions, and the mother's need for her boy, he might have passed by and said nothing, he replied in substance as follows: "No, sir. That isn't the way the government works. My orders are to bring in every child of school age, and that's what I'm going to do. It is up to the people at the fort to take care of them." At that time, in 1928, on account of the spread of trachoma, certain schools on the reservation had been denominated "Trachoma schools" and all infected were transferred to them while, conversely, all uninfected children were sent away to nontrachoma schools. The superintendent at Fort Defiance was therefore overwhelmed by scores of strange, sick children, with no extra appropriation to care for them—his hospital all built but not a single bed provided, distracted parents rushing in to find their little ones; but his stockman was never too busy to stop and carry on his "kid snatching." The heartbreak and misery of this compulsory taking of children was never more fully exemplified than on my recent visit to Lee's Ferry, Arizona, where old Jodie, or Joe Paiute, lives. He is the last of his people in that part of the country and he and his wife had ten children. But as they came of school age they were taken away from him, and of the first eight all but one died in school. One daughter survived and was sent to Riverside. But like all of them she was given a white person's name, her Indian name was not adequately recorded, and though he had tried to find where she is, the school had lost track of her.

While working for me, Jodie informed me that the truck was soon coming over to take his little boy and girl, the last two children of ten. His wife, he said, sat and cried all the time and he asked me what he should do. I told Jodie and I tell the world that a mother has a right to her children. They are hers, and since the others had all died or been lost he should take these and his little band of sheep and hide far back in the mountains. Poor old Jodie said nothing and I suppose by this time his children are shut up in school. And every year in that school, as in most others, there are epidemics of influenza and other diseases. Very likely his last two will die. In special cases like that I think the government should relent and allow them to grow up wild. And in all cases where the parents object or the children are afraid to go, I think the child catchers should be called off. I have heard too many stories of cowboys running down children and bringing them hogtied to town to think it is all an accident ... It is a part of the regular system where the Indians are shy and wild—and no matter how crowded the buildings are, the children are caught, just the same.

My reason for submitting these facts is that no government employee, no matter how kind-hearted, would dare to mention the practice, while the traders and white residents on the reservation are even more compelled to silence. Yet it is a condition easily solved if day schools are installed and transfers to distant schools abolished. If they could see their children every day, as we see ours, the mothers would gladly send them to school. But if they are torn from their arms and transported far away, given strange names and taught an alien tongue, the mothers will sit like old Jodie's wife and weep and watch the road.[8]

TESTIMONY OF JULIA C. CARROLL

MRS. CARROLL, MATRON. ... So the matron walked me up to the big girls' building and she said: "Mrs. Carroll, when you came this afternoon I saw you over in the guest chamber with a lot of the Indian girls talking to you. That is one of the things the superintendent will not allow. You are not to talk so much with the children. They are Indians and you cannot trust them." I said, "Miss Dushay, I came out here from Mr. Garber's office and he told me to be kind to the Indian children; ..." I said, "However, if it is Mr. Davis' desire, I will certainly not do it." Mr. Davis sent me a letter that I was to go into the dining room and supervise the children taking their meals.

MR. GLAVIS. Tell us what food was furnished to the children there.

MRS. CARROLL. There were four or five hundred children or over to be fed, all the way from 2 or 3 years of age to grown men. They had bread but no butter; half cooked oatmeal with no milk; the sloppiest coffee I ever saw. And there was not enough bread. There were children 4 or 5 years old holding their little hands out and saying: "Mrs. Carroll, will you please see if you can get another piece of bread for me; I am so hungry." That went through like a knife, being a mother. I went to the bakery, and there was lots of bread, rolls piled up, but everything was locked up. I went to Mr. Walker and I said to him: "What is the matter with this school? These children are hungry; they have not enough bread." He said: "They have what Mr. Davis gives them and no more."

MR. GLAVIS. Did you refer the matter to Mr. Davis—the superintendent?

MRS. CARROLL. I met Mr. Davis coming out of the dining room, met him face to face. I said, "Mr. Davis, I think it is a shame the way you treat these children. They do not get enough to eat." He whirled around to me—and he carries a stick—and he said, "I want you to distinctly understand that I am the superintendent here, and I do not want any meddlers; and if you are going to come here and meddle, I will see that you are put out of here."

MR. GLAVIS. Did Mr. Davis own any farms there?

MRS. CARROLL. He owns two of the most beautiful farms. What does he do? He takes boys from the school and takes them out on the farm to work, and the assistants are so afraid of him that they mark those children as present when they are not there at all. I am absolutely sure of it. They work on his farm and do his work. And he takes the Government machinery; and takes the stuff out of the commissary to feed those Indian children on his own farm.

MR. GLAVIS. Were the children punished?

MRS. CARROLL. Oh, punished! They were beaten up like dogs. They were beaten up so that I saw little children beaten up there until, honestly, it is a surprising thing that they have such an institution anywhere conducted by white men over Indian children. I have seen those children beaten up until the blood would flow out of their noses. This brute would conduct a religious ceremony and when he got out he would beat and club those little Indian children. It is a positive shame.

When he was talking to the little Indian children about going home for their vacation I thought everybody was trying to be funny, everybody laughed; and there was a little girl who got very bad treatment from the Indian Bureau; and Mr. Davis, because he could not make her sign a paper against me, compromised that girl's good name, and said she was not decent; and the night of June 10, when he found out that the little girl lived—he went to the other dormitory which no man has any right to go into the girl's dormitory after 10 o'clock at night, and made that girl get out of bed and come downstairs, and he struck her and knocked her down with his fist, and she clung to the handle of the umbrella.

There is a window in the sitting room that the curtain does not come down, and Mrs. Livermore told me, "I saw Davis go in the girl's dormitory at 10 o'clock at night, and I wondered what he was doing, and I peeked in the window and I saw him knock that girl down with his fist, and saw him beat her with the umbrella;" and in the morning I saw Sarah, and I said, "Sarah, what is the matter with your face?" There was a great big blue mark. The girl is almost white. She said, "Mrs. Carroll, I am afraid." I said, "Have you been hit?" She said, "Yes." I said, "Who hit you?" "Mr. Davis." "What did he hit you for?" "I do not know. He came into the dormitory last night and I came down to that room, and he hit me;" and she said, "Will you mail a letter for me?" I said, "Yes." She said, "Well, Mrs. Carroll, he told me that if I told my parents that he would beat me every day." I tell you, you men have no idea what is going on out there at that Genoa School. He is a brute.

Then I wrote to Mr. R. L. Spalsbury, Lawrence, Kansas, and told him the conditions. He is over this Indian school. Over him is a gentleman by the name of Peairs, who I thought was a polished gentleman when I heard of him. Well, I think it must have been Mr. Peairs that sent Spalsbury out there, and he came out to investigate that very business, and he never came to question me. He was going around the country with Davis in his automobile being wined and dined, and having a good time. I got angry, and I said in the dining room one day when he was there eating, I said, "Mr. Spalsbury, do you intend to ask me any questions?" He said, "I will meet you at your room." He came over, and I told him what I thought. He went right straight and told Mr. Davis! What kind of a man do you call that for an investigator? Should not that have gone straight here to the Indian Bureau?

Mr. Davis sent for me to come to his office, and he sat in a big chair, and when I walked in he said, "I do not want you on these premises. I am going to get you out of here. I am going to transfer you, because you had no business to write that letter." I said, "My letter has come back to you?" He said, "Yes, it has." I said, "Alright; I have told the truth;" and he said, "Write this statement, that you made a mistake." I said, "No; I will not do anything of the kind."

Then the matter came up of the beating of that little Sarah, and I sent a letter to the Indian Bureau, and Mr. Burke answered and told me he would have an investigator there, and Mr. Spalsbury came again.

MR. GLAVIS. The same investigator who had been there before?

MRS. CARROLL. Yes. He came again. In the meantime a boy by the name of Mackey had been working down on Davis' farm, and he came to me on Wednesday for some clean clothes, and I gave them to him, and he said, "Mrs. Carroll, there is no use in you trying to do anything for these Indian children. The Indian Bureau is not going to pay any attention to you. That is the way they do with everybody. The only thing for you to do is to try to get your congressman or somebody interested, and go over the head of the Indian Bureau, because it has been going on too many years. I have been beaten up for little things. Even if I do not go out onto his farm to work, I am punished and whipped." I said, "Where does he keep the whip?" He said, "Down in Mr. Johnson's desk; a big cat-tail whip and another whip. It looks like he cannot beat them hard enough, and he takes a loaded blacksnake whip, and he has got little pieces tied to it with string." I said, "Do you mean to tell me that any white man could do a thing like that?" He said, "Yes." I said, "I am going down there to find it." Mr. Johnson had to go away, I think they put him on some other reservation to beat up some other children, and I opened Johnson's door and there was the big cat-tail, slashed down, and on the ends of it, where it ran down in little strips it was tied in little knots. He could not beat them hard enough without cutting into the flesh.

MR. GLAVIS. You say you saw these whips?

MRS. CARROLL. I took them out and I carried them down to Father Borah, and I said, "Father Borah, this is what happens here." I went down and took them away from there and sent them to Mr. Carroll. I said, "You hold these things. I do not intend to stay here. I am coming home, and we will get this whole thing before Congress. It is no use going to the Indian Bureau at all." I sent them home. Not long after I heard that they were going to have a new man out there and investigate matters, and I wanted to have those things there, and I sent home to Mr. Carroll to ship those things right back to me, which he did. He took them to the Department of Justice and they referred them back to the Indian Bureau, and nothing was done, except very suave, polite letters from [Commissioner of Indian Affairs Charles] Burke saying that he was going to do this and do that.

I wrote to Mr. Peairs and told him the condition there, and he promised help, but he went right to Davis and told him everything. This girl remained there in disgrace, and she is pure as a lady; and afterwards I was kicked out of the Indian Bureau.

MR. GLAVIS. Is this the letter announcing your dismissal?

MRS. CARROLL. Yes. If you do not do something about this you are going to have more trouble than this. Mr. Davis sent William Johnson to Miss Schenendore's room—she is an Indian girl. Now in my presence William Johnson said, "Miss Schenendore, Mr. Davis wants to talk to you. Your conduct has been so bad here with ———— that it is a disgrace. You have brought yourselves to such a disgraceful point here that the nice women on the place do not feel like they want to associate with you and Mrs. Carroll." I said, "Look here, William Johnson, what have I done wrong?" He said, "You have disrupted the morals of the whole school."

Miss Schenendore went over to see Mr. Davis and she came back and she said, "Mrs. Carroll, there are only two things I can do. He wants me to swear that you are a liar—in plain English, 'liar'—and that you have influenced me in such a way that I will have to leave unless I sign a paper to that effect, and I refused to do it." Then the scoundrel sent for me. "Now," he says, "I have just gotten through with Miss Schenendore, and she has got to leave or resign; and as for you, I am going to have you put out if I can, because I do not want you; you are too much of a meddler." I said, "I am only telling the truth, and you do not want to hear it." He shook his fist in my face, and I said, "If you were a man of any common decency, if I had my two sons here, they would wipe the floor up with you, and I am not afraid of you."

SENATOR WHEELER. Do you know, Mr. Burke, if Mr. Davis owns the farms?

MRS. CARROLL. He owns two.

MR. BURKE. I think he owns a farm in that vicinity.

MRS. CARROLL. He has two, because I have been to both of them. I hired an automobile and went out there, and while I was out there he had Indian children at work there on his farm.

SENATOR WHEELER. You say he took the food from the Indian—

MRS. CARROLL. Yes. I want to get that in right now. Mr. Spalsbury took four Indians in a room and took their affidavits that when Davis went and stole food from the commissary these boys helped to take it out on the farm and feed the children.

I have got something else to tell you. This boy who then worked out on the Davis farm, that day that Spalsbury was there he came in that afternoon, and Davis took him in his office and the boy told me the next day, "Mrs. Carroll, I do not know what I have signed, but last night they brought me in from the farm after Mr. Spalsbury was here and Davis scared me so; I saw the closet door open and this great big blacksnake whip"—another torture—"I did not know what those two men were going to do with me there. They frightened me so. Mr. Davis gave me a paper to sign and I signed it. I do not know whether it is against you or for you, but, I think it is against you, and he ordered me off the place and I have to leave today."

SENATOR WHEELER. Do you know whether he paid these boys that worked on his farm or not?

MRS. CARROLL. He certainly did not pay them when they were suppose to be in school; but through the summer time, I think, to keep some of the boys there, he paid them 10 or 15 cents an hour; but he kept the money. They had to go to him for the money.[9]

TESTIMONY OF INA M. LIVERMORE

MR. GLAVIS. Something has been said about the boys working on Superintendent Davis' farm.

MRS. LIVERMORE. I know that to be a fact, positively.

SENATOR WHEELER. Tell us what you know about that.

MRS. LIVERMORE. Thursday was bath day for the boys; they would come to me for their bundle of clean clothes. But the boys would come in Saturday evening or Sunday morning. Naturally I enquired as to why they had not come on Thursday evening and I was informed by the boys they had been working on Mr. Davis' farm and could not come in. They were taken out Monday mornings and brought back Saturday evenings.

THE CHAIRMAN. Was that during schooltime?

MRS. LIVERMORE. Yes sir; that was during schooltime, in the spring of the year.

MR. GLAVIS. Did you make any complaint about that?

MRS. LIVERMORE. I did not make any complaint. I asked some of the employees whether it was permissible. I had not supposed it was. I was informed if I sent a complaint to the Indian Bureau my complaint would come back to Mr. Davis' desk and he would proceed to get rid of me in some way or else make me sign a statement I was mistaken.

SENATOR WHEELER. Do you know anything about his taking food and other materials away from the Indian school?

MRS. LIVERMORE. Of course, I only know what I saw. We saw his car every sabbath morning backed up to the back of the commissary and it was said that he took things, but I couldn't say; the clerk said to me. He made the remark just like this: "I am the only one that knows about that." I could tell, of course. I was in the Indian service. I had two boys depending on me and I could not afford to do anything that would jeopardize my position.

SENATOR WHEELER. What was the condition of the dormitories at the school when you were there?

MRS. LIVERMORE. When I was there the boys' building was in a very deplorable condition. For one thing, there was perhaps 9 or 10 beds in the basement. I went there in February, and those boys were afflicted with bed dampening. Those beds were filthy, absolutely. Mr. Johnson, the disciplinarian, took the boys out when they went with their basketball team. I cannot recall where they went, but they went on their trip every spring, and Mr. Mumblehead, who was appointed to take his place, I asked his assistance and we got the beds dried up and got sheets and fixed the beds up. Then he got in touch with the night watchman and had those boys wakened every night to try and clear up that condition. When Mr. Johnson got back he got orders from Mr. Davis to move those beds out of the basement—it was warm down there—and move them out on a glassed-in porch. Now, it is not very warm in Nebraska in March.

SENATOR WHEELER. Now as a matter of fact, they know around those places when an inspector is to come, do they not?

MRS. LIVERMORE. They know. His mail comes three or four days before he does. So his approach is heralded.

SENATOR WHEELER. When they know the inspectors are coming around they just clean up and fix up things do they not, for the benefit of the inspector?

MRS. LIVERMORE. Yes, sir; exactly.

SENATOR WHEELER. As a matter of fact, the inspector very seldom sees anything excepting what the superintendent wants him to see; is that not true?

MRS. LIVERMORE. Yes sir. There were boys out there on his farm when Mr. Spalsbury was there. One of the teachers complained to the disciplinarian about one of the boys in her room being out. You see, the Indian Bureau expects those teachers to pass those children every year, and this teacher asked where the boy was; he had not been in school. She was told he was out on Mr. Davis' farm. She says, "It is too bad, because I do not see how I can pass him if he is not in school." Mr. Johnson spoke this way: "Mr. Davis, he is the boss; it is his orders." Another thing, when he pulls that off right in front of Mr. Spalsbury's nose, I am not going to say anything.

SENATOR WHEELER. What do you know about his beating up the children out there?

MRS. LIVERMORE. Well, the case of Helen Parker—she was one of my girls. She came to me at noon. She had been sent over to us. Her face was all bruised and swollen; her dress was all covered with blood. They had tried to remove the traces of the blood. She came to me and I got her clean clothing. She told me Mr. Davis told her there would be no need for her to write to her people because she would not be allowed to send out any letters. It was perhaps a week or ten days before it cleared up.

THE CHAIRMAN. Do you know anything about him beating up other children?

MRS. LIVERMORE. Only by hearsay. When I was in the boys' building I used to hear the children crying. They said Mr. Johnson used a hose on them.

THE CHAIRMAN. You never made any investigation?

MRS. LIVERMORE. I never made any investigation because I did not feel like it was really worth while. As I say, I could not jeopardize my position. When I was ready to leave I wanted to leave with a good, clean record. That is all.

SENATOR WHEELER. What do you know about the food that was given to these children out there?

MRS. LIVERMORE. Well, they did not get good food. I would not want my children to eat the food they got. In the mornings they generally had a cereal; that is oatmeal, and I think it was sweetened a little. Bread and no butter. What they did with all the milk and butter that all of those cows gave I do not know. They had milking machines there. I really couldn't say how many they had, but they were permitted to have butter once a week and that was on Saturday for dinner. That is the only butter I ever saw.

THE CHAIRMAN. Did the children have milk to drink every day?

MRS. LIVERMORE. No sir. The smaller children occasionally had milk in the evening. It looks like with all the cows they had and the milk—the boys had to get up early to milk—it looks to me like there should be some milk and butter. I think they were supposed to have milk and butter once a week.

COMMISSIONER BURKE. When you came to Washington, did you visit the Indian Office to discuss these things.

MRS. LIVERMORE. No sir, I did not. I did not think it was worth while, to be perfectly frank with you. As I say, I have been working to establish myself permanently in the Government. I have been in Washington four years. On account of my age it was hard for me to get a permanent position, and that is what I had been working for, and at last I succeeded in getting a position and that has been my chief aim.

THE CHAIRMAN. I take it from what you have said, Mrs. Livermore, from the conversations you had at the time with these various employees of the department in the Indian Service that you felt it would do no good to report these things that you have spoke of to the department; that they would not take any action, anyway?

MRS. LIVERMORE. That was just the opinion I had. Mr. Davis had been there for a number of years—I think they said 14—when I went there, and he sent those boys out on the farm every spring and, I was told, the employees said he had been sending them to his own farm; but there was another farm that he let them go to out there.

COMMISSIONER BURKE. I was going to ask you if it is not the custom to let boys go out at times when they are not in school to work on farms and earn money?

MRS. LIVERMORE. They might have been, but this is when they should have been in school.

COMMISSIONER BURKE. Well, they do go out, do they not?

MRS. LIVERMORE. In vacation time.

COMMISSIONER BURKE. Yes; and at other times during the week, Saturdays and days they are not required to be in school they are permitted to go out and earn money for spending money, is that not true?

MRS. LIVERMORE. That might be the case; I could not say positively, because they needed all the children they have there to help with the work. The work there was suppose to be done—

COMMISSIONER BURKE. They did work on other farms than Mr. Davis'?

MRS. LIVERMORE. I was told there was one other person that they said Mr. Davis used to let the boys go to work for.

SENATOR WHEELER. They took them out of school and let them work on farms?

MRS. LIVERMORE. Yes, sir. I figured they were not only defrauding the Government, but they were defrauding the children of their education.[10]

The Product

Plain and simple, most Indian schools failed to produce what they promised: an educated individual who was fully assimilated and ready to take his or her place in American society. As then-former Commissioner of Indian Affairs Francis Leupp wrote in 1910, the Indians did not fail in their quest for an education but the educational system failed the Indians.

I have never made any secret of my somewhat radical views as to the general limitations which it was advisable to set upon the education of young Indians by the Government; and wherever they have been published they seemed to strike a responsive chord among readers who really knew the red race and had no private interests to serve. But a few well-meaning friends who have not had an opportunity to study the field at close range, and have let theory usurp the place of practical acquaintance, are still full of faith in the "higher education" as a panacea for most of the ills of a backward people. If it is so desirable a thing for white youth, they ask in all sincerity, why not for the Indian?

The analogy fails at a good many points. The Indian boy, brought from the camp in early childhood, and passed from one institution to another till he receives his final diploma as a graduate in theology, or a bachelor of arts, or a doctor of medicine, goes to begin his life—where? To New York, or Boston, or Philadelphia, where philanthropy flourishes? If so, the chances are that he will die of homesickness, or starve. As a speaker at church or society meetings, for a while he may prove an attraction for persons to whom an educated Indian is a novelty, but such occasional appearances do not constitute livelihood; even the white altruists will go on employing white lawyers and white physicians, and will probably prefer the religious ministrations of a white clergyman. Moreover, in an Eastern city the Indian is at the same disadvantage socially as professionally; though no racial antagonism raises a barrier against him, neither does any natural bond attach him sympathetically to his environment. I am speaking now not as a theorist, but from personal observation of a number of cases.

Possibly, then, he had better settle in Chicago or St. Louis, Minneapolis or Omaha—cities so recently in the frontier zone that they still retain some of its more liberal atmosphere. I have seen it tried. One experimenter is today subsisting by his wits, borrowing from every chance acquaintance upon whose kindness he can impose, and never paying; another is pretending to practice his profession in an obscure way, but actually living on philanthropic subsidies; a third, who has attempted a series of callings since failing at the one for which he was especially educated, ran up a debt of $400 with a trustful landlady, and took some three years to pay an installment of $100 on it, though spurred by persistent appeals and threatened with legal proceedings. These illustrations are typical. I can at this moment think of only four successes, each outweighed by a score of conspicuous failures.

Is there nothing left for the professional Indian man to do? He can go back to his own country. What awaits him if he does? A little better welcome, perhaps, than he found in the East, but not enough to satisfy his aspirations for leadership. If he is a physician, he has to meet deadly competition with white physicians in any white community, while among his own people the old medicine men fight him with a venom they hardly dare display toward a Caucasian, for they can hold him up to scorn as a renegade. If he is a lawyer he stands a larger chance, but the persons who bring him cases usually do so because they hope to use him as a lure for other Indians in some scheme they are working; and all his surroundings, including the local standards in professional ethics, combine to put his probity to a cruel test. As a minister he may find employment for his talents in missionary work, but in this field he labors, as a rule, under white superiors and subject to their discipline.

Even where he has made a failure, we ought not to blame the Indian. It is his unbalanced white friends who are accountable. He was in no position to get a perspective view of his own situation, and to discover that, however much good raw talent there was in his race, the time was not yet ripe for its utilization in certain fields. The doctrinares with whom he has been thrown have sounded in his ears "the benefits of an education" till the phrase has taken on a wholly fictitious meaning in his mind. What is this education, he asks himself, which white people crave so much because of the advantage it gives its possessor over his fellows? It must be something which, once acquired, will absolve him from further need of hard work, so that he has only to sit still and spread his lap and let fortune fill it with prizes.

Indeed, where his instruction is carried no further than the graduating course at a huge non-reservation school, the chances are that he has no real conception of its practical side till the truth is driven into it by the hard knocks of experience. I asked a group of Indian school graduates once, soon after their commencement exercises, what each expected to do on entering the outer world. Three-fourths of them, embracing both boys and girls, had no definite expectations or ambitions. A few thought they would like to be missionaries. A rather dull-appearing boy believed that "the Government ought to give him a job." Another lad had made up his mind to be a musician and play in a band. Only one in the entire class has decided to go home at once, take off his coat and help his father cultivate their farm. Not one had perfected himself in any skilled trade. I venture a guess that if these young persons, instead of receiving a routine mental cramming with material foreign to their normal element, had been taught merely the essential rudiments of book-learning, but also how to do something with their hands well enough to earn a living with it, every one would have had a better start in life. As it is, I doubt whether any except the farmer and the musician will ever amount to anything. One of the brighter members of the party, whom I have met since, has certainly not improved in the interval.

We hear a great deal about the way the "educated" Indian degenerates after he returns to his reservation. There are, unhappily, too many illustrations of this to justify denial or permit evasion. But what can you expect? Take a boy away from the free open-air life of an Indian camp, house him for years in a steamheated boarding school in a different climate, change all his habits as to food, clothing, occupation and rest, and you risk—what? Either undermining his physique so that he sickens at the school, or softening it so that when he returns to the rougher life he cannot keep up the pace. Morally, too, he has a hard struggle to sustain himself, for he has no social background at home against which to project his new acquirements. The old people laugh at his unIndian ways; most of the young people, even those who have had some teaching near home, feel estranged from him; his diploma finds him nothing to do; and he despises the old life while in no condition to get away from it. Can a less happy fate be conceived than such suspension between heaven and earth? Is it wonderful if a lad not over-strong lets go his hold, and slips back to a last state which seems vastly worse than the first? With a girl, the chances of evil are yet greater, for reasons which must be obvious.

But there is another side to this picture, which saves the courage of those of us who are toiling at the Indian problem; the returned student never does, as a positive fact, fall back quite so far as the point where he began. His outward condition may be worse, but he has learned a lesson. He will start his children, if any come to him, on a much better plane than he started on; and he will try to see that they receive a training more practical than that which proved a broken staff in his own case. He realizes that if he had not been carried so far up, he would not have had so far to fall; that if he had devoted the energies of youth to learning how to shoe a horse, or build a house, or repair wagons, or manage a stable or a dairy, or something else which he could have continued to do after his return home, he might have remained of humbler mind, but he would have grown richer in character and in purse. He would have done more for his race, also; for every time we miseducate an Indian, and the poor fellow pays the penalty of our philanthropic blunder by going to pieces, a lot of shallow sophists shout: "What did we tell you? Anything done for an Indian is thrown away!" It is another shot for the adversary's locker.

How are the Indians to live, inquires someone, unless we educate them to compete with the whites? That is exactly what I wish to see done; but let us study fitness in all things. You would not think of teaching a young man to dye wool in order to prepare him for work in a cotton factory. You would not train a boy as a glass-blower and then put him in an iron foundry to practice his trade. Yet what you are doing with the Indian every day is not less inconsequent. Now suppose, instead of persisting in this folly, you inquire what there is for a young man to do after he has finished his schooling, and adapt your teaching to that? You may not make so brave a showing in your paper statistics of the Indian's "educational progress," but you will make a big difference for the better with the Indian himself, and that is of more importance.

Individualize and specialize: there is your fundamental motto. If a boy is to be a farmer, train him in those things which are absolutely essential to the equipment of a farmer at the outset, and then put him at farming as a hired laborer. His work under such conditions will teach him what life really means, as well as how to reduce his theory to practice. If he is to be a mechanic, train his fingers at school, and then send him into an outside shop to get his bearings in his trade. What he needs is practical rather than showy instruction.

The boarding-schools are suppose to take children of a somewhat more advanced age and intelligence than those who are gathered into the day schools, and to give them a more extended course of study. They also supply a definite need on reservations where it is impractical to extend the day-school system beyond its present dimensions; as for example, where the Indian families are so thinly scattered over a large area that it would be out of the question for any considerable number of children to walk daily to one school, or where the parents are engaged at an occupation like sheep-herding, which requires them to shift camp from season to season. The design kept in view by the advocates of the non-reservation boarding schools, in carrying the children hundreds of miles away from home and trying to teach them to sever all their domestic ties and forget or despise everything Indian, is to surround them with white people and institutions for the whole formative period of their lives, and thus induce them to settle down among the whites and carve out careers for themselves as the young people of other races do. This theory has always had its attractions for a certain class of minds, but in practice it has not worked out as expected.[11]

8

THE MERIAM REPORT

In 1925 Commissioner of Indian Affairs Charles Burke declared that the federal Indian school system was the most efficient and effective way of educating Indians. To support his assertion, Burke stated:

> Its results are now unmistakable and the best argument for its continuance through some years to come. It has enabled the Indians to make greater progress than any other pagan race in a like period of which there is written record. Of the 347,000 Indians in the United States, approximately two-thirds speak English and nearly 150,000 can read and write that language.[1]

Burke's high opinion of the Indian school system was far from universal. Critics of the Indian Bureau held that the Indian policies advanced over the past decades had failed to achieve their intended result: assimilation of the Indians. Angie Debo, in her 1970 political history of the American Indians, wrote, "After more than a generation of destruction of the Indian spirit by forced acculturation and exploitation ... it began to dawn on some good people ... that perhaps the Indians were not exactly prospering under it."[2]

Increasing criticism and charges of failed policies pressured Congress to make a thorough evaluation of Indian policy and Indian conditions. In 1923 Secretary of the Interior Hubert Work appointed the Committee of One Hundred to evaluate and make recommendations as to the state of Indian affairs. Divided by political differences and the absence of a unifying concept, the committee failed to make any substantive recommendations or changes in Indian policy.

A Comprehensive Survey of Indian Education

Urged on by a group of eastern philanthropists who called themselves the "Friends of the Indians," Secretary Work in 1926 authorized the

Institute for Government Research to make a comprehensive survey of Indian affairs. Headed by Lewis Meriam, the institute conducted seven months of field work, thoroughly examining the social, economic, legal, and health conditions among the Indians as well as the state of Indian education. Education was considered in the broadest sense possible; no aspect was left untouched. The institute's report, *The Problem of Indian Administration,* was published in February of 1928.[3]

The Meriam Report, as the study came to be called, described deplorable conditions in all areas of Indian affairs. "It seems as if the government assumed that some magic in individual ownership of property would in itself prove an educational factor, but unfortunately the policy has ... operated in the opposite direction," the report concluded.[4]

Because the Meriam staff viewed the Bureau of Indian Affairs primarily as an educational agency, the report emphasized educational reform. The Indian Bureau's chief responsibility, in the opinion of the survey team, was to see that the Indian people were absorbed into mainstream America or, at a minimum, fitted to live in a standard of decency alongside the dominant culture. Thus, the report urged the promotion of health, advancement of reservation economies, the maintenance of family and community life, and the extension of education to adults. The report also recognized the need to prepare white communities to receive the Indians.

The report identified the boarding school as the dominant feature of the Indian school system, but noted that such schools made inadequate provision for the care and education of the Indian children. In particular, the Meriam staff criticized the poor diets, overcrowded dormitories, inadequate medical attention, and the work-study (platoon) program. Low salaries for teachers were given as the principal reason why education in the Indian schools was not equal to that in non-Indian schools. In addition the uniform curriculum, the strictly routine school work, the placement of students in schools hundreds of miles from their homes, and the restrictive discipline and institutional nature of the schools all served to hamper the growth of the Indian children.

To correct the deficiencies the Meriam Report urged "a change in point of view." The report recommended that the Indian Bureau discard the long-held theory that it was best to remove Indian children from their homes. Instead, the Meriam report urged the Indian Bureau to adopt the "modern point of view" and educate Indian children in their communities, where they could be near their families.

The Meriam Report brought changes to the Indian Bureau, and fostered a new philosophy in Indian education, that is, bringing education to the Indians rather than bringing the Indians to education. In 1929 W. Carson Ryan, the Meriam staff's educational specialist, became the director of education for the Bureau of Indian Affairs. Using the Meriam Report as his guide, Ryan sought to develop a more responsive education system by organizing community school systems on the reservations. Ryan was also instrumental in the general reduction of the Indian boarding schools after 1929. For the first time federal Indian education policy took into account family life. The impact of the report was ephemeral, however. By 1945 the Indian Bureau had returned to most of its old educational practices.

The Problem of Indian Administration

FUNDAMENTAL NEEDS
The most fundamental need in Indian education is a change in point of view. Whatever may have been the official governmental attitude, education for the Indian in the past has proceeded largely on the theory that it is necessary to remove the Indian child as far as possible from his home environment; whereas the modern point of view in education and social work lays stress on upbringing in the natural setting of home and family life. The Indian educational enterprise is peculiarly in need of the kind of approach that recognizes this principle; that is, less concerned with a conventional school system and more with the understanding of human beings.

Recognition of the Individual It is true in all education, of people situated as are the American Indians, that methods must be adapted to individual abilities, interests, and needs. A standard course of study, routine classroom methods, traditional types of schools, even if they were adequately supplied—and they are not—would not solve the problem. ... Indian tribes and individual Indians within the tribes vary so much that a standard content and method of education, no matter how carefully they might be prepared, would be worse than futile. Moreover, the standard course of study for Indian schools and the system of uniform examinations based upon it represent a proce-dure now no longer accepted by schools throughout the United States.

A Better Personnel ... The surest way to achieve the change in point of view that is imperative in Indian education is to raise the qualifications of teachers and other employees. After all is said that can be said about the skill and devotion of some employees, the fact remains that the government of the United States regularly takes into the instructional staff of its Indian schools teachers whose credentials would not be accepted in good public school systems.

Salary Schedules Better personnel cannot be obtained at present salaries, which are lower than for any comparable positions in or out of the government service. In many of the positions, however, it is not so much higher entrance salaries that are needed as high qualifications and a real salary schedule based upon training and successful experience. Public school systems long ago learned that good teachers could be attracted partly by good entrance salaries, but even more by salary schedules assuring increases to the capable—a principle already written into law by Congress, but apparently never made effective in the Indian Service.

The Question of Cost Although high entrance salaries are not the essential factor in getting and keeping better employees, it would be idle to expect that a better educational program will not cost money. It will cost more money than the present program, for the reason that the present cost is too low for safety. ... Cheapness in education is expensive. Boarding schools that are operated on a per capita cost for all purposes of something over two hundred dollars a year and feed their children from eleven to eighteen cents worth of food a day may fairly be said to be operated below any reasonable standard of health and decency. From the point of view of education the Indian Service is almost literally a "starved" service.

EDUCATION AND THE INDIAN PROBLEM AS A WHOLE

That the whole Indian problem is essentially an educational one has repeatedly been stated by those who have dealt with Indian affairs.

Importance of Home and Family Life ... "However important may be the contribution of the schools," says Dean James E. Russell, "the atmosphere and conditions of the home are, especially in the early days of the child's life, the primary determinant in the development of the child, and, since it is the parents who determine these conditions and create the atmosphere, it is they who are of necessity the most important educational factors in the lives of their children." A recent statement adopted by representatives of many nations places education for family and community as a first requisite in any educational program.

More than Mere Schooling Necessary The Indian educational program cannot simply take over the traditional type of school; it must set up its own objectives, finding out in general and for each reservation or tribal group the things that need to be done. ... As tools the three R's still have a place for the Indian, as for others, but they should by no means be the main objective, and, moreover, they cannot be taught to Indian children in the usual conventional way. Confusion on this point in the leadership of Indian education has led to an unjustifiable insistence by Indian school staffs upon learning English as the main objective of the elementary school. Even in the acquisition of this language tool, the older methods are relatively ineffective with Indians. Of what use is a classroom drill and technique with children, some of whom may never have spoken a word in school because of shyness? In such cases what the teacher has to deal with is a home and family condition far more important than any mere skill in speech.

Adults in the Education Program No matter how much may be done in schools, or how much the educational program may center about the school, as it very well may, a genuine educational program will have to comprise the adults of the community as well as the children. Several of the superintendents have realized this keenly, and have started adult education campaigns of one sort or another that are deservedly praised in various parts of this report. Such a community program must include, as Commissioner Burke says, teaching how to farm; it must include a thorough campaign to eliminate illiteracy; it must teach interdependence and reliance upon their own efforts to a people who have been largely miseducated in this direction for several generations.

Education and Other Indian Business At present it is not at all unusual to see the schools teaching one thing and the school plant and agency exemplifying something else. This is especially true in health teaching, where a conscientious teacher will be found instructing her children in the necessities of a good simple diet, and the school dining room will be violating most of the principles laid down, serving coffee and tea instead of milk and seldom furnishing the vegetables and fruits called for in the sample menus the children have learned in the classroom.

Undesirable Effects of Routinization The whole machinery of routinized boarding school and agency life works against the kind of initiative and independence, the development of which should be the chief concern of Indian education in and out of school. What all wish for is Indians who can take their place as independent citizens. The routinization characteristic of the boarding schools, with everything scheduled, no time left to be used at one's own initiative, every movement determined by a signal or an order, leads just the other way. It symbolizes a manner of treating Indians which will have to be abandoned if Indians, children and adults alike, are ever to become self-reliant members of the American community.

Can the Indian Be Educated? It is necessary at this point to consider one question that is always raised in connection with an educational program for Indians: Is it really worth while to do anything for Indians, or are they an "inferior" race? Can the Indian be "educated"?

The question as usually asked implies, it should be noted, the restricted notion of education as mere formal schooling against which caution has already been pronounced; but whether schooling of the intellectual type is meant or education in the broader sense of the desirable individual and social changes, the answer can be given unequivocally: The Indian is essentially capable of education.

Evidence of Intelligence Tests Like members of other races, the Indian has recently been subjected to intelligence tests. Without entering into the objections sometimes raised to these attempts to measure inherent ability, it may be said at once that the record made by the Indian children in the tests, while usually lower on the average than that of white children, has never been low enough to justify any concern as to whether they can be "educated," even in the sense of ordinary abstract schooling. T. R. Garth of the University of Denver ... concludes that "because of differences in social status and temperament" even the differences in intelligence quotients probably lose much of their significance.

Experience of Teachers and Others The experience of teachers in the public schools having Indian children is almost exactly what one would expect from these experimental data. ... Indian children, in both government and public schools, are usually abnormally old for their grade, but statistics collected during the present investigation show that this over-ageness is almost wholly a matter of late starting to school, combined with the half-time plan in use in government boarding schools. By far the great majority of public school teachers who have Indian children in their classes say that there is no essential difference in ability; that on the whole they get along satisfactorily and do the work. Once language handicaps, social status, and attendance difficulties are overcome, ability differences that seemed more or less real tend to disappear.

Indian Psychology The submissiveness of Indian children to boarding school routine, the patience of Indians under difficult conditions, their willingness to surrender, at times, their most cherished cultural heritage, ... whether certain Indian characteristics of today are racial or merely the natural result of experiences—and the probabilities are strongly in favor of the latter assumption—it is the task of education to help the Indian, not by assuming that he is fundamentally different, but that he is a human being very much like the rest of us, with a cultural background quite worth while for its own sake and as a basis for changes needed in adjusting to modern life. ...

Over-Age Children and Attendance The heavy "over-ageness" among present Indian school children reflects the failure to get children into school during the past dozen years. Of 16,257 Indian pupils studied in detail in the present investigation, only 1,043 were at the normal grade for their age, 2,170 were one year retarded, 2,951 two years, 3,125 three years, 2,491 four years, 1,778 five years, 1,160 six years, 665 seven years, and 801 eight years or more, with only 264 pupils ahead of their normal grade. That this over-ageness is not, however, due primarily to slow progress as much as it is to failure to get children into school is shown by the fact that 4,192 have reached the grade appropriate for the number of years they have been in school, and 6,199 others are only two years or less behind the point where their years of schooling would normally put them. This is almost exactly the discrepancy between attendance and grade that is normally found in state school systems.

Illiteracy Among Indians Another customary measure of extent of schooling is the amount of illiteracy. Here again there are conflicting figures, but the census returns make possible some rather striking comparisons. Whereas the rate of illiteracy for the entire United States was 6 per cent in 1920 for Indians of sixteen states having large Indian populations it was nearly 36 per cent. In three of the sixteen states the Indian illiteracy rate exceeded 60 per cent, as compared with rates only a fraction of this for other groups that usually show high illiteracy, namely, rural population and foreign-born whites. ...

THE EDUCATIONAL PERSONNEL OF THE INDIAN SERVICE

Properly equipped personnel is the most urgent immediate need in the Indian education service. At the present time the government is attempting to do a highly technical job with untrained, and to a certain extent even uneducated, people. It is not necessary to attempt to place the blame for this situation, but it is essential to recognize it and change it.

Amount of Training for Teachers Standards for teachers and school principals in government schools should be raised to the level of at least the better public school systems. At present only a comparatively small number of the teachers and principals in the Indian Service could qualify on this basis. ... There is even some evidence that the Indian Service is receiving teachers who have been forced out of the schools of their own states because they could not meet the raised standards of those states. The national government could do no better single thing for Indian education than to insist upon the completion of an accepted college or university course, including special preparation for teaching, as the minimum entrance requirement for all educational positions in Indian schools or with Indian people.

Salaries Abnormally Low The uniform elementary salary of $1,200 in the Indian Service should be compared with the salaries of elementary school teachers in the fifty-nine cities studied by the National Education Association, which in 1926 ranged as high as $3,400, with a large number between $2,800 and $2,900, and a "median" salary of slightly over $2,000.

One result of the low salaries is the amount of turnover in some of the schools. In one school visited in March 1927, there had been twenty-six teachers since September for the eight school rooms. One room up to that time had ten different teachers. Only two of the eight rooms had in March the teachers they started with in September. What this means for morale and educational progress, is easy to see.

Methods of Appointment American school heads make a practice of selecting most of their teachers for the following year between February and June, thereby assuring themselves of experienced teachers who have made good and also of the best new candidates available from the colleges, universities, and teacher-training institutions generally. In contrast to this, Indian Service examinations have been held comparatively late, and appointments not made until so far along that most of the good candidates have already accepted positions. Again, the modern school head almost invariably interviews the candidate in action or gets first-hand information from qualified persons who have. It may not be possible under government conditions to do the thing on such a personal basis as this, but it would be highly desirable if competent heads of schools in the Indian Service could have the same opportunity public school superintendents and heads of private schools have of seeing to it that a teacher is selected who fits the special conditions of his employment.

Chief Changes Needed in Personnel Provisions

1. Superintendents of reservations as well as of schools should be held to at least as high qualifications as superintendents of public schools or directors of extension work.

2. The principles of the salary schedule should be applied to the Indian education service, so that professionally qualified teachers and other members of the educational staff entering the service can count upon salary increases for capable work.

3. The present "educational leave" should be extended to cover at least the six weeks required for a minimum university summer session.

4. There is a need for a definite program of pre-service training for Indian school work.

5. Personnel standards will have to be raised for other employees as well as for members of the strictly "teaching" staff.

6. More attention will need to be paid to service conditions aside from compensation.

The difficulties of getting and retaining qualified employees for the educational service are not confined to salary and salary schedules, important though these are. It would be difficult to find an educational work where the hours are as confining, the amount of free time as nearly nil, the conditions of housing as poor, as in the Indian educational service. In the boarding schools the teachers and other staff persons are almost literally on a twenty-four hour service basis, seven days in the week. The summer school provision recently made means that teachers are obliged to teach in the summer session without additional pay—a condition that obtains, so far as is known, nowhere else in the United States and one that could only be justified by high compensation. In the day schools the teachers are obliged to go almost entirely without any of the congenial companionship that is an essential to morale.

THE COURSE OF STUDY FOR INDIAN EDUCATION

... No course of study should remain static; it should be constantly revised in terms of children's needs and aptitudes; and no course of study should be made uniform in details over a vast territory of widely differing conditions. These are the chief difficulties with the present course of study for Indian schools, which was originally prepared in 1915, and is now very much in need of revision.

Suggestion Rather than Prescription Present-day practice regards a course of study as mainly suggestive rather than prescriptive. It usually lays down certain minimum requirements, or may suggest minimum attainments; but it is careful to leave considerable latitude to the teacher and to local communities. It is doubtful if any state nowadays in compiling a course of study even for its comparatively limited territory would do what the national government has attempted to do, that is to adopt a uniform course of study for the entire Indian Service and require it to be carried out in detail. The Indian school course of study is clearly not adaptable to different tribes and different individuals; it is built mainly in imitation of a somewhat older type of public school curricula now recognized as unsatisfactory even for white schools, instead of being created out of the lives of Indian people, as it should be; and it is administered by a poorly equipped teaching force under inadequate professional direction.

Program versus Actuality The Indian school course of study contains excellent statements about the "use and scope of the library," but there are in fact practically no libraries worthy of the name in the Indian Service, almost no provision for acquiring worthwhile new books, and few if any trained librarians or teacher-librarians to carry out the plans.

A Special Curriculum Opportunity The special curriculum opportunity in Indian schools is for material based upon the ascertained needs of Indian boys and girls and adapted to their aptitudes and interests. Such excellent opportunity exists for community civics based upon both Indian and white community life instead of the old-time "Civil Government," long since abandoned in better American public schools and especially meaningless for the Indian, who needs to have his own tribal, social, and civic life used as the basis for an understanding of his place in modern society. Interesting opportunity abounds for Indian geography as a substitute approach for the formal geography of continents, oceans, and urban locations; for Indian history as a means of understanding other history and for its own importance in helping Indians understand the past and future of their own people. The possibilities of Indian arts would make a book in themselves; already in one or two places, notably among the Hopis, Indian children have given a convincing demonstration of what they can do with color and design when the school gives them a chance to create for themselves. There is such a chance to build up for the Indian schools reading material that shall have some relation to Indian interests, not merely Indian legends, which are good and susceptible of considerable development, but actual stories of modern Indian experiences, as, for example, the success or failure of this or that returned student; how this particular Indian handled what he did in the "Five-Years' Program." These are real things that Indians are experiencing and that have everyday significance for them.

School Organization in the Indian Service

In an effort to furnish Indian boys and girls with a type of education that would be practical and cost little the government years ago adopted for the boarding schools a half-time plan whereby pupils spend half the school day in "academic" subjects and the remaining half day in work about the institution. Some of the best educational programs for any people have been built upon some such provision of work opportunities. As administered at present in the Indian Service, however, this otherwise useful method has lost much of its effectiveness and has probably become a menace to both health and education.

Half-time Plan not Feasible for all Students If the labor of the boarding school is to be done by the pupils, it is essential that the pupils be old enough and strong enough to do institutional work. Whatever may once have been the case, Indian children are now coming into the boarding schools much too young for heavy institutional labor. Indian Office reports speak of the introduction of labor-saving devices as if they were an accomplished fact, but actually little has been done in this direction; there is no money. In nearly every boarding school one will find children of 10, 11, and 12 spending four hours a day in more or less heavy industrial work—dairying, kitchen work, laundry, shop. The work is bad for children of this age, especially children not physically well-nourished; most of it is in no sense educational, since the operations are large-scale and bear little relation to either home or industrial life outside; and it is admittedly unsatisfactory even from the point of view of getting the work done. To make a half-day program feasible, even for older students, a plan of direct pay for actual work is probably better.

A Full-Day Educational Program Needed In Indian schools, as in all good modern school systems, a full-day educational program should continue through the first six years or grades. This should not be a mere three R's academic program which would be just as bad a mistake as the present system, but one that will offer to all pupils abundant provision for play and recreation, work activities of a useful and educational nature, and creative opportunities in art and music. This should be followed by a semi-industrial junior or middle school period of approximately three years with plenty of industrial choices and specific vocational training for chronologically older boys, the content of which shall be determined by general educational aims rather than by the needs of the institution or even vocational aims except in the case of older children. This in turn should be followed by three years of senior high school work, specifically vocational for some students, sufficiently general in the case of others to leave the way clear for further education in college and university for students who show that they could profit by it.

The Platoon Plan "The boarding school program," says the 1926 report of the Commissioner of Indian Affairs, "has been so modified that there shall be assigned each week one half-time for classroom instruction, one-fourth for vocational instruction, and one-fourth for institutional work details of pupils. The school program is essentially the platoon system of organization."

... anything that will release Indian boarding school children from what the Commissioner of Indian Affairs himself appropriately calls "noneducational routine labor" is a step in the right direction. At one school visited the heads of the work departments objected at first to the plan because it gave them the children for only two-hour work periods instead of four, but they later in the year withdrew their objection because, as they said, they found the children did as much labor in two hours as they had previously done in four, and the morale was better. Of course production aims should not control in the education of Indians, any more than they should in the education of whites, but the entire half-day plan has been controlled by the necessity of production, and the platoon plan will not be able to develop into what it should unless an educational rather than a production aim is definitely accepted for Indian education and the funds are provided to get it.

INDUSTRIAL AND AGRICULTURAL EDUCATION
A glance at some of the work-activities of the boarding schools will illustrate the need for a more thorough understanding of vocational possibilities. Harnessmaking is still carried on in many of the schools; in at least one school visited there was harness-making but no automobile mechanics. It is true that recently shoe-repair machinery has been introduced into the harness shops in the effort to replace the vanishing trade of harness-making with that of shoe-repairing, but even here there will be little likelihood of vocational success unless careful preliminary study is made to determine what the actual opportunities are in shoe-repairing and unless supervision and direct help can be provided to the young Indian in setting up in business. Again, a good deal of excellent printing work is done at a few of the schools, in some cases under well-prepared printing instructors using modern material. ... The printing trades are highly organized, and, however good a craftsman the Indian printer may be, unless the way is paved for him to enter union ranks through regular apprenticeship, his way is made unnecessarily hard. ...

Vocational Agriculture From some points of view agriculture is the most important vocation for which Indian schools could give vocational training.

It is already the occupation of the majority of Indians; the schools usually have land, and the Indian himself generally has an opportunity to apply on his own land what he learns in school. On the other hand, agriculture at an Indian school is rarely taught in terms of what the Indian boy will need when he gets out. The old notion persists that farming is a desirable occupation into which more people should be sent, whereas the Department of Agriculture has recently issued warnings to the effect that there are already too many persons engaged in certain kinds of agriculture. ...

... At one school, Chilocco, the important step has been taken of furnishing a limited number of boys with enough land apiece to reproduce individual farm management conditions, but even here it has not been possible to press the opportunity to the point where this might become a thoroughly workable vocational agricultural project.

Vocational Training for Girls The work opportunities of an Indian school offer few opportunities for specific vocational training for girls. ... The contrast between the valuable home economics work in some of the better schools and the mere drudgery of the institution is often striking.

Half-Time and Vocational Training In order to make the half-time program of the Indian boarding school approximate successful cooperative part-time plans of vocational training elsewhere it will be necessary to investigate outside occupations where Indian boys and girls might find a place; to confine the plan to older and more advanced students for whom a specific period of vocational training is clearly the next step; and to employ as directors and teachers of trades persons professionally trained for such work at least to the level of federally-aided public vocational schools of secondary grade. Employment in real adult situations outside would also bring payment for actual service, thereby giving part of the much-needed reality that is lacking in a school where pupils work but are not paid for working and cannot see the relation between labor and life.

The Outing System The nearest approach in the Indian Service to the cooperative part-time plan is the so-called "outing system," which, originally established at the old Carlisle School, Carlisle, Pennsylvania, is still praised by the graduates of that institution wherever one finds them. Its possibilities for specific vocational training have hardly ever been given a fair trial. Whatever it may have been in the past, at present the outing system is mainly a plan for hiring out boys for odd jobs and girls for domestic service, seldom a plan for providing real vocational training.

HEALTH CONDITIONS AT THE SCHOOL
Old buildings, often kept in use long after they should have been pulled down, and admittedly bad fire-risks in many instances; crowded dormitories; conditions of sanitation that are usually perhaps as good as they can be under the

circumstances, but certainly below accepted standards; boilers and machinery out-of-date and in some instances unsafe, to the point of having long since been condemned, but never replaced; many medical officers who are of low standards of training and relatively unacquainted with the methods of modern medicine, to say nothing of health education for children; lack of milk sufficient to give children anything like the official "standard" of a quart per child per day, almost none of the fresh fruits and vegetables that are recommended as necessary in the menus taught to the children in the classroom; the serious malnutrition, due to the lack of food and use of wrong foods; schoolrooms seldom showing knowledge of modern principles of lighting and ventilating; lack of recreation opportunities, except athletics for a relatively small number in the larger schools; an abnormally long day, which cuts to a dangerous point the normal allowance for sleep and rest, especially for small children; and the generally routinized nature of the institutional life with its formalism in classrooms, its marching and dress parades, its annihilation of initiative, its lack of beauty, its almost complete negation of normal family life, all of which have disastrous effects upon mental health and the development of wholesome personality: These are some of the conditions that make even the best classroom teaching of health ineffective.

Physical Education and Recreation Modern emphasis in physical education is upon the recreational and play-type of activity rather than upon the formal and military. In accordance with this principle playground apparatus has been installed at Indian schools and directions have been issued from the Washington office intended to provide recreational opportunities for all school children. Lack of qualified personnel, however, has made it possible to develop this program only partially. The result is that Indian schools for the most part have as the only system of physical training applicable to all pupils a scheme of military drilling that is largely obsolete even in Army training camps. Whatever the advantages of military drill for boys of high school age few advocates of military training would find any value for girls and little children in the formal type of drill insisted upon in most Indian boarding schools.

HEALTH CONDITIONS IN THE BOARDING SCHOOLS
The desirable cubage per child for dormitory construction is usually estimated at six hundred cubic feet. Indian schools in most instances fall far below that figure. The percentage of window space to wall space is low in Indian schools, and hence ventilation is often unsatisfactory. In some instances this is aggravated by the practice of nailing down windows in girls' dormitories. The only section assured of adequate ventilation are porches, and generally they are not ideal, as several sides of the porch are exposed.

The problem of housing is so serious that a few of the numerous instances should be mentioned. The Pipestone School has a new porch on the boys' dormitory which is said to give adequate space. This porch in itself is adequate, but in building it, a large dormitory was deprived of three windows, leaving only a single outside window for about thirty-five beds, which were separated from one another by only a few inches. The three windows between the new porch and the old dormitory are still in place, thus allowing at best the window space of one and a half windows. The inner rooms were very poorly lighted, and the air was greatly vitiated.

The overcrowding of rooms with beds is not the only problem. In a few instances, two children were in a single bed, not because they preferred it to keep warm during the cold nights, but because no room was left to place additional beds. A single instance might have been excused but in one case as many as thirty children were accommodated two in a bed.

Every available space that will accommodate beds is often pressed into service. Thus children are frequently quartered on attic floors, in closely placed beds, with the same lack of light and air. Not infrequently in these attic dormitories the fire hazard is serious. In a school recently renovated, for example, approximately seventy girls were quartered on the third floor of a building of temporary construction. The only fire escape for this floor was located off a store room at the rear of the building. The entrance to this escape was securely locked and the matron kept the key. In case of a fire coming up the stairway, it would be impossible for these girls to escape through the windows onto the roof. Locked fire escapes and nailed windows were sometimes found in girls' dormitories. The explanation offered was that such measures are necessary to keep the sexes separated.

The main sanitary sections are usually located in the basement of the dormitories, making it necessary for the pupil to go down from one to three flights of stairs at night as well as in the day time.

Many dormitories, especially those occupied by boys, are not provided with night toilets on the upper floors. These facilities on the upper floors are generally locked during the day. The Indian Office reports that the present plans will provide more toilet facilities on upper floors.

The Pullman towel system has been installed in nearly all schools, but its effectiveness varies. Apparently about as many towels are used improperly as are used properly. The explanation of misuse is generally the limited supply of towels, necessitating the issue of one to each child either daily or at the designated wash periods. If a child wishes to wash between periods he must make a special request for a towel, which involves the problem of locating the matron, or use available soiled towels, or toilet paper, or nothing. ... The containers are frequently not locked, thus permitted the child to take a soiled towel if clean ones are not at hand.

Tooth brushes are supplied usually by the school ... Apparently the same brush serves for a long time, as the majority appeared much used. A tooth powder is supplied in one can for all children, unless the pupils can purchase individual tubes. This practice is unsanitary because many brushes come in contact with the top of the can. In some schools, the children keep their tooth brushes in their individual lockers, a plan much better in principle than the hanging of dozens of brushes according to numbers on a rack, even though the rack is screened and the rows are staggered to prevent contamination by dripping.

The Indian is often criticized for not accumulating possessions. His lack of this trait is cited as an indication of his general improvidence, and unquestionably his lack of desire for possessions is one of the factors in making him content with a very low standard of living. Certainly the boarding school is making no attempt to change this condition. The Indian boy in a typical boarding school could not possess much more than the clothes on his back, because there is no place to keep other things.

Other Buildings Next to the dormitory, the student perhaps uses the school building more than any other. As a rule, the school rooms and buildings have not been planned in accordance with the best practices in white communities. In only a few could the lighting and ventilating be given a high score. A large number of schools still have non-adjustable seats. In the few schools where adjustable seats were found, no effort was made to adjust them because adjustment is regarded as impractical under the half-day plan of instruction. Two or more groups of children must use the same classrooms, and therefore some seats would have to be adjusted twice daily. The majority of the classroom buildings are not provided with sanitary facilities.

Recreational Facilities Playgrounds and their related activities are not given their due place in the programs of the school children. Some agency officers believe that the child's surplus energy should be expended in some productive labor. Consequently, the playground area and equipment is often curtailed. Greater stress is placed on teams than on individual pupils, and as a result the provisions for individual play and recreation in Indian schools are far below the standards in our public schools.

Care of the Child Thus far an attempt has been made to picture in a very sketchy manner the multitude of difficulties inherent in the average Indian boarding school from the standpoint of the child's environment, not including personnel. The most important factor, however, is the care of the child. With intelligent administration and supervision of a school, it is often possible to overcome to a degree very inferior accommodations and equipment, though in many Indian boarding schools it could not be accomplished under present conditions. For example, nothing will correct overcrowding except providing additional space or restricting the number of pupils. Adequate sanitary facilities are dependent upon good equipment. A proper balance in recreational, school, and labor activities is dependent upon space, equipment, intelligent personnel, and a proper apportionment of the child's time.

Obviously one of the most important items in the care of the child in these schools is the food supplied, and yet in many if not most schools it was found to be limited, not only in variety but also in amount.

Generally speaking, however, the children are not given a balanced ration, and in some instances the food supplied is actually insufficient in quantity. At Rice School, to cite an extreme example, the average amount spent for food was nine cents a day. The dietary was examined at first hand for three successive days, and it was obvious that the children were not receiving an adequate amount of food even of the very limited variety supplied. Malnutrition was evident. They were indolent and when they had the chance to play, they merely sat about on the ground, showing no exuberance of healthy youth.

At several boarding schools visited the officers in charge would offer the explanation that Indian children do not like vegetables, milk, eggs, and other articles of diet, because they never have them at home. A child quite naturally does not like anything he never has had. Tastes for certain foods must be developed. It is just as much a responsibility of the boarding school to teach the child to appreciate a proper dietary as it is to teach him reading, writing, and arithmetic. It is true that dietary facts are generally taught in the school room, but this effort at formal instruction is more than counteracted by the daily meals placed before the child. What is the use of telling a child he should eat fruit, vegetables, and milk, when some of them are never available, and teaching him that he should never drink coffee when coffee is regularly served in the dining room?

In some schools the child must maintain a pathetic degree of quietness. In fact, several matrons and disciplinarians said that they did not allow the children to talk. The loud laughter and incessant din of young voices heard three floors above the dining room at the St. Francis Catholic School on the Rosebud Reservation was an attractive contrast. At Chemawa the children are seated in what are termed "family groups." At each table are boys and girls of different ages, with a big boy at one end and a big girl at the other. If brother and sisters are in the school they sit together. Here the children talk freely, although the bell is sounded as a caution if the matron thinks the noise too great. This arrangement seemed to the survey staff far better than that usually found. In some schools the segregation by sex and age is carried out so meticulously that one table in the boys' half of the dining room contains the smallest boys in the school, and a corresponding table on the girls' side contains the smallest girls. Frequently these little ones can scarcely manage the heavy pitchers and serving dishes. The youngsters charged with the duty of serving the others struggle manfully and get through this task after a fashion, though sometimes a six or seven year old child cannot make a satisfactory distribution of the food.

Some may contend that the poor diet served the Indian children is adequate because so many of them are at or above the normal weight, as computed on the standard height-age tables. To the student of nutrition the weight of a child is but one of the many factors to be taken into consideration in evaluating his nutrition. The Indian child, long subjected to a diet with an excess of starchy foods, frequently has a flabby, unhealthy fat that is sometimes mistakenly assumed to indicate good health. On stripping the child the body is mute evidence of the fallacy of such an idea. The winged scapulae, pot-belly, stooped shoulders, and the general lack of tone and healthy color in the skin give unmistakable evidence of malnutrition. The Indian child frequently suffers from diseases influenced by a deficient diet, notably tuberculosis and possibly trachoma.

Daily Activities ... Generally speaking, the Indian child's day begins at 6 a.m. and continues for the smaller children in some schools until 7 p.m., and for the older children from 9 or 10 p.m. Theoretically one-fourth of the older child's time is devoted to industrial activities, supposedly educational, and not connected with the routine labor of the school. In practice much of the industrial work is undertaken for production and not for education.

The laundries are perhaps open to the most serious criticism. As has been pointed out, the amount of labor spent is far greater than necessary, a waste due to the old, inefficient equipment. Practically all this work requires the child to stand. The monotonous ironing of simple dresses and shirts for hours is frankly production work, and is not necessary to teach the child the simple processes involved.

The methods practiced in disciplining children are often unwise. More than once members of the survey staff have seen small children standing in corners for long periods as a punishment for minor offenses.

Medical Care of the Child ... The most extreme instance of neglect in respect to physical examination was found at one of the day schools. Approximately ninety children were enrolled there at the time of the visit. The teachers and the public health nurse reported that the physician examining these children spent not more than two hours and that he never used a stethoscope or counted a pulse or took a temperature.

In a few schools vision charts were available ... records show a large percentage of visual defects requiring corrective glasses, but it is a rarity to see Indian children wearing glasses. The excuse offered is that they break them. Observation of children in classrooms and while reading indicated that a considerable proportion need glasses.

Not only are innumerable defects overlooked, but there is not enough specialized personnel to make the necessary corrections.

Recommendations

1. Immediate steps should be taken materially to improve the quantity, quality, and variety of food served Indian children in boarding schools.

2. The production of milk should be increased so that the average daily supply will be at least one quart per capita.

3. The definitely malnourished child should be provided with a fuller and more specialized diet than that furnished others.

4. Material improvement should be made in the preparation and serving of food, both for the children in normal health and those below standard.

5. The over-crowding at present found in many boarding schools should be corrected promptly, preferably by providing for more Indian children in schools near their homes, either Indian Service day schools or public schools. A minimum of six hundred cubic feet per pupil in dormitories is recommended. Beds should be at least four feet apart. Not more than one child should sleep in the single thirty-six or forty-inch beds provided. At least ten square feet of floor space per capita without furniture should be provided for "rough house" games.

6. Much more adequate medical care should be given the children. Since so many Indian children are below normal, thorough physical examinations should be made of all children at least twice a year and more frequently for those found below standard.

7. The question of the amount and nature of the work required of boarding school children should be given serious consideration. At several schools both the amount of work required and its nature appear to be an important factor in explaining the low general health condition.

8. Material improvement should be effected both in the toilet facilities themselves and in their use. The equipment should be at least sufficiently modern in design to be

effective, and it should be kept in practically perfect order.
The minimum standards should approximate: lavatories
one to four pupils; waterclosets one to six; showers one to
ten; baths one to six where showers are not used; where
both baths and showers are used one to ten.

RELIGIOUS EDUCATION

Among Indians much of the missionary work is still almost exclusively
confined to the purely evangelistic side. Thus at one school visited the
children attended religious services for two hours Wednesday evenings,
two hours Thursday evenings and twice on Sunday. Even the fact that the
preaching was better than average cannot save this type of religious
education from defeating its own purpose, especially with the compulsory
attendance feature that is attached. The boys and girls of this and other
Indian schools need a real program of religious education, which would
include relatively little forced church-going and Sunday-school attendance but a large amount of scouting, club work, and other activities that
will help make religion part of their daily lives and connect with their
homes. Few of the missionaries of the Indian field are equipped by training
or experience to make the personal and community contacts that are
essential in a modern program.

Judged educationally, current religious efforts among Indians fall down at
precisely this point; knowing little of Indian religion or life, many missionaries begin on the erroneous theory that it is first of all necessary to destroy
what the Indian has, rather than to use what he has as a starting point for
something else. The fact that some of the denominations have apparently
sent to many Indian jurisdictions weaker than average workers brings it
about that instead of the broad handling of the religious background that
one finds on other mission fields, involving recognition and even apprecia-
tion of the religious impulses and traditions of a people, the Indian missionary
is only too likely to be a person who, however honest his intentions and earnest
his zeal (and there are places in the Indian field where even these must be
questioned), puts most of his energies into non-essentials. One finds him
fighting tribal ceremonies without really knowing whether they are good or
bad, interfering with the innocent amusements of agency employees, or
fussing over matters affecting mainly his own convenience. It is hardly to be
wondered at that after many years of work this type of missionary has little
to show in building up personal character among Indians or developing the
religious life of the community.

ADULT EDUCATION

No educational program is complete that does not include efforts to reach
adults as well as children. This is especially true with Indians, where the rate
of adult illiteracy is abnormally high; where economic salvation is largely
dependent upon better agricultural methods; where health conditions are

serious, and where a boarding school policy in education has tended to leave the adult members of the family isolated from necessary social change.

Community organization of social life for Indians, based upon the principle of participation by Indians themselves, is also a real need. The government has in effect destroyed Indian tribal and community life without substituting anything valuable for it. Tribal councils are seldom utilized by the superintendent of an Indian reservation, though they are one of the best natural training schools for citizenship.

Community Participation Indians do not as a rule have even the community participation involved in parent-teacher associations and school-board membership. Most superintendents of reservations and agency employees generally do not understand the fundamental educational principle that the Indian must learn to do things for himself, even if he makes mistakes in the effort. They do not seem to realize that almost no change can be permanent that is imposed from above, that no "progress," so called, will persist and continue if it is not directly the result of the wish and effort of the individual himself.

THE NON-RESERVATION BOARDING SCHOOL

Although the present Indian Office policy rightly favors elimination of small children from the non-reservation boarding schools and the admission of Indian children wherever possible to public day schools, the boarding school, especially the non-reservation school, is still the most prominent feature of Government Indian education. Of the 69,892 Indian children reported by the Indian Office as enrolled in some kind of schools in 1926, 27,361, or slightly less than two-fifths, were in government and other boarding schools; and of the 26,659 enrolled in government schools, 22,099, or more than four-fifths, were in boarding schools, about evenly divided between non-reservation and reservation schools.

Place of the Non-Reservation School Whatever the necessity may once have been, the philosophy underlying the establishment of Indian boarding schools, that the way to "civilize" the Indian is to take Indian children, even very young children, as completely as possible away from their home and family life, is at variance with modern views of education and social work, which regard home and family as essential social institutions from which it is generally undesirable to uproot children.

... Indian parents nearly everywhere ask to have their children during the early years, and they are right. The regrettable situations are not those of Indians who want their children at home, but of those who do not, and there is apparently a growing class of Indian parents who have become so used to being fed and clothed by the government that they are glad to get rid of the expense and care of their children by turning them over to the boarding school.

Entirely too many children are already crowded into the non-reservation boarding schools. Many of the schools regularly enroll one-fifth more than their rated capacity, and the "rated capacity" of an Indian school is in excess of ordinary standards. Members of the survey staff were repeatedly told at schools with a rated capacity of around 850 that it was the practice to enroll a thousand or more, even if there was no place to put them, so that the average attendance would meet the requirements for securing the necessary Congressional appropriation. If this is true, the situation should be clearly presented to the Budget Bureau and to Congress, so that better methods of financing may be adopted.

Needed Changes While non-reservation boarding schools are not the place for young children, there is an admitted value for older children quite apart from the special opportunities here suggested, namely, in furnishing new contacts and in adjusting adolescents to conditions different from those found on the reservation or within the narrow boundaries of the community or the tribe. If the schools are to be what they should be in this and other respects, however, very great improvements will have to be made. Almost without exception Indian boarding schools are "institutional" to an extreme degree. ... Much more attention should be given to boys and girls as individuals rather than in the mass. This will necessitate rooms for two to four students, for example, rather than the immense open dormitory system that prevails so generally; much more adequate health care than is now provided; small classes; less of the marching and regimentation that look showy to the outside visitor but hide real dangers; better qualified teachers, matrons and other workers.

RESERVATION BOARDING SCHOOLS
Many of the statements just made with regard to the non-reservation boarding schools apply to the boarding schools on the reservation, except that not quite such large numbers are involved, and the schools are somewhat nearer to the homes of the Indians. Both of these advantages are offset, however, by the fact that recently the reservation boarding schools have become in some cases as large and unwieldy as many of the non-reservation schools, with even greater lacks in trained teachers and other workers, especially because of their isolation, and the children are often so far away from their homes that there is almost as little opportunity for maintaining family life as in the non-reservation schools.

Place of Reservation Boarding Schools The number of reservation boarding schools shows a commendable tendency to decrease, as public school provision begins to be made. There were only fifty-nine of these schools in 1926, as compared with eighty-five in 1916. The number of pupils has increased, however, without facilities to take care of them having increased in anything like a corresponding manner, the result being that congestion is often worse than at the large schools, and housing and health conditions bad. Ultimately most of the boarding schools as at present organized should disappear.

The changes suggested in the non-reservation boarding schools will have to be made in the smaller boarding schools on the reservation, whether maintained, transformed or eventually abolished. In some cases the public might take over the boarding schools for ordinary public school purposes, but in most cases the government plant is not as good as a local community would insist upon in building a new public school. One advantage that ought to be utilized in improving or modifying these boarding schools is the fact that even with the distances that prevail on Indian reservations the reservation boarding school is usually smaller and less institutional, is closer to the parents whose children it has, and has better opportunities for developing normal social life.

MISSION SCHOOLS

From the earliest time the national government has accepted the cooperation of private citizens and private agencies in many of its activities, and there is no reason why it should not continue to do so in the Indian education enterprise. Without attempting to review the long history of missionary efforts for Indians, it would seem that at the present time mission schools might be justified on at least four different grounds; first, as needed supplementary aid to existing facilities; second, to do pioneer work not so likely to be done by public or government schools; third, to furnish school facilities under denominational auspices for those who prefer this; and fourth, to furnish leadership, especially religious leadership, for the Indian people.

Government Supervision In general the principle has been accepted in the United States that parents may if they prefer have their children schooled under private or denominational auspices. There is no reason why Indian parents should not have the same privilege. Equally definite, however, is the principle that in return for the right of parents to educate their children in private and denominational schools of their own choosing, the community shall hold these schools to certain minimum standards. In the case of Indian mission schools the national government should exert its right, as most of the states now do, to supervise denominational and other private schools. It is important, however, that this supervision be of the tolerant and cooperative sort rather than inspectional in character. Furthermore, the surest way to see to it that private schools are kept on a high plane is for the government to set a standard to which only the best private schools can attain, and to have as its educational representatives persons whose character and professional attainments necessarily command respect.

GOVERNMENT DAY SCHOOLS

Except for sections where good public schools are open to Indians, the government day schools offer the best opportunity available at present to furnish schooling to Indian children and at the same time build up a needed home and community education. That this opportunity has only been partially realized is due to the usual deficiencies both in quantity and quality of personnel.

A Home and Community Enterprise The chief advantage of the day school for Indians, whether maintained by the national government or the state, is that it leaves the child in the home environment, where he belongs. In this way not only does the home retain its rightful place in the whole educational process, but whatever worthwhile changes the school undertakes to make are soon reflected in the home. The boy or girl from boarding school goes back to a home often unchanged from what it was, and the resulting gulf between parents and children is usually more or less tragic. In the day school, on the other hand, the youngster is in the home and community far more than in the school. Some connection is bound to exist between the home and the school, frequently constant and close connection; ideas of cleanliness, better homekeeping, better standards of living, have their influence almost immediately in the home and community.

Need of the Day Schools The weaknesses of the government day schools are the usual weaknesses of the Indian Service: Low training standards and lack of qualified personnel to work with the families from which the pupils come. a few notably good teachers are found in the government day schools for the Indians, but the average is low. It has already been pointed out that with salaries and certification requirements as they are now in the public schools of most states, only those teachers as a rule will apply for the Indian Service who cannot meet the newer state requirements. This applies with special force to the day schools, which are usually in very remote places and lack the attractiveness of surroundings characteristic of some of the non-reservation boarding schools. There are exceptions, of course, including a few who by preference teach Indian children and a few others who go into the Indian Service in order to "see the country" or get the benefit of a certain climate, but for the most part the teachers in the day schools do not appear to reach even minimum accepted standards of education, professional training, and personality. Day school teachers should be at least graduates of good normal schools and preferably of colleges and universities. Furthermore, the one chief opportunity of the day school, that of working with the homes, is missed if the teacher lacks social understanding and if qualified workers of the visiting teacher type are not provided.

PUBLIC SCHOOLS AND INDIAN CHILDREN
The present plan of the government to put Indian children into public schools wherever possible is commendable as a general policy. It will be necessary to make certain, however: (1) That the step is not taken too hastily in any given situation and as a mere matter of temporary saving of money; (2) that the federal authorities retain sufficient professional direction to

make sure the needs of the Indians are met; (3) that the ordinary school facilities are supplemented by health supervision and visiting teacher work— types of aid most needed at present among Indians; (4) that adult education and other community activities are provided.

Advantages of the Public School Like the government day school, the public school has the great advantage that the children are left in their own home and family setting. In addition (and many Indians regard this as especially important) attendance of Indian children at the public school means that the Indian children usually have a chance to associate daily with members of the white race. Any policy for Indians based on the notion that they can or should be kept permanently isolated from other Americans is bound to fail; mingling is inevitable, and Indian children brought up in public schools with white children have the advantage of early contacts with whites while still retaining their connection with their own Indian family and home. This would seem to be a good thing for both sides.

Furthermore, admission of Indian children to public schools involves the important principle of recognition of the Indian by the state. Many of the difficulties of the Indian at present are that he is regarded as in the twilight zone between federal and state authority; the state's welfare activities, usually in advance of what the national government is doing for the Indian, are not available for him because he is regarded as "a ward of the government." Once the Indian child is admitted to the public schools with other children, the community begins to take a much more active interest in him as a citizen. Parents of other children become excited, for example, over the health conditions of Indians, if only for the selfish and natural reason that the health of their own children may be affected. In ruling that the Indian child must be admitted to the public schools the California courts have taken the broad ground that any other action would be a violation of the state's constitutional guarantees of equal educational opportunity. If the states are ever to amalgamate the Indians justly and effectively with the rest of their citizenship, they should begin by taking the responsibility for educating Indian children in the public schools.

Danger in Too Rapid Extension That the government will put Indian children too rapidly into public schools is a real danger, or at least it may fail to follow them up properly when the change takes place. Small though the per capita for Indian boarding schools is, even this is a larger amount than the cost for tuition in a public school. The temptation is therefore a very real one for the government to save money and wash its hands of responsibility for the Indian child. The rapid increase in public school attendance in the past few years suggests that the government has perhaps been more concerned with "getting from under" and saving a little money than with furnishing Indian children the kind of education they need.

School Social Workers To hand over the task of Indian schooling to the public school without providing public health nurse service, family visiting, and some oversight of housing, feeding, and clothing, results unfortunately for the Indian child, especially the fullblood. He becomes irregular in school attendance, loses interest, feels that he is inferior, leaves school as soon as possible; or, in some cases, he is regarded by the white parents as a disease menace, and is barred from school on that ground, though often a little attention by a public health nurse or the school family case worker would clear up the home difficulty and make school attendance normal and regular.

HIGHER EDUCATION AND THE INDIAN

More and more Indian youth will go on for education of college and university grade. Already hundreds of Indian men and women are in higher educational institutions; the University of Oklahoma has nearly two hundred students with some Indian blood, and the increasing number of Indian boys and girls in high school will undoubtedly lead to a corresponding growth in applicants for college admission. This should be encouraged, not, however, by setting up special institutions of higher learning for Indians, but by furnishing adequate secondary schooling and scholarship and loan aids where necessary for Indian students.

Adequate Secondary Education Needed At present the chief bar to the provision of higher education for such Indians as could profit by it is lack of adequate secondary school facilities. Only recently have any of the boarding schools offered schooling beyond the tenth grade. Furthermore, the secondary work offered at these schools would hardly be accepted by most reputable universities throughout the United States. This is not primarily because of the half-day industrial plan, though this affects the situation somewhat, but mainly because of the difficulty so frequently referred to in this report, namely, low standards of personnel. Almost the first requisite for an "accredited" high school, whether the accrediting is done by the state or by regional associations, is that the teachers shall be graduates of standard four-year colleges with some professional preparation in education courses. So far as can be ascertained no government Indian school meets this minimum requirement. Indian boys and girls who graduate from these schools at present find it practically impossible to continue their education in acceptable colleges and universities, because the colleges cannot take them even when there are people interested in Indian youth who would provide the funds.

SCHOOL PLANT AND EQUIPMENT

For the most part the buildings and equipment of government Indian schools are below the standards of modern public schools. The Indian Service has some goodlooking school plants; there are a few creditable buildings erected by student labor, and there is some ingenious use of very limited resources, as in the Hopi day schools; but most of the school buildings are unattractive and unsuited to present-day educational needs.

Furthermore, a policy of patching up out-of-date structures, combined with insufficient repair funds, puts the government school plants at a serious disadvantage.

Too Many Old Buildings One of the difficulties of the Indians school service has been the habit of turning over for school use abandoned forts and other government property (in 1882 Congress enacted legislation which set aside abandoned military facilities for Indian educational needs). There is almost never any real economy in this practice; the recently established Charles H. Burke School at Fort Wingate, New Mexico, for example, has already cost more than adequate new school buildings would probably have cost, and the army barracks and other structures there will never make satisfactory school buildings. Military plants of this sort usually date from long before the modern period of lighting, ventilation, and conveniences, and they are often of poor construction, necessitating continued and expensive repair bills.

Machinery and Other Institutional Equipment Indian schools are conspicuously lacking in the various types of auxiliary equipment that are characteristic of the best modern schools. The chief needs are: (1) Modern school furniture, of the movable type, especially for kindergarten and elementary schools; (2) libraries, laboratories, books, and laboratory equipment; (3) play and athletic facilities for the mass of the pupils. The meagerness of most Indian school classrooms is that of American schools of thirty or forty years ago or of the poorer country schools in remote districts today.

ADMINISTRATION OF INDIAN EDUCATION

If Indian administration is to be effective it will need to have closer relations than have ever existed before with other federal agencies in education and welfare. A number of federal bureaus and boards do work that is directly related to the needs of the Indian Service and their aid should be enlisted. In the same department with the Indian Office, to use the most striking example of need of cooperation, is the United States Bureau of Education, which already has qualified specialists in the types of work in which Indian Service needs are greatest, namely, health, rural education, industrial training, agricultural education, adult education, primary schooling, secondary education, and other fields.

FINANCING THE INDIAN EDUCATIONAL PROGRAM

The educational program recommended in this report will necessarily cost more than the present educational program. ...

How much money will be required to make the changes suggested in this report? While exact figures are impossible because of several varying factors, it seems quite certain that a well-staffed educational program for the Indian Service will cost approximately twice what is now paid.

Amount Suggested Is Small Doubling the amount of funds for government Indian education does not involve the expenditure of large amounts of money. The Indian education expenditure is one of the smallest items in the national budget. The procedure suggested is based on the principle that it is good business to spend sufficient amount to get satisfactory results, rather than to do a half-hearted, unsatisfactory job. Spending the recommended amount will not create an ideal educational service; it will, however, bring Indian education up nearer the level of better educational work in the United States, and it should make possible a certain amount of pioneering and leadership in education that one would like to associate with the efforts of the national government.

In the long run the nation will settle the Indian problem or not by its willingness to take hold of the issue in a responsible and business-like way. … The major problems of the Indian, health, social and economic development, as well as education in the more restricted sense of schooling, are all in need of the kind of handling that comes from people who are qualified by special training. It takes more money to get qualified people than is at present paid in the Indian Service, but on the other hand the work of qualified people brings assurance that the task will be effectively done. The nation has a right to expect that Indian education as a special governmental function will eliminate itself in a comparatively few years; this can come about if funds for an adequate program are provided.[5]

THE NAVAJO–HOPI REHABILITATION ACT

THE HISTORY OF education among the Navajo, particularly after 1868, epitomizes that of other North American tribal groups. To recap briefly, the U.S. Army in 1863 destroyed the Navajo's economic base and forced the tribe on the "Long Walk" to Bosque Redondo (Fort Sumner), New Mexico. In 1868, in a treaty that allowed the Navajos to return to northeastern Arizona in exchange for a promise to stop raiding, the federal government had to provide a school and teacher for every thirty Navajo children who attended school and also make attendance mandatory for all children between the ages of six and sixteen. The education provision was to continue for a minimum of ten years.[1]

While the compulsory attendance provision alienated many Navajos, some of whom refused to send their children to off-reservation boarding schools, the United States government failed to provide an adequate number of schools. As described in detail in Chapter 7, Navajo children were often kidnapped and sent to boarding schools throughout the West. This only increased Navajo reluctance. In many cases the Navajos resisted such abduction of their children by fleeing to the more remote areas of the reservation. The resistance of many Navajos to education continued until World War II, when returning Navajo veterans, having been exposed to the complexities of the world and the need for education, stimulated the desire for education among the tribe.

Back to Boarding Schools

World War II greatly disrupted the entire Indian school system. Decreased funding left many schools understaffed and poorly maintained. The day schools that reform-minded Commissioner John Collier valued were devastated. Needed improvements and repairs could not be made. Enrollment declined during the war years, decreasing from 25,839 in 1941 to 22,770 in 1945.[2] By the mid-twentieth century, Congress had had its fill of cultural pluralism. With American involvement in World War II diverting attention from domestic problems and creating a wave of patriotism, Congress, also influenced by the conservative backlash to the New Deal policies, shifted back to its old view of rapid assimilation of the American Indians.

The 1940s saw government opinion shift back to pre-Meriam Report policies. The House Select Committee on Indian Affairs criticized reservation day schools for adapting their school programs to the needs of the Indian children and reservation way of life. The solution to the "Indian problem," according to the committee, was a return to off-reservation boarding schools. According to the committee, "The goal of Indian education should be to make the Indian child a better American rather than to equip him simply to be a better Indian."[3] In 1944 the committee's report concurred. Its report stressed moving away from the more costly day schools and returning to boarding schools. The committee reported: "If real progress is to be made in training Indian children to accept and appreciate the white man's way of life, the children of elementary school age who live in violently substandard houses on the reservation should be encouraged to attend off-the-reservation boarding schools."[4] The Bureau of the Budget also frowned on authorizing additional reservation schools.[5]

Also in 1944 the Bureau of Indian Affairs hired University of Texas rural education specialist George Sanchez to evaluate the state of education among the Navajo. In 1948 Sanchez recommended the construction of new schools on the reservation as well as increased funding to meet the needs of the children who were not provided with any educational facilities.[6] A second study, conducted in 1945 by George Boyce, Director of Navajo Education for the Bureau of Indian Affairs, concluded that the students should be boarded in off-reservation schools, preferably in public schools.[7]

In the post–World War II years, Congress became increasingly aware of the seriousness of the Navajo educational and economic situation. Beginning in 1946, hearings and reports concerning the status of Navajo education were annual events. No one doubted the seriousness of the crisis, although Congress and the Bureau of Indian Affairs were of the persuasion that to relieve the situation many thousands of Navajos would have to relocate off the reservation, either to the Colorado River Indian Reservation, which had agreed to accept a certain number of families, or to urban centers where the Indians would presumably acculturate more quickly. It was in response to the economic and educational crisis that Congress drew up the Navajo–Hopi Rehabilitation Act of 1950.

Navajos Request Reservation Boarding Schools

Henry Chee Dodge, chairman of the Navajo Tribal Council, speaking at the 1946 Navajo education hearings before the Senate Committee on Indian Affairs, stressed the need for education and the Navajo's preference for on-reservation schools. Not only did Chairman Dodge stress the necessity of education, but he also desired that the education be provided on the Navajo Reservation. Of critical importance to the Navajos was an education that would allow them to compete with non-Indians on or off the reservation. Of key importance is Dodge's assertion that Navajo's needed and preferred on-reservation boarding schools; day schools were as useless as no school at all, he said.

We have many children of school age who have attended no school at all and there are no facilities provided for them to go to school. The facilities provided leave us with 14,000 children of school age on the reservation for whom no schools are provided. Referring back to 1868, provision was made by the Government whereby they would provide a teacher for every thirty children of school age and we would like to ask that it be fulfilled as soon as possible.

The reasons for the establishment of schools, particularly on the reservation proper, are that we have an area on the eastern portion, outside the reservation where there are 13,000 Navajos living. They need to be provided with schools for their children. I would like to leave it to the committee to consider the best possible places to establish the schools for these 13,000 outside the reservation.

I said we need schools to accommodate 14,000 Navajo school children of school age. Not only do we need to have them taught English, but they need to be educated to such an extent that when they are through with schools on the reservation they will be able to compete with white people. At the present time all of them are growing up to the same state as many of our old people—uneducated and unable to compete with the outside world off the reservation.

As I recall it, from the 1868 agreement, it was understood that the Government would educate the Navajo children. That has been intended for a hundred years now. Since 1868 to the present time there are few Navajo Indians who understand the English language and carry on a conversation in other than Navajo. We would like to have a beginning in the near future for these Navajo people so we can see in 15 or 20 years that the Navajos will learn to talk English and be able to get around outside the reservation. We do not want it to take another 100 years to begin. We would like to have it taken up now and have a beginning.

The cost of establishing all these schools on the reservation of the Navajos will be expensive. But the longer we talk about it and the less action we take in the accomplishing of it will only make it more expensive for the people. From 1868 to the present is a long time. Much money has been wasted and there are no results shown, and there is no evidence that this particular appropriation to educate the Navajos has been properly used. We are asking that these schools be boarding schools where they will stay for the school periods. That means they will send their children there to board and room.

We have had an experiment with day schools on the reservation. For the last 12 years day schools have been established on the reservation. We have not a single product of that day school whereby we can point to one or two as a result of the experiment. It does not work with the Navajo people. This is due to the fact that the Navajos do not live in villages but in all directions from these day schools and most of them at a great distance and since there is no provision to get them to these schools it is a hardship to walk these distances and when they discovered it was just a hardship, especially during the cold weather, they could not keep it up.

From past experience with day schools, our tribe has taken it upon themselves to say they cannot take their children to day schools. It is a hardship and sickness to keep that going and we cannot show in the last 12 years a single product of that day school. They tried to go there and could not carry it out. We want to replace that with the boarding schools and that is what we are pleading for our people. They have delegated us to tell you about this desperate situation. That is the weighty matter we have brought to you for your consideration and I hope you may be able to give us an answer that something could be done about it.[8]

Dodge's plea went unheeded. In 1946 the Indian Bureau established the Special Navajo Education Program, for adolescent Navajos who had little or no education. Implemented at Sherman Indian School in Riverside, California, the program had three goals: (1) to prepare Navajo children to live in the non-Indian world, (2) to teach basic education skills to ensure the student the ability to make a living off the reservation, and (3) to teach vocational skills.

In 1948, however, it was estimated that only one-fourth of all Navajo children were enrolled in school. As part of an investigation into the state of Navajo education, a fact-finding trip was organized. In the following selection two members of the team report what they found. Their report was presented at the 1948 hearings before the Senate Subcommittee of the Committee on Interior and Insular Affairs.

THE CRISES IN NAVAJO EDUCATION

The educational situation of the Navajo Tribe of Indians in New Mexico was brought to the attention of the State department of public education when statements were publicized that there are thousands of Navajo children for whom no school facilities are available. Also, it seemed to be the impression of some persons that large sums of money had been spent for Indian education, the results possibly not being commensurate with expenditures; and that the system of education might or might not be a satisfactory and successful one. There also has been considerable public discussion of the possibility that the Navajo Indians, spurred by their war experiences, might seek and obtain the franchise, in which event the large number of illiterate persons who would come into the electorate is a concern to the State.

Our attention had been called to the reports of the Interior Department, Office of Indian Affairs, that the median years of schooling for the Navajo Tribe in New Mexico is only nine-tenths of 1 year, some 80 percent of the tribe being illiterate in the usual definition of that word and about 57 percent unable to speak the English language.

In order to get first-hand information on the situation, a trip to the Navajo Reservation was arranged ... we spent an intensive week visiting a number of two-room elementary schools and all of the classes and school plants in four of the eight boarding schools.

According to the Navajo Agency reports, the reservation covers approximately 14,500,000 acres and the Indians occupy also about 3,000,000 acres outside the reservation boundaries, most of the latter in New Mexico. There are approximately 55,000 Navajo Indians and their population is increasing at the rate of about 2 percent, or 1,000 persons annually. This large annual increase indicates about 17 percent more children of school age are in the Navajo population than in the nation generally, hence a greater proportionate need for school facilities is indicated. It is appalling that schools do not even exist for three quarters of school-age Navajo children.

The poor economic situation of this tribe is beyond the belief of the average American and is rapidly approaching a crisis. Government reports show that during the year 1940 the overall per capita income of the Navajo was about one-tenth as much as that of the overall American (approximately $82 each including the value of home-grown and home-consumed products as compared with a national average of $861).

Navajo Economic Situation Critical During the war, some 3,600 Navajo men and women did valiant duty in the armed forces and about 15,000 were intermittently off the reservation doing war work. The activities provided sources of income which contributed temporarily to improvement of Navajo economic conditions for able-bodied families, but with the close of the war about $7,000,000 annually, or 67 percent of all current income, has been lost to the Indians, who now return to the economic crisis of 1940. Few reservation resources exist, and even with their full development little satisfactory economic improvement can be expected excepting through adequate education.

It has been estimated by the Indian Service that there are at least 20,000 Navajo children of school age, about one-half of whom live in New Mexico. (About 22 percent of the reservation is in New Mexico.) There are school facilities for only 5,500 of these children, some 3,500 of which are in day or community schools in 1944-45 and 2,000 in boarding schools. The capacity of the latter, by Army standards, is only 1,580, but for the last two or three years 2,500 children have been crowded into these schools. Not more than 1,760 of the day school seats have ever been filled because of lack of roads to bring the children in, and since the war, this number has decreased to 1,300. About 500 Navajo boys and girls are being educated by the churches of the United States in mission schools on or near the reservation.

About 12,000 Children Out of School Our first concern was for the thousands of children for whom there are no schools. We observed in traveling over the reservation many children of school age herding sheep, carrying water, playing around the hogans or otherwise occupied out of school. Upon inquiry we found that many of these children had applied for admission and even walked to school over long miles, only to be told there was no room for them and that they would have to remain out of school. The Ramah teacher informed us that six times as many children applied for enrollment as the facilities would accommodate. At Chinle and many other places, when announcement was made that enrollment would take place for 2 days, sufficient children appeared in less than 1 day to fill the school, so others had to be turned away although some children were insistent and kept coming back in an effort to force themselves into the classes.

Existing Schools Not All Operated That only one Navajo child in four can be in school became more shocking when we learned that of the 49 Government day schools on the reservation, 19 have been closed at different times during the war period for lack of funds or lack of personnel. We did not have an opportunity to check cost data or budgets. In our observation, however, we saw no evidence of waste of money during the war period, but there was ample evidence of need for more adequate appropriations. Many of the costs for feeding, housing and other care of children are not properly classifiable as "education" and in our opinion should not be computed as such.

There are three general types of Government schools on the reservation; walk-in day schools, boarding schools, and "community" schools. These last were built originally as day schools, serviced by bus which brought the children from their scattered hogans over distances as far as 40 miles away. The Navajo Indians do not live in villages. The busses proved unsatisfactory in many instances because there were no roads or very poor ones and because of the mobility of the people. The Navajos seasonally move their flocks of sheep between summer and winter ranges, move to wooded areas for winter fuel, go pinon-nut picking in the fall and otherwise travel about more than other groups. As the busses wore out they were not replaced. In many areas, parents were so eager that their children attend school that they met in groups and at their own expense built crude dormitories from the materials at hand, in which to house the children overnight, and convert the day schools into community boarding schools.

Day School Attendance Irregular Attendance, which had been very poor when the children were attempting to travel by bus or walk in, became more regular as soon as the children were housed at the community school. The hogan dormitories at first had only dirt floors, were very small, had no beds and were extremely crowded, but the Indians themselves enlarged and improved the facilities somewhat. Now most of these hogan dormitories have floors and there are usually beds. However, schools are so crowded that it is not uncommon for four children to sleep in each of the double deck single beds. In one school we visited, where beds were not available, the children over-flowed each night into the hallways of the school, where they slept on pads.

Housing of the children at the school site makes an added burden and responsibility for the teacher. When weather is bad, as it quite frequently is in this country, or when parents are unable to come for the children, she must care for the boys and girls over Saturday and Sunday as well as during the other 5 days of the week.

Curriculum Corresponds Closely to Public Schools We found that much scientific study and research has been done to develop a curriculum to meet the needs of all pupils attending the schools. We secured copies of curriculum material, inquired into their development and visited 36 classrooms in operation, besides the vocational shops. Well-chosen teaching materials have been provided for the teachers to enrich pupils' learning and aid in the development of accurate concepts about the world in which all people live. The curriculum corresponds very closely to that of many of the Southwestern States, especially of the public schools of Arizona and New Mexico where there is a non-English speaking group to be considered. This curriculum has been evolved only within the last several years, and it is still in the process of development, which development is being pursued along sound and acceptable academic techniques and procedures. Efforts are constantly and successfully being made to improve the curriculum and efforts are being made, also successfully, to take the children where they are and have them proceed at the maximum of their ability during the entire time they are in the school environment.

Major Emphasis on Healthful Living The professional supervisory staff at the Navajo agency is doing good work to acquaint and help teachers with the many problems of teaching, problems which are much more complex on the Navajo reservation than in an average school system.

Major emphasis is placed on healthful living at all times. The scope of health education has been so developed as to show children how to live better lives, not only in the humble native hogans but also in the type of homes found in modern society. Everything relating to health—fresh air, bathing, care of teeth, care of hair, clean clothing, care of the home, clean beds properly made, accident prevention—is being taught objectively to the children. From the youngest 6-year-old to the oldest boys and girls, the children are actually performing these tasks under courteous, kind supervision and demonstration.

Community School Teachers Heroic Most of the community schools visited were two-room schools. Few individuals employed by the American public elsewhere would even consider performing the long hours of confining work being done by the teachers of these reservation schools. They must rise at sun-up, see that the Indian assistant builds the fires, see that the children are up and brushed, combed, and dressed for their morning meal, and that breakfast is prepared and served to about 55 children. Then housekeeping duties must be performed by the children, to clear away the dishes, make their beds, clean the hogan dormitories and report to class. This is made particularly difficult because of the constant change in children, as new ones come in who are unable to speak the English language, and who are usually without toilet training or any knowledge of personal care.

All the clothing worn by the boys and girls must be laundered, both washed and ironed, then mended by the children themselves with the aid of the teachers and the woman assistant. After the morning duties have all been performed, the teacher is ready to start her day in the classroom. Here the problems are difficult and complex. Shortage of school facilities, plus economic need of the parents to keep the children home to herd sheep, make for intermittent attendance—the Begay family for example may decide to send Mary to school this year, then next year John comes to school, and the year after it will be Ben's turn to have a year of education. Ages of the children in a room range from 6 up. Some of the oldest ones may have been in school only 1 or 2 years, or possibly for the first time, and it is necessary to separate them into at least three or four ability groups. The groupings are arranged on the basis of social ability. Having an older child come into school for the first time is a problem we encounter in the public schools, although it is much more prevalent on the reservation where there is no compulsory education and where the facilities are so inadequate that only one fourth of the children can be in school.

Simple Dormitories for Community Schools We were told that the Government is building low-cost dormitories at three of the day schools which were too distant for us to visit. The Government should take the responsibility for erection of modern dormitories with adequate facilities for training these children in comfortable home living. These should not be of an institutional type; nor should they be crude, unfinished, cold, uncomfortable temporary structures such as have been erected by the Indians themselves. It is most commendable that the parents of these Navajo children arose to the occasion to build dormitories when the United States Government was occupied otherwise. ...

At Ganado we saw a walk-in day school, where no dormitories have been provided for the children to stay overnight. Some of the children walk as far as 8 miles and attendance is extremely irregular at this school. When boys and girls can attend, many of them are so exhausted and hungry from the long walk that they are not capable of performing good school work.

In general, in our visits to day and community schools, we found the architecture and condition of the plants satisfactory, excepting for the need for dormitories. Some of the schools that have been closed and which we urge be reopened soon, must be reconditioned. Some original installments were never completed and plumbing, heating plants, and other equipment have deteriorated from nonuse. We saw one fine school closed in the Twin Lakes area although there are hundreds of children in that section out of school.

Boarding Schools We visited four of the eight boarding schools. The plants were aged and decrepit, and not originally built for the service they are now rendering. Some were old army quarters built from 30 to 60 years ago and then converted into boarding schools. Walls are crumbling, plaster is off, electrical wiring is in bad condition; At Chinle and Tohatchi we saw walls so weak that roofs had to be supported by inside and outside braces, and some buildings had been abandoned or partially abandoned because they were unsafe.

The atmosphere of the dormitories at the boarding schools is reminiscent of a poor orphan's home of two decades ago, with bare iron beds crowded together. Because of overcrowding it is impossible to conform with proper health requirements for spacing beds to obtain proper air ventilation and sanitation. Barrenness of dormitories is due partly to lack of space and also to total lack of such furnishings as dressers, chairs, mirrors, etc. Also the condition might be attributed in at least one instance, to the regimented attitude of the matron in charge. The only place a child has for any personal possessions is usually a tiny cubbyhole in a multiple open-shelved cabinet in a hallway.

There are no facilities for the segregation or isolation of sick children. At Fort Defiance, the dormitory toilet facilities are the only ones available for use of children during school hours, although this necessitates travel from the school for a distance of more than a block. This seems to be the prevailing boarding school situation.

Recommendations

1. In order to properly finance the education of 20,000 Navajo Indian school children, adequate appropriations are essential to build the school facilities required as well as to operate and maintain them in the future.

2. An adequate budget must be provided to operate the schools now in use, to reopen and keep open the schools now closed, to erect suitable dormitories, and to convert day schools into community schools.

3. The condemned and damaged buildings at boarding schools should be replaced or renovated as required, with whatever enlargements or new plants are necessary.

4. A complete building program must be financed and carried out to provide and then operate additional elementary and secondary schools to educate all children for whom there are now no school facilities, as well as such vocational training and high schools as may be required.

5. Provisions should be made so that substitute teachers are available; at present there is no provision for a substitute in case a regular teacher must be absent from the class.

6. There should be school nurses, and in all other ways we believe the boys and girls of the Navajo Reservation are entitled to and should have educational facilities that meet present-day requirements such as are considered essential for rural education in all other parts of the United States. They are entitled to such an education not only because of the promises of their treaty with our Government but in their own right as promising young American citizens.

> *Mary Watson,*
> Director of Elementary Education,
> *Gail Barber,*
> Director of Arts and Crafts,
> New Mexico State Department of Public Education.[9]

Government Pushes Off-Reservation Boarding Schools

By 1949, 1,650 Navajo children were attending boarding schools in Chilocco, Oklahoma; Phoenix, Arizona; Carson, Nevada; Albuquerque, New Mexico; Chemawa, Oregon; and the Cheyenne–Arapaho boarding school in Oklahoma. In 1950 a seventh school—the Intermountain Indian School in Brigham City, Utah—was established, enrolling over twenty-two hundred students by 1952.

The Special Navajo Education Program did not solve the problem of inadequate educational facilities on the Navajo reservation. In 1948

Secretary of the Interior Julius Krug consolidated the Sanchez and Boyce studies and proposed a long-range program for Navajo rehabilitation. The forward to Krug's report detailed the goal of the bureau.

> The program provides, in essence, adequate education, health, and other public service facilities, the development of physical and other subsistence resources on the Navajo Reservation, and assistance in obtaining stable employment or occupation off the reservation. The complexity of the problem faced in preparing and executing a comprehensive program is well established. In recent years the Navajos have become the Nation's foremost Indian problem. The social and economic assimilation or adjustment of so large a minority group could never be, at best, a simple matter. Today, too, the Navajos are facing, for the first time, these difficult questions. How are the people to live with white Americans? What alien ways must they learn if they are to survive? Navajos will be encouraged to seek work off the reservation as soon as they acquire sufficient training. Navajos now regularly employed off the reservation will be discouraged from returning to the reservation.[10]

The Navajo–Hopi Plan

Out of Secretary Krug's report came the Navajo–Hopi Rehabilitation Act of 1950. The act outlined a comprehensive program to conserve and develop tribal resources and to generate employment on and off the reservation. Of the nearly $90 million appropriated over a ten-year period, $25 million was allocated to education. Acting contrary to the Sanchez report the Indian Bureau emphasized off-reservation boarding schools to hasten assimilation and save money. Many Congressmen and Indian Bureau officials believed that, as Navajos relocated from the reservation, the crisis would be solved by simple subtraction.

A Major Miscalculation

In the following selection from the 1948 Navajo–Hopi rehabilitation hearings, George A. Boyce, director of Navajo education, and William Zimmerman, assistant commissioner of Indian affairs, proposed the construction of a limited number of educational facilities on the Navajo reservation on the assumption that many Navajos would relocate off the reservation within a few years and the critical need for schools would subside. Under critical questioning Boyce and Zimmerman admitted that their recommendations would not meet the educational needs of all the Navajo children. Zimmerman pointed out his belief that Congress probably would not fund any long-term building projects since many of the schools, in his opinion, would eventually sit empty. It is important to note that two Congressman participating in the hearing were sharply critical of the bureau's efforts and recommendations.

MR. BOYCE. You have had pointed out to you that the Navajos have a great health problem, a great economic problem, and while I may be biased as a school teacher in putting unusual faith in education, I don't think it is too much to say that better health and better use of resources, better citizenship, better training for off-reservation employment—in fact, all aspects of Navajo progress, depend on education, and in education in its broadest sense, not merely learning how to spell "cat" and that 2 and 2 is 4. So that in those terms we start with people who are not only illiterate in the vernacular sense but almost completely ignorant of life in an industrial society and whose premises of thinking and thought patterns are definitely different from those in the surrounding society. Therefore, these people need universal education—that is, every child needs an education. Many adults who never had any schooling need some educational services, and they need a very good education. Certainly, after waiting all these years it would be little enough to give them the best kind of schools that we know how to build and certainly it is going to take the best know how under the best conditions that we know how to provide.

We have on the reservation school seats for about 4,500 to 5,000 in Government schools. Now some of those seats are not occupied because in the day schools, for example, where we have 60 seats we are sleeping children in 30 of them, or the equivalent of it. In other words, where we have two classrooms with 30 seats each, we are using one classroom with mattresses on the floor or castoff beds as a dormitory, so that at present our actual facility is considerably less than those 4,500 seats. Some schools are closed and those seats, therefore, are fictitious to that extent. The seats in the boarding schools are very inadequate seats. The dormitories are overcrowded, toilets and sanitary facilities are obsolete and inadequate. So we say we have 4,500 seats, plus or minus, but it is with a big "if" and under very serious limitations. So one of the first proposals is to make fully available all of the seats that we have and to make somewhat decent the seats that we have by including sanitary installations, eliminating some of the over-crowding and some of the generally hazardous conditions.

The road system proposed is only a skeleton road system of main roads to the schools so that we can get supplies in and out, and it does not include just trails out to the hogans where the people will be living. We subscribe to a child walking to school if it is within walking distance over terrain that he can walk across. That is our first proposal.

Our second proposal is to modernize the plumbing, the lighting, the electrical wiring, and things of that sort in our larger boarding schools. We now have to add some temporary dormitories in some instances, permanent dormitories in others, so that we can at least walk by the beds in the dormitories. We can reduce the cross infection for any contagious diseases by having a proper distance between the beds in the dormitories.

We also propose in some of these community schools where there is sufficient water to undertake some enlargements so that in some instances where we have a 2-teacher school or 60 seats to add on another room with the necessary classrooms, dormitories, quarters, and the like. So the program as it now stands in those terms will give us on the reservation no more than 8,500 seats. Some of those are uncertain because we included in the estimate those that we are not building or proposing now because of the inadequate water. Otherwise we won't be able to use all the seats that we have in those schools. Our most optimistic hope is to bring the present Government seats up to about 8,500; with an estimated 1,000 mission school and small public school seats, that would give us on the reservation about 9,500 seats. Children from 6 to 12 in the first six grades and age range would be given preference. We estimate that we have at least 12,000 children in that age range. This program also proposes to make some additional seats available in some of the non-reservation boarding schools, such as at Albuquerque, Phoenix, in California and Oklahoma, and some more or less temporary construction on the Colorado River project.

MR. FERNANDEZ. I am wondering why the program was cut down to $25,000,000 when other estimates all indicate that it would cost a great deal more, and why it was cut down to take care of only 9,000 children when double that amount should be provided for—and provided for now. What right have we to say to the Navajo people, "We will educate only half of your children?" If we have an obligation to educate them, we have an obligation to educate them all, to provide schools for all of them and not for only 50 percent of them.

MR. BOYCE. What we have recommended in this case has been that the Government do what is in this program in the first 3 years, the ten-year education construction program, and the program as now phrased makes the statement that we will review every two or three years further possibilities and needs. I think it should be understood by the committee and all those interested in Navajo education that this is, therefore, in terms of dollars and in terms of seats and not a complete Navajo education program.

MR. FERNANDEZ. That ought to be made very clear not only to the Government but to the country, that this program does not anticipate a complete job at all. Mr. Sanchez made a thorough study and estimated it would cost about $85,000,000 excluding the road construction. Here we are calling for the expenditure of $25,000,000, which admittedly takes care of less than half of those who are without schools. Now then, certainly to take care of the full amount it will cost at least $50,000,000 and may I say right now that in studying the history of this reservation and the programs that have been presented heretofore in the years from 1920 on, I think around 1919, that a program was put forth and in that program only about one-third were ever contemplated and not anywhere accomplished. And time after time we see it is the same thing. We take care of only one-third or one-half and let the rest go. You are never going to finish the problem unless we face the facts, and the Congress ought to know the facts and face them.

MR. ZIMMERMAN. We are faced with these alternatives, either we say to Congress, "You provide structures for a total population, which admittedly is in excess of what the area will support, with the result that at some future time you are overbuilt as to your schools, or you build for the population on the reservation which, according to the best estimates, will remain permanently on the reservation and make subsequent provision for that excess population." The location of other schools in addition to those suggested in this report would necessarily depend on the developments in the next few years. If a thousand families go to the Colorado River Reservation, if a thousand families move away to urban areas, or whatever developments may be, those developments will materially change the situation. There is one other factor that seems to me to be clear. Maybe I underestimated the generosity of Congress, but I don't believe the Congress will feel justified in spending 80 or 100 million dollars on boarding schools which we would have to confess would be temporary institutions.

MR. FERNANDEZ. Wouldn't it be better to guess wrong in favor of the Indians than to guess wrong and find ten years from now we are in exactly the same situation we are now?

MR. BOYCE. We don't know where the Navajos will be four or five years or any number of years from now, and it is squarely up to Congress as to whether or what shall be done for the 4,000 we see remaining on the reservation, and the ten thousand beyond that we have as children today. I know that you can project the Navajo condition another fifty years. For every day that goes by with any child that is not in school, the 10 year-old that is not in school today, 50 years from now will be a 60 year old Navajo adult who has had no schooling.

MR. BARRETT. I would like to make this plea at this time. We need these schools badly. I believe this is the poison spot of America. It is a poison spot because the lack of education of the people is a menace to all other people around them. I would like to make this plea. We need these schools and we need the program. For the love of God give us enough money and enough people to do the job.[11]

A Navajo's Plea

The letter that follows, written by Navajo tribal member Jacob Morgan to the Senate Subcommittee, stressed the necessity of education as the top priority of the Navajo Nation. The education sought, moreover, was one that was equivalent to a state curriculum rather than the standard government Indian school curriculum. This implied opportunities for higher education, which were deemed necessary to many Navajos since most of the federal Indian schools were not accredited; therefore, most colleges in the United States would not accept Indian students from the non-accredited Indian schools. Without an appropriation to provide an education for all Navajo children, Mr. Morgan opined, the past seventy-eight years of "non-education" would prevail upon the Navajo once again.

With your permission I should like to present a very short statement regarding Senate Bill 2363 on promotion of the rehabilitation of the Navajo and Hopi Tribes of Indians. I shall speak for the Navajos.

The greatest need of this very large tribe is school and education above all things. I fully realize that if my people are expected to get along, help themselves in the world as law-abiding citizens they have first got to acquire education. There is no way around it.

Now, for the information of the honorable committee, I should like to review very briefly the growth of our Navajo schools to show some weakness there. After the return of our people from 4 year's captivity at old Fort Sumner, New Mexico, a school was first proposed to be established at Fort Wingate, New Mexico, but the same year it was transferred to Fort Defiance, Arizona. At first only 30 children were enrolled out of probably nearly a thousand. Four years later (1874) a new schoolhouse was built for 128 pupils, but only 84 were taught. The school began to struggle along until finally, in 1879, the number of pupils went down to 15. In the year 1880, a larger boarding school was established. At the time I entered Fort Defiance, in 1889, there were only about 56 pupils. And now, after 78 years, our tribe has increased to over 60,000 and there are over 12,000 children growing up without education. For this number of children we now have 6 boarding schools with a capacity of not more than 300 pupils and we did have about 40 or more day schools built up after the old Mexican style but half of them are closed and boarded up and I cannot tell how many boys and girls are attending these now. At any rate, those in authority say 5,000 boys and girls are now in school, while more than 7,000 are out of school. How long are they going to wait for opportunity?

For a number of years, some of us have been advocating that all our schools be put under the State's courses of studies rather than to struggle along with the Department's progressive education. Why don't we have some good high schools at several points on the reservation with regular State courses of study? I know our ideas about these things have been scoffed at by those who want to keep the Indians down, but I am determined to bring before your honorable committee that we need and should have advanced education. Some people say to do this is to push the people into civilization too fast. To the contrary, if these people are not being pushed along toward better education there will be another 78 fruitless years. In these days it is not too fast for anybody to learn to do what is good and useful. Learning better things by doing is better than seeing our boys and girls "go back to the blanket," as the saying is.

Now there is a proposal of a 10-year program. I see by that program the Bureau would plant industries or small factories on the reservations. If that is the idea, then why not go back to the old system of training like we used to have: Carpenter, blacksmithing, wheelwright, shoe and harness making, painting, farming, engineering and electrical work for the boys; and for the girls, sewing, dressmaking, cooking, laundering, nursing and so forth. If these are reopened in all our boarding schools to give our young people the very best opportunities, I am sure a part of the $90,000,000 now proposed for rehabilitation will be wisely spent.

To be sure, our people are in dire need of well-prepared, educated men and women for leadership in all lines of work, and leaders must come forth from our Navajo schools. If a Portuguese or even a Jap can be recognized to receive college education in our country, most certainly we Navajos are entitled to the same. I want to state to the committee that in the last 78 years our people have been trying to get along fairly well on the crumbs that fall from the table of higher levels of learning.

Education must largely depend on good health. Those in authority must look far beyond the horizon of the future to keep in mind that in this fast-changing world our people must be shown the way to good health, for education and health must go hand in hand together. Health depends on pure water. I hope a portion of the $90,000,000 will be set aside for this purpose. We also need two all-year-round roads running east to west across the length of the reservation, and two roads to run crosswise north and south. These roads if constructed will prove to be a help in reaching the most remote places. Now gentleman of the committee, these items I have mentioned to you, to my mind are the most essential to the welfare of the Navajo people. I am sure the Navajos will appreciate all these besides the need of education. Thank you.[12]

Despite the attention focused on the Navajo situation and the passage of the Navajo–Hopi Rehabilitation Act, thirteen thousand Navajo children were not in school in 1954. That year Congress enacted the

Navajo Educational Emergency Program, which called for the construction of elementary schools and additional public schools, the expansion of boarding schools, and the establishment of bordertown dormitories for Navajo students in bordertown public schools. As part of this effort the Bureau of Indian Affairs provided a number of temporary trailers to be used as schools. However, because of the shortage of educational facilities, many Navajo children continued to be sent to boarding schools throughout the West. Elementary school children were sent to boarding schools as far away as Albuquerque, New Mexico. [13]

Although most Navajo children were in school by the late 1950s, there remained a shortage of facilities because far fewer Navajos than expected relocated from the reservation. By 1969 there were still four thousand to eight thousand Navajo children not attending school, largely due to a lack of facilities.

THE PUBLIC SCHOOLS

THE MOVEMENT TO place Indian students in public schools began in 1891 when the federal government paid public school systems ten dollars per quarter for each Indian student enrolled. The purpose of placing Indians in public schools was to "render the specific Indian School unnecessary as speedily as possible, and to substitute for it the American public school."[1] In 1894 Commissioner of Indian Affairs Daniel Browning noted, "It is in full accord with the desire of the nation to do away with the Indian problem by assimilating the Indians in the body politic of the United States."[2] Several years later the Indian Office began to admit non-Indian children into the Indian schools as "an easy way to integrate the two cultures."[3] By 1909 three thousand Indian students were enrolled in contract public schools in California, Nebraska, South Dakota, and Utah. An additional 818 students were enrolled in non-contract public schools in twelve states.[4]

Federal Assistance for Public Schools

In 1934 Congress enacted the Johnson–O'Malley Act, which granted the Secretary of the Interior authority to contract with "any State or Territory, or political subdivision thereof, or with any State university, college, or with any appropriate State or private corporation, agency, or institution, for the education of Indians in such State or Territory."[5]

The Johnson–O'Malley Act established two important concepts. First, the law made it possible—at least in theory—for Indian tribes or organizations to incorporate under state law and then contract with the interior department for educational services; such authority, however, was not made statutory until the passage of the Indian Self-Determination Act in 1975. Second, the act reaffirmed the continuing legal responsibility of both the federal government and the states to provide education for

Indians. While the federal responsibility was based on treaty and statute, the states' responsibility lay in their obligation to educate all residents.

Because most public schools are supported by property taxes and Indian lands are non-taxable, the original intent of the Johnson–O'Malley Act was to provide federal subsidies in lieu of taxes. Some states were also willing to assume part of the responsibility for educating Indian students. Although the law specifically called for the protection of Indian culture and enhancement of cultural studies, most public schools failed to provide any substantive programs for Indian students. Community hostility and school administrator's indifference to Indian needs trickled down to many of the public school teachers. Indian children—at the expense of their own cultural heritage—were taught the culture, history, and values of the dominant society. As recently as the late 1960s, Indian children in some schools studied history from books that depicted Indians as savages. High dropouts rates or apathy usually resulted from this type of miseducation.

The public school movement gained momentum in the 1950s with the passage of Impacted Aid legislation which comprised a pair of laws. The first, Public Law 81-815, provided federal funds for the construction of schools in areas affected by federal activities, such as military bases or other federal lands that are nontaxable. Since Indian reservations were federal trust lands, the legislation was applied to Indians living on reservations. The second law, Public Law 81-874, provided money for the operation and maintenance of schools affected by federal activities. Indians living off the reservations were excluded from these laws; in later years legislators expanded the laws' coverage.

The intent of the Impacted Aid legislation was to abolish state contracting under the Johnson–O'Malley Act and, by withdrawing federal support for Indian-only education, promote equality among Indian children and non-Indian children in public schools. However, Amendments to the Impacted Aid legislation not only expanded the use of federal funds in Indian education but allowed school districts to obtain Impacted Aid subsidies while retaining Johnson–O'Malley funding.

The Elementary and Secondary Education Act of 1965 extended federal financial assistance to local educational agencies that served a large numbers of low-income families. In amendments, Indians were made eligible for special educational needs programs. Later amendments, such as Title VII, added bilingual education programs for Indian children. In schools with few Indian students the special programs provided did not necessarily meet the needs of the Indian children.

In the selection that follows, from *Education and the American Indian: The Road to Self-Determination, 1928–1973,* Margaret Connell Szasz traces the history of Indian education in the public schools and argues that, with few exceptions, Indian educational policy focused on acculturating Indian children, even though the federal subsidy laws held the retention of Indian culture as their main objective. Thus, it was common for school districts, particularly before the mid-1960s, to misuse Johnson–O'Malley funds that were designed to enhance Indian educational needs, by applying them to programs for the school at large, often benefiting non-Indian students more than Indian students.

EDUCATION AND THE AMERICAN INDIAN

Although some Indian children attended public school before the end of the nineteenth century, the federal government did not begin to contract for this type of education until 1891. In the first years that contracting was done, Bureau leaders were not convinced that the transfer of pupils to public schools was practical. After ten years of contracting, they admitted that "notwithstanding the incentive of $10 per capita offered by the government, indifferent results were obtained." Public schools for Indian pupils, they concluded, are valuable "only when they are located in sections favorable to the coeducation of the races." Given the difficulty of contracting during this early period, this conclusion was realistic. Nonetheless, public school enrollment began to climb after the turn of the century. By 1928, the year of the Meriam Report, public schools had already surpassed federal schools by a significant margin in number of Indian students enrolled.

The forty years between 1930 and 1970 witnessed the greatest increase in public school enrollment in the history of Indian education. In 1930 federal schools accounted for 39 percent of total enrollment of Indian children in school, while public schools accounted for 53 percent. By 1970, public schooling had jumped over three times, from 38,000 in 1930 to 129,000 in 1970, which meant that 65 percent of all Indian children in school were attending public school. Those who attended federal schools in 1970 accounted for only 26 percent of Indian children in school, or a total of about 51,000.

During much of this period the Education Division played a prominent role in the transition to public schools. From 1930 to 1953 it was the sole federal agency responsible for funds allocated to public schools for their Indian pupils. Carson Ryan had recognized the trend toward public education as early as 1928. In the Meriam Report he observed that the policy of placing Indian children in public schools was to be "commended."

When Ryan became Education Director he retained this attitude. His quarrel with public school enrollment was not with the theory but with the method of funding by the federal government. Funds were provided to school districts for their Indian pupils to the extent that the districts incurred a loss of revenue from non-taxable Indian lands. ... Although the federal government did not "contemplate paying the entire cost for the education of Indian children," it was willing to make up the loss that their enrollment would entail.

However, the system of payment was unnecessarily complex. Rather than contract with each state for a single annual tuition payment to cover all of the Indian children in the state, the Department of the Interior went through the tedious process of dealing with each school district. This meant, in effect, that it was negotiating hundreds, even thousands, of contracts each year. Ryan thought this was not only "administratively absurd" but also a "violation of every principle of Federal-State relationship in education." The federal government "should not be dealing directly with local communities in this fashion," Ryan said, "it should be dealing directly with the states."

As soon as he took office, Ryan began to implement this idea. Within a matter of weeks he began negotiating with a number of states on the Bureau's plan to consolidate its public-contract operations in several states. Ryan suggested that in each of these states the Bureau appoint a supervisor who would serve as a liaison between the Indian Service and the state departments of education.

Despite the awkwardness of the arrangements, those states that cooperated with the Bureau's Education Division during this early period were among the earliest to sign state contracts with the federal government. The difficulty of reaching a compromise that suited both levels of government gave an advantage to states that had some experience in working with the Bureau. The situation within the state itself, however, also contributed to the early completion of some contracts. In both Washington and California, for example, by 1934, Indian education was already controlled by the state divisions of instruction. This situation had shifted the responsibility for Indian education to state officials and had forced them to develop a state policy as well as a system of revenue. One of the last states to sign a contract with the federal government was New Mexico, which had been unable to direct the education of its Indian pupils since it had a large number of federal schools. On the other hand, Arizona, which had an even greater Indian population, was one of the first four states to sign a contract. The great majority of Arizona's Indians lived within the Navajo Reservation, which meant that they could not attend public schools in any case. Consequently, Arizona moved quickly to form a state plan for educating the small number of Indians who lived within access of the public schools, and sought a federal contract to implement this plan.

The diversity of conditions among the states with significant Indian populations was compounded by an even greater diversity among school districts within each state. Although the Bureau was fully aware of the problems this created, Congress was extremely slow to pass the necessary legislation, and it was not until April 16, 1934, that the Johnson-O'Malley Act was passed. JOM, as the legislation came to be known, established the legality of state contracts by authorizing the Secretary of the Interior to enter into contracts with any state or territory that had legal authority to do so for education, medical attention, agricultural assistance, and social welfare. Thus, after providing funds to public schools for some forty years, the Bureau was finally given the authority to centralize its contracting on a federal-state basis.

The year 1934 marked the high point in good relations between Congress and the John Collier administration. In the first six months of this year, two of the most important pieces of legislation of this administration were passed: The Indian Reorganization Act and the Johnson-O'Malley Act, both of which would have a profound effect upon the Indian people. However, the net effect of the two measures was neither the sudden separatism feared by some nor the rapid assimilation feared by others. The heritage of Indian-white relations and of federal Indian policy served as an effective barrier to change, and change was also slowed by the critics of the new policies ... Although the federal government had been supporting Indian education for more than fifty years, Congress still begrudged these appropriations. In 1935, for example, debate in the House of Representatives raised the question of legitimacy of appropriating funds for Indian children when general school funding was in dire need because of the Depression. Supporters of special funding for Indian children pointed out that the need of public schools made it even more necessary to give them added funds for the new pupils. The increased Indian enrollment had already overcrowded the schools beyond the capacity of local or state funding. To turn back to boarding school education was unrealistic, however, for the per capita cost would be more than tripled should the government "build Indian schools and attempt to run them on a departmental basis." Thus Congress was committed, albeit unwillingly, to an expanding aid program for public school education.

The Johnson-O'Malley program was predicated on the assumption that state and federal administrators could work together toward a common goal. Even before the act was passed, however, Bureau education leaders were concerned about this relationship. When state administrators became aware of its built-in difficulties, they hastened to establish independent control, a hostile reaction that forced Bureau leaders to relinquish their aid and direction much earlier than they had originally planned.

Bureau educators were very dubious about the motives of the state public-school systems. Principally they feared that public schools were more interested in the money that Indian enrollment would add to their school budgets than in the Indian pupils themselves. They knew that many schools were in serious financial difficulty and were all too eager to receive additional funds. The challenge for Bureau educators was twofold: Could they retain sufficient control over the funding and administration of public-school programs to insure that the type of education needed by Indian pupils would be provided? Given the trend of increasing state control of JOM programs, could they teach state administrators the unique approach necessary for Indian students before the states took over? The history of the

JOM program, from its inception to the 1950s, is, to a great degree, an account of the Bureau's failure to cope with this challenge.

... Diplomacy was the unwritten guideline for Bureau communication with state departments of public instruction, but the tone of the correspondence made it apparent that extensive experience in administering a system spread over a vast area and compounded by a multitude of tribal situations bred a superior attitude on their part. In most cases, the state appeared to them to be a novice, which with proper guidance might emerge as an able director of its own Indian education.

Despite this assumption of superiority, Bureau education leaders soon discovered that they were also learning things. ... State conditions seemed to exist in an infinite variety, and each had to be dealt with individually. Variety itself was not a new phenomenon for the Indian Bureau, but variety compounded by the administration of a separate bureaucratic entity was.

... In the 1936 *Annual Report* Collier listed the most important controlling facts: type and quality of schools actually maintained; amount of money needed to maintain a suitable school adapted to the needs of Indian and white children; amount and value of nontaxable Indian lands; methods of taxation; amount of state support for education; basis of distribution of state support; maintenance and capital outlay costs; changing legislation affecting school finances; distribution of Indian children; and attitudes of whites toward Indians. Collier frankly admitted that these factors created the "ever-changing problem" of "determining what part the Federal Government should assume in support of public schools."

... In contract negotiations it was imperative that the Bureau be well informed about each of these conditions in the state concerned. In some states with large Indian populations, such as Arizona, few of the Indian children attended public schools; in Oklahoma, on the other hand, more than three-fourths of the Indian children were enrolled in public school. At least one state—Oregon—derived about 60 percent of public-school revenue from local funds, which enlarged the responsibility and authority of local school districts, while others depended almost entirely on state income. Sources for state income also varied tremendously, from poor states like New Mexico where the property tax accounted for less than one-fourth of the state revenue, to more wealthy states where it provided a significant portion of state income. If the budget was dependent upon property taxes, the amount of nontaxable Indian land within a community was a determining factor in the ability of the school district to raise money for the schools. In such cases, the amount of Indian land was in direct proportion to the financial need of the school district: the greater the amount of nontaxable land, the greater the need of the district. However, if funding came from sources other than property tax, then theoretically the impact of nontaxable

Indian land on the school budgeting should be less significant, and, in turn, JOM funding would be proportionately smaller.

Many of the problems that arose in the federal-state relationships were present in the initial contracts. Between 1934 and 1941 four states negotiated contracts with the Department of the Interior: California (1934), Washington (1935), Minnesota (1937), and Arizona (1938). With the exception of Minnesota, all of these states experienced difficulties either in their contract negotiations or in the implementation of their contracts. In each relationship the circumstances were different, but there was a common thread through the discontent—that of the federal government asserting too much authority over a system that had already developed a jealously guarded autonomy. The federal bureaucracy might be older and more extensive, but it was being duplicated on a smaller scale by the expanding bureaucracies of state government. ...

California served as the advance guard by completing its contract in the same year that the JOM program went into effect. ...

... Many California Indians were satisfied with the JOM program. But if this was the case with the Indians, it certainly was not true of some of the state administrators who found it necessary to work with Mary Stewart, the Bureau appointee who held the position of Superintendent of Indian Education for the state. An experienced educator, Mary Stewart had been with the Indian Service for seven years when she received the California position. A number of factors combined to make this experience perhaps the most difficult in Mary Stewart's career with the Indian Service. One of the reasons she encountered so much antagonism may have been her approach, which Willard Beatty, head of the Bureau's Branch of Education, later described as both a "frank and fearless presentation of the facts" and a "quiet but firm insistence that steps be taken to correct irregularities." Her forthright attitude was not calculated to ease the problem of state autonomy, which in any case was blown up out of all proportion by egoistic state administrators. ...

Beatty, with his customary perceptiveness, understood the dilemma of state education administrators who found it necessary to maintain, at any cost, the image of independence (even to the point of making a Bureau liaison appointee like Stewart feel like a "clerk"). Despite his support, however, the strain of the relationship must have proved too great. By 1941 Mary Stewart had retired from the Indian Service and by 1942 the Bureau position of Indian superintendent in California had been abolished. The Indian Service continued to maintain a watch over its "interests" in the state, but it no longer took an active hand. ...

... During the first five years of the state contract in Washington difficulties were few, particularly when compared with California. Homer L. Morrison, a Bureau employee and Superintendent of Indian Education, developed a good rapport with state and county administrators. Washington's Superintendent of Public Instruction, who had been on good terms with Bureau educators for a number of years, handled the situation without excessive demands for autonomy. When a new state Superintendent of Public Instruction was elected, however, the relationship suddenly became strained. ... As a result, the Bureau found it expedient to appoint a new Superintendent of Indian Education. The new superintendent was forced to step into the "rather delicate situation" of appeasing both the critics of the old policy and the demands of the new Superintendent of Public Instruction, who was anxious for the state to assume full direction of JOM funds.

Again, Willard Beatty's diplomacy was called upon to smooth over the situation. He was aware that the newly elected Superintendent of Public Instruction based her argument for autonomous control of funding on the situations in California and Minnesota. In each of these states the director of Indian education was appointed by the state, and the Bureau had assumed the capacity of advisor. In Washington State, however, Beatty had little confidence in the ability of the person whom the state superintendent wished to appoint. Although he modified his stand to the extent that he granted further control of the program administration to the state appointee, he saw to it that the reins of control remained in the hands of the Bureau employee. Within a few months, the beginning of the war, the resignation of this second representative of the Bureau, and the cutback of federal budgets enabled Beatty to transfer the direction of the Washington contract to the Bureau superintendent in Oregon. The latter was then responsible for a more economical district, which included Oregon, Washington, and northern Idaho.

In spite of Beatty's deft handling of the question of Bureau control, he predicted that assumption of state control in Washington was merely a matter of time. In 1941 he wrote, "We have looked forward to a gradual diminution of the total federal contract and its ultimate elimination as the state aid payments to districts reach a point of adequate support." Beatty's primary concern was that the state be fully prepared for the total commitment, once it was made. At least one state—California—still was not prepared when termination of JOM went into effect. Despite the shortcomings of federal control, it might have been advantageous to maintain federal supervision in some states, even if only in an advisory capacity.

Minnesota proved to be an exception to the pattern of uneasy rapport established between the first two contract states and the Bureau. From the early thirties, Minnesota had an exceptionally well run Department of Education. When Samuel Thompson visited the state for contract negotiations, he quickly decided on a positive recommendation and wrote to Beatty, "There is no state within my knowledge where the head of the state school system and his right-hand man have either the knowledge or the interest in the education of Indian children as is to be found in the State Department of Public Instruction in Minnesota." When a state had already attempted to plan its education program around the needs of both Indians and whites, the Bureau reasoned, there was no necessity for Bureau control. Therefore, the Indian Service fully supported the state's choice of O. R. Sande as administrator of the JOM contract. As an experienced education administrator, Sande was praised by Samuel Thompson, who observed that he had "always been interested in the Indians and for a number of years has given a large part of his time to looking after the Indian children."

In the estimation of Bureau leaders, the early years of Minnesota's contract proved to be as successful as the Education Division had expected. In 1941, when Collier summarized the four state contracts then in existence, he concluded that the Minnesota JOM program was the "most efficient." The program "has produced greater advantages to the Indian people," he pointed out, "and as a result has furnished a better educational program to the white children also in attendance at these schools."

The Arizona contract was much smaller than the others and consequently was less of a burden for the Bureau, which could brush aside the usual dispute over who should manage and distribute JOM funds. The Education Division would keep in "close touch" with the state, Beatty advised the Superintendent of Public Instruction, but "your office would take over the distribution of tuition funds to the several districts." Thus one of the basic causes of conflict was avoided.

By the end of the 1930s the precedent for state contracting was well established. The Bureau had negotiated four contracts and others would soon follow. Bureau education leaders nevertheless remained skeptical of state control. Since they viewed public schooling for Indian children as a compromise at best, they regarded the independence of state educators as stretching this compromise. Some years later Beatty admitted that in many ways Bureau education was superior to that of public schools. Ryan had also questioned the advisability of transferring Indian students to public schools without extensive follow-through on the part of the Bureau. In the Meriam Report he recommended that the Indian Service "supplement the public school work by giving special attention to health, industrial and social training and the relationship between home and school." He concluded, "The transition must not be pushed too fast."

This attitude was a significant comment on the esprit de corps of the Bureau in the 1930s. During the Indian New Deal the infusion of new leadership introduced a fresh approach. In the case of Ryan and Beatty, it may have been more optimistic than it was realistic. Under their guidance the Education Division began to demonstrate a concern for the value of Indian cultures and for the possibility of modifying the Bureau school system to meet the needs of those cultures and, consequently, of the individual student. When these ideas began to be implemented in the 1930s, the Education Division reasoned that Bureau education was geared more to the needs of Indian students than was the public-school education. A number of education administrators who worked with the states were deeply concerned about the weaknesses of the public school systems. Their experience convinced them that most public school administrators had very little background in developing special programs for a unique group such as the Indian students, and they feared that the students would be seriously affected by this lack of understanding.

This concern was sufficiently great to reach the level of policy statement. In the 1934 *Annual Report* Collier indicated that the Bureau was fully cognizant of the poor conditions of the schools where Indians would probably be enrolled. These were the schools that were "especially hard-hit by the depression," and as a result they tended to drop the newer courses—"health and physical education, shop work, home economics, art, music"—which, according to Collier, were the "real fundamentals." Since the Bureau had already begun to include these courses in the curricula of its schools, it was naturally reluctant to transfer Indian children to public schools without some assurance that a "modern type of education" would be provided. Collier concluded, however, that public schools offered other advantages that made the transfer advisable. This was the dilemma of education leaders confronted with giving up students to an inferior system.

During the next few years, Bureau education employees who worked directly with public schools continued to weigh the values of public school education against those of Bureau education. They were in a position to observe the built in faults of the public school system, but the awkward nature of their divided responsibility—as liaison between the state systems, with their competing local districts, and the Bureau of Indian Affairs—made it exceedingly difficult for them to improve the existing structure. As one employee who had recently been transferred to a superintendency of state Indian education wrote, "I have been almost completely baffled for answers to the problems of needed corrections for evident weaknesses."

One aspect of public schooling that cried out for improvement was the attitude of teachers and administrators, particularly in rural areas. Whereas Bureau educators suggested that new Indian pupils might need individual guidance, rural teachers who had to conform to the attitudes of the local populace often found it difficult to regard their Indian pupils with even ordinary civility and kindness. The indifference of their administrators to the underlying causes of Indian behavior also discouraged teachers from developing a sympathetic attitude. As one state Indian superintendent wrote, the teachers "simply mirror the attitudes of those who control their professional destinies and so they can be even more difficult to convert than the community itself." There were many exceptions, however. In Nevada in the mid thirties several communities flatly refused to allow Indian children to attend their public schools. But on the Flathead Reservation in western Montana, Indians had begun attending public schools shortly after the turn of the century, and the idea of barring Indian children from these schools ran contrary to several decades of experience.

Many Bureau educators were convinced that most public schools were unsympathetic toward Indian children, and whenever they compared the two systems public education came out a poor second. As Willard Beatty concluded, "school for school, the teachers of the Indian Service are superior in training and character to those found in many small rural public schools." Beatty was basing his conclusions upon the efforts of his own administration, and there is no question that during his term of office teachers received better training than under any other administrator. The in-service training program was highly successful and the efforts to encourage Progressive Education within the Indian Service were so well known by the late thirties that one state director of public instruction, in the process of negotiating a contract with the Department of the Interior, commented, "With the progressive and practical ideas of education that Willard Beatty has we can get ideas across to our public school people by learning what is being done in Indian Education." Beatty's own teachers may not have been as uniformly Progressive-minded as he wished, but unlike many rural school teachers, they did have the opportunity to keep abreast of current trends in education and to receive special training for teaching Indian children.

In its efforts to prepare the public schools for the programs that would meet the Indian student needs, the Education Division attempted to respond to the tremendous variety of conditions within the states and in the individual school districts. In some areas, the greatest needs were physical—transportation, school lunches, even clothing and shoes. It was not unusual for Indian families to send their children to federal schools primarily because these needs were supplied. Transfer of their children to public schools did not lessen the need. Nonetheless, the Bureau was reluctant to extend this aid to children in public schools.

Most Indian parents could provide clothing, but many were dependent on school lunches, which were often the only nourishing meal of the day for their children. On at least one occasion a sympathetic teacher used this program as a means of educating the children about the values of a balanced diet and how to plan, purchase, and cook meals. ... In some areas, such as the remote stretches of the larger reservations among the Dakota Sioux or the Navajo, the greatest physical problem was transportation. From these areas the boarding schools had filled their quotas during the assimilation period. They had also been the proving grounds for the community day school experiment of the 1930s, which failed because of transportation difficulties and other problems during World War II. On the perimeters of these reservations, where white towns rubbed shoulders with Indian land, some children could be enrolled in public school if transportation could be provided for them.

The physical needs of the children were important, but sometimes other needs were equally urgent. These were more easily ignored. If children needed busing to school or a free meal or a pair of shoes, it was fairly obvious. If they needed special guidance in order to adjust to a new environment, or to determine vocational training; if the relationship between the family and the school needed the assistance of a social worker; if the children would benefit from courses on Indian history or from bilingual courses—these needs were less easily recognized. One source of this problem was lack of communication. Parents had little idea of what went on in the schools, since many of them had not attended school or had dropped out. As far as Indian parents were concerned, there was little community direction of the school; any "community" direction came from the white community. Nor did the Indian students speak out about their needs; they felt that their teachers and their non-Indian classmates had little sympathy for them. They were taught the culture and history of mainstream, non-Indian America, and from this perspective they learned that they were nonentities, or worse, "savages," as outdated textbooks continued to describe them even in the 1960s.

In the first years of JOM contracting Bureau leaders expressed a guarded hope that special programs for Indian students would be implemented through the public school system. In Oklahoma, George C. Wells, one of the most enthusiastic state directors of Indian education and an Indian Service employee, outlined a number of suggestions which would have been sound advice for most communities involved with Indian education. These included a system of close supervision and in-service training of rural teachers (in cooperation with the state); use of health workers and social workers in Indian communities; training to properly equip Indians to serve as teachers, physicians, nurses, and so on; a program to make both whites and Indians more conscious of the contributions the Indian has made to civilization; and an increase of the part played by Indians in working out their own problems.

In formal policy statements the Bureau perpetuated an optimism not unlike that of the Oklahoma supervisor. In the same year that JOM was enacted, Collier wrote that the Indian Service would not transfer "extensive and important Indian educational work to the states or to their subdivisions except where careful preparations have been made." By this time, the Education Division knew that most of the hoped for gains from such changes would "eventuate only when adequate replacement arrangements are set up." In the next few years the truth of this statement was proved, but often through the unhappy discovery that replacement arrangements simply could not be made.

There are only scattered indications of successful adaptation of Bureau programs. When the Genoa Boarding School in Nebraska was closed, the Bureau tried to help the children by sending social workers to work with the families and providing a physical-education instructor at the Winnebago-Omaha Agency, which supervised the area. At local schools, the Bureau helped to introduce shopwork and to strengthen home economic programs. In the state of Washington, which had transferred all Indian children to public schools before the JOM Act was passed, the Superintendent of Indian Education also attempted to adapt Bureau principles to public schools. He planned to employ four visiting teachers paid by the Indian Service to relieve congestion in an overcrowded community school. With public school cooperation, he was also introducing vocational education in schools that had never before offered these courses. In addition to the standard tuition payment, in some parts of the state the federal government provided funds for books, supplies, and clothing. Reports from other areas indicate that the Bureau's major success in attempting to establish programs for Indian pupils was in vocational education and in meeting the children's physical needs. Interest in courses related to Indian culture was rare.

Thus the Education Division was generally unsuccessful in its effort to influence public school education. When the states began to administer federal funds, they were no longer directly responsible to the Bureau. The failure of the bureau to maintain control in the 1930s and early 1940s meant, therefore, that it had lost its opportunity to affect the public schools. The primary weakness in the JOM program that prevented the Education Division from implementing its ideas can be summarized as follows: the poor quality of teachers and administrators; the hostile attitudes of communities; the public schools' greater interest in funding than in the Indian students themselves; the diversity of conditions among and within the states; and the difficult relationships between state and federal administrators. All of these led to a type of education ill suited to the needs of the Indian children.

Despite the numerous shortcomings of the JOM program, Indian enrollment in public schools continued to grow in the post-war years. By 1953 there were 51,000 Indian children in public schools, 31,000 of them in schools that received JOM funds. The number of participating states had jumped to fifteen, and individual districts in other states as well as the Territory of Alaska were also in the program. Most states administered the federal funds themselves.

The year 1953, which was the nineteenth year of the JOM program, was a dividing line for Indian education in public schools. It marked the end of a single federal program to aid public schools and launched the new sources of aid that would take more and more of the burden away from JOM itself. However, the new legislation had no immediate effect on the use of funds established by JOM. Although public schools often received additional appropriations through the new programs, they continued to use them in their general school budgets.

In 1950 Congress passed two bills that became known as the "federally impacted area" legislation (Public Law 874 and Public Law 815). These laws were intended to provide federal funds to compensate school districts for the financial burdens placed on them by federal activities. P.L. 874 was to provide funds for general operating expenses, in lieu of local taxes; P.L. 815 was to provide funds for school construction in federally impacted areas. When these laws were passed, they were not applied to Indians; they were intended primarily for areas that supported military installations. In 1953, however, they were amended to include Indians. In the case of P.L. 815, a further section (14) was enacted to enable the federal government to provide funds to school districts where there was a need for additional facilities for Indian enrollment.

In the case of Public Law 874, the legislation took a more complex twist. Before it was amended in 1953, it was the subject of extensive debate between the state education administrators and the U.S. Office of Education under the Department of Health, Education and Welfare. Many state officials objected to a mandatory transfer of funding from JOM to Public Law 874, in the event that the latter was amended to include Indians, because they preferred the flexibility of the JOM program. JOM was funded according to school district need, that is, according to the "tax exempt land and Indian children to educate." Public Law 874 would be funded according to entitlement: "Only children whose parents lived on or worked on trust land (would be) considered for Federal aid." In other words, the amount of funds a district would receive would be based on the "specific number of eligible Indian children." There was some question as to whether this numerically based formula was a wise criterion for funding, and whether the Indian child might not suffer in the long run. One other reason for state opposition was that state departments of public instruction were familiar with the JOM program. They had come to rely on these funds and, in many cases, administered them independently.

The outcome of this debate was an amendment that tried to please everyone. Although it permitted Indian children to receive funds from Public Law 874, their eligibility would be determined by the state in which they resided. The governor of each state that held a JOM contract would decide whether he wanted to transfer to Public Law 874 funding, but transfer meant a cutoff of JOM funds. This amendment became known as the "governor's clause."

For the next five years Public Law 874 remained unchanged. Most states remained opposed to the new form of funding, and only two of them transferred. In 1957, at a meeting of state Indian education administrators, with one exception the states voted in favor of the governor's choice clause.

Despite this mandate of state opinion, in 1958 Congress passed a second amendment to Public Law 874 requiring all JOM states to transfer to Public Law 874. This was not, however, the mandatory change that state educators had feared in 1953, for it did not terminate the JOM Act. In some states, under certain conditions, school districts would be eligible for both types of funding. The new amendment stipulated that states must apply for Public Law 874 funding as their primary source of aid. If this assistance was equal to or greater than the previous JOM funding, then the latter contract would be canceled. On the other hand, if the total funding under Public Law 874 did not equal that of the previous contract, then JOM funds would make up the difference. Public Law 874 was intended to provide the basic support for these children, hitherto provided by JOM; and JOM was now to be used only for special needs.

In many cases the passage of this amendment meant additional funds for school districts, but still the measure created a great deal of concern for state education administrators. Their immediate problem was adjusting their budgets for the fiscal year 1958-59. Since Congress did not pass the measure until August 13, it became law after all of the state budgets under the JOM program had been approved for the fiscal year. An even tougher problem was complete revision of the state plans. Under the JOM program each state submitted an annual state plan that outlined its Indian education program for the coming fiscal year. These plans would have to be completely altered in accordance with the new system of funding. The Bureau also had to revise its program, since it was now responsible for avoiding duplication of aid.

Less than ten years later these state plans had to be revised again. On April 11, 1965, Congress enacted the Elementary and Secondary Education Act. In theory, this measure was totally different from either the Johnson-O'Malley Act or the impacted-area legislation. JOM and Public Law 874 were intended to meet the financial need of the school districts. The Elementary and Secondary Education Act was intended to meet the "special education needs of children of low-income families." In other words, the Elementary and Secondary Education Act marked the first official recognition of the special needs of the children to whom it applied. For more than thirty years the federal government had refused to acknowledge that there was any need other than the financial aid it provided to the school districts themselves. Belatedly, this legislation recognized that the children themselves should be considered.

Almost all Indian children were to benefit directly from Title I of this new legislation, since funding was to be allocated according to the number of children in the school district whose families were either receiving Aid to Families with Dependent Children payments or had an income of less than $2,000 per year. If they failed to qualify under these conditions, they would probably be eligible through the stipulation that provided for all students who attended schools with high concentrations of "educationally deprived" pupils from low-income families. There was really no question that Indian students were qualified for aid from Title I. Most of them were from low-income families and most of them displayed the characteristics of the educationally deprived. Not only were they well below average in achievement and well above average in the dropout rate, but also a significant number of them were convinced that they simply could not achieve.

Title I funding, like the impacted-area legislation, fell under the direction of the U.S. Office of Education. Unlike the earlier legislation, however, it was not administered by this office. Rather, the Bureau of Indian Affairs submitted its proposal for projects to the U.S. Office of Education, which usually approved them, and then the Indian Office administered the program. In 1969 the funding was broken down: a little over half of the money was allocated for in-service training, teacher aides, and pupil personnel services; the remainder went to curriculum development, enrichment, language arts, health and food, kindergarten, and mathematics and science.

By the mid 1960s, the federal government was providing three sources of funding to public school districts for their Indian enrollment. The impacted-area legislation was carrying the brunt of the burden with an appropriation of $505,900,000. By comparison, the other two programs operated on very low budgets. The Johnson-O'Malley program was the second largest, with state contracts for 1969 totaling only $11,552,000. Title I of the Elementary and Secondary Education Act totaled $9,000,000. Theoretically, this apportioning of funds was justified by the intent of each program as it was written. Thus the program to assist with basic maintenance and operation expenses, that is Public Law 874 and Public Law 815, should have received the heaviest funding, and the programs to provide supplemental and special assistance, that is JOM and Title I, should have been funded sparingly. However, even if this had been the case, critics of this division of the funds countered that the needs of Indian students required much more extensive funding on supplementary programs.

As had been true for the Johnson-O'Malley legislation, there was a wide gap between the intent of the more recent legislation and its implementation. In theory, the remolded JOM program and the innovative Title I program were geared to meet the needs of Indian students; in practice, a large portion of this funding was used for basic operating expenses. Many school districts channeled JOM and Title I funds into their annual budgets for the entire school system and used the funds so widely that they were not even sure where they went, and impacted-area funds came to be similarly misused. In other words, these special funds, which totaled about $530 million in 1969 and which Congress intended for Indian students, usually were spent for all of the students in the school districts, and in some cases non-Indian students benefited more from them than Indian students.

By the 1960s, then, it had become apparent that the concern of Bureau leaders in the 1930s over public school funding for Indian education had been justified. Their prediction that the state school systems would be more interested in the additional money than in the Indian students had proven correct. This situation continued to exist for so many years largely because those who were directly affected by the aid—Indian pupils, parents, and communities—had never been consulted. Throughout most of this period the question of Indian involvement was not even raised.

In the late 1960s young Indian leaders, eager to change the condition of their people, saw federal funding for public schools as a likely target. Interest in JOM programs began to be kindled in widely scattered parts of the country. In at least three states—Nebraska, North Dakota, and South Dakota—the intertribal Indian groups acquired the right to review all JOM budgets before they became final. In New Mexico, the newly formed National Indian Leadership Training program launched an active campaign to educate parents of children in public schools. If parents were acquainted with JOM procedure, National Indian Leadership Training personnel reasoned, they could begin to take an active part in determining what programs their children needed.

Two reports—*Indian Education: A National Tragedy—A National Challenge* and *An Even Chance*—as well as the National Indian Leadership Training project, pointed out similar weaknesses in the federal funding programs. They agreed that, regardless of the beneficent intent of the legislation, the Indian child had been denied the benefits intended for him. The most serious weakness was identified as the failure to encourage Indian participation—if Indian parents had been consulted, they would have had the opportunity to correct the other weaknesses. First among these was the lack of proper accounting for funds. Of the three programs, Title I required the most detailed outline for the annual budget. Both Johnson-O'Malley and Public Law 874 were notorious for the freewheeling atmosphere in which funds were guaranteed each year. The annual state plans required for JOM programs did not even provide a standard form. Another problem, at least in New Mexico, was that JOM budgets were completed before the general school budgets. This was very convenient for public school administrators because it allowed them to apply JOM funds to any part of their budget where there was a need. A JOM budget might list four teacher aides, while in practice the school system actually hired only one, who served non-Indian children equally. Before these funds were spent properly, they had to be accounted for.

The failure of federal aid between 1928 and 1973 is illustrated dramatically by the tragic effect it had on Indian children in public school. Throughout these four decades, one of the most persistent problems was that of poor attendance and high dropout rates. Lack of motivation, general defeatism, and a seminomadic pattern of existence—all of these combined to make the Indian child feel there was no reason for attending or continuing school. Consequently, the Indian level of achievement remained well below the national average.[6]

11

THE KENNEDY REPORT

THERE ARE MORE than five hundred federally recognized Indian tribes and communities in the United States and many unrecognized tribes, each with different cultural values and attributes, political and social organizations, and histories. In light of this diversity, the difficulty of educating Indians in systems outside tribal control that remain insensitive to cultural differences is readily apparent. When Indian students were placed in public schools under the assumption that such schools would facilitate the students' assimilation better than segregated federal schools, the system failed. The failure of the public schools to educate and assimilate Indian students was the focus of a special Senate subcommittee investigation in 1968 and 1969.

The subcommittee published its findings in a report entitled *Indian Education: A National Tragedy—A National Challenge.* Begun under Senator Robert F. Kennedy (and completed under Senator Edward M. Kennedy), the report was an indictment of both the public and federal schools' failure to provide Indian children with an education equal to that provided for non-Indians. The failure of the public schools, the report concluded, stemmed from the schools' curricula, attitudes, values, and dogmas, all of which at times denigrated American Indians and Indian culture. Lack of Indian control through elected boards of education also prevented Indian communities from influencing the education of their children. As a result, many Indians became alienated by a school system that seemed to have little concern for Indian needs and desires.

The report also concluded that, by perpetuating commonly held stereotypes that Indians were inferior to whites, public school administrators and teachers were responsible for cultivating a self-fulfilling prophecy; that is, many Indian students came to believe the stereotypes. Indian participation and control over their children's education was essential, the report concluded; without that control, most Indians experienced a feeling of powerlessness and a sense of despair, leaving many Indian children feeling as if education were an enemy, rather than a friend.

Little Progress in Forty Years

The Kennedy Report repeated many of the stinging criticisms that had been made in the Meriam Report forty years earlier. School dormitories were still overcrowded and student life was overly regimented and harshly disciplined. In addition, most off-reservation boarding schools had become "dumping grounds" for students with social and emotional problems. Apathetic teachers—one-quarter of whom said they preferred not to teach Indian students—set goals of socialization rather than education, trained students in obsolete vocations, and held students accountable for the teachers' own deficiencies.

The Kennedy Report was significant in that it illustrated the recurring failure of the public and federal school systems' attempts to assimilate and educate Indian children. But rather than recommending an educational system controlled by Indians the report merely urged more Indian involvement in the current system. By making the assumption that all social and economic ills facing the Indian people were educational in nature, the report concluded that Indian involvement in the educational system would serve as a cure-all.

Notwithstanding its shortfalls the Kennedy Report was instrumental in effecting several changes in Indian education. Funding for Indian education was increased, bilingual programs were expanded, a National Indian Advisory Board was established to review Indian education programs, Indian boards of education were created at the local level, stipends for higher education were increased, and tribally controlled community colleges were established. Despite the changes, however, the educational system remained a non-traditional and non-tribally controlled institution.

INDIAN EDUCATION: A NATIONAL TRAGEDY—A NATIONAL CHALLENGE
(THE KENNEDY REPORT)

The American vision of itself is of a nation of citizens determining their own destiny; of cultural differences flourishing in an atmosphere of mutual respect; of diverse people shaping their lives and the lives of their children. This subcommittee has undertaken an examination of a major failure in the policy: The education of Indian children. We have chosen a course of learning as obvious as it has been ignored. We have listened to the Indian people speak for themselves about the problems they confront and about the changes that must be made in seeking effective education for their children.

The responsibility for the education of Indian children is primarily in the hands of the Federal Government. Of the 160,000 Indian children in schools—public, private, mission, and Federal—one-third are in federally operated institutions. In addition, the Federal Government has a substantial responsibility for Indian children enrolled in public schools. To a substantial extent, then, the quality and effectiveness of Indian education is a test of this Government's understanding and commitment. Has the Federal Government lived up to its responsibility? The extensive record of this subcommittee, seven volumes of hearings, five committee prints, and this report, constitute a major indictment of our failure.

> • dropout rates are twice the national average in both public and Federal schools. Some school districts have dropout rates approaching 100 percent;

> • achievement levels of Indian children are 2 to 3 years below those of white students; and the Indian child falls progressively further behind the longer he stays in school;

> • only 1 percent of Indian children in elementary schools have Indian teachers or principals;

> • one-fourth of elementary and secondary school teachers—by their own admission—would prefer not to teach Indian children; and

> • Indian children, more than any other minority group, believe themselves to be "below average" in intelligence.

What are the consequences of our educational failure? What happens to an Indian child who is forced to abandon his own pride and future and confront a society in which he has been offered neither a place nor hope? Our failure to provide an effective education for the American Indian has condemned him to a life of poverty and despair.

The cold statistics illuminate a national tragedy and a national disgrace. They demonstrate that the "first American" has become the "last American" in terms of an opportunity for employment, education, a decent income, and the chance for a full and rewarding life. There are no quick and easy solutions in this tragic state of affairs; but clearly, effective education lies at the heart of any lasting solution. And that education should no longer be one which assumes that cultural differences mean cultural inferiority. The findings and recommendations contained in this report are a call for excellence, a reversal of past failures, and a commitment to a national program and priority for the American Indian equal in importance to the Marshall plan following World War II.

There is so much to do—wrongs to right, omissions to fill, untruths to correct—that our own recommendations, concerned as they are with education alone, need supplementation across the whole board of Indian life.

The cold figures mark a stain on our national conscience, a stain which has spread slowly for hundreds of years. They tell a story, to be sure. But they cannot tell the whole story. They cannot, for example, tell of the despair, the frustration, the hopelessness, the poignancy, of children who want to learn but are not taught; of adults who try to read but have no one to teach them; of families which want to stay together but are forced apart; or of 9 year old children who want neighborhood schools but are sent thousands of miles away to remote and alien boarding schools.

We have concluded that our national policies for educating American Indians are a failure of major proportions. They have not offered Indian children—either in years past or today—an educational opportunity anywhere near equal to that offered the great bulk of American children.

The pattern of Federal responsibility for Indian education has been slowly changing. In 1968, for example, the education of Indian children in California, Idaho, Michigan, Minnesota, Nebraska, Oregon, Texas, Washington, and Wisconsin was the total responsibility of the State and not the Federal Government.

In 1968, there were 152,088 Indian children between the ages of 6 and 18; 142,630 attended one type of school or another. Most of these—61.3 percent—attended public, non-Federal schools with non-Indian children. Another 32.7 percent were enrolled in Federal schools, and 6.0 percent attended mission or other schools. Some 6,616 school-age Indian children were not in school at all. The Bureau of Indian Affairs was unable to determine the educational status of some 2,842 Indian children.

What concerned us most deeply, as we carried out our mandate, was the low quality of virtually every aspect of the schooling available to Indian children. The school buildings themselves; the course materials and books; the attitudes of teachers and administrative personnel; the accessibility of school buildings.

A few of the statistics we developed:

> • forty thousand Navajo Indians, nearly a third of the entire tribe, are functionally illiterate in English;

> • the average educational level for all Indians under Federal supervision is 5 school years;

• more than one out of every five Indian men have less than 5 years of schooling;

• in New Mexico, some Indian high school students walk 2 miles to the bus every day and then ride 50 miles to school;

• in one school in Oklahoma the student body is 100 percent Indian; yet it is controlled by a three man, non-Indian school board;

• only 18 percent of the students in Federal Indian schools go on to college; the national average is 50 percent;

• only 3 percent of Indian students who enroll in college graduate; the national average is 32 percent; and

• the BIA spends only $18 per year per child on textbooks and supplies, compared to a national average of $40.

PART 1: NATIONAL TRAGEDY

HISTORICAL FINDINGS

I. Policy Failure

The dominant policy of the Federal Government towards the American Indian has been one of coercive assimilation. The policy has resulted in:

• The destruction and disorganization of Indian communities and individuals.

• A desperately severe and self-perpetuating cycle of poverty for most Indians.

• The growth of a large, ineffective, and self-perpetuating bureaucracy which retards the elimination of Indian poverty.

• A waste of Federal appropriations.

II. National Attitudes

The coercive assimilation policy has had a strong negative influence on national attitudes. It has resulted in:

> • A nation that is massively uninformed and misinformed about the American Indian and his past and present.

> • Prejudice, racial intolerance, and discrimination towards Indians far more widespread and serious than generally recognized.

III. Education Failure

The coercive assimilation policy has had disastrous effects on the education of Indian children. It has resulted in:

> • The classroom and the school becoming a kind of battleground where the Indian child attempts to protect his integrity and identity as an individual by defeating the purposes of the school.

> • Schools which fail to understand or adapt to, and in fact often denigrate, cultural differences.

> • Schools which blame their own failures on the Indian student and reinforce his defensiveness.

> • Schools which fail to recognize the importance and validity of the Indian community. The community and child retaliate by treating the school as an alien institution.

> • A dismal record of absenteeism, dropouts, negative self-image, low achievement, and ultimately, failure for many Indian children.

> • A perpetuation of the cycle of poverty which undermines the success of all other Federal programs.

IV. Cause of the Policy Failure

The coercive assimilation policy has two primary historical roots:

> • A continuous desire to exploit, and expropriate, Indian land and physical resources.

• A self-righteous intolerance of tribal communities and cultural differences.

FAILURE OF THE PUBLIC SCHOOLS

General Analysis

To thousands of Americans, the American Indian is, and always will be, dirty, lazy, and drunk. That's the way they picture him; that's the way they treat him.

A Kansas newspaper in the middle of the 19th century described Indians as "a set of miserable, dirty, blanketed, thieving, lying, sneaking, murdering, graceless, faithless, gut-eating skunks as the Lord ever permitted to infest the earth, and whose immediate and final extermination all men, except Indian agents and traders, should pray for." The subcommittee found anti-Indian attitudes still prevalent today in many white communities. In every community visited by the subcommittee there was evidence among the white population of stereotyped opinions of Indians.

Superior Court Judge Robert L. Winslow of Ukiah, California, told the subcommittee that in Mendocino County, California, there was a "common feeling that Indians are inferior to non-Indians." A study of Indian-white relations in Ukiah said that whites generally looked upon Pomo Indians as "lazy, shiftless, dirty, biologically and culturally inferior." A Pomo Indian testified, "Some think the Indian is not very much or probably not even human." A Southwest study found many people convinced that Apaches were hostile, mean, lazy, and dumb. An Oklahoma principal said of his Indian students, "(they) are even worse than our coloreds and the best you can do is just leave them alone."

The basis for these stereotypes goes back into our history—a history created by the white man to justify his exploitation of the Indian, a history the Indian is continually reminded of at school, on television, in books and at the movies. It is a history which calls an Indian victory a massacre and a U.S. victory an heroic feat. It is a history which makes heroes and pioneers of goldminers who seized Indian land, killed whole bands and families and ruthlessly took what they wanted. It is a history which equates Indians and wild animals, and uses the term "savages" as a synonym for Indians.

It is this kind of history—the kind taught formally in the classroom and informally on the streetcorners—which creates feelings of inferiority among Indian students, gives them a warped understanding of their cultural heritage and propagates stereotypes.

The manner in which Indians are treated in textbooks—one of the most powerful means by which our society transmits ideas from generation to generation—typifies the misunderstanding the American public as a whole has regarding the Indian, and indicates how misconceptions can become a part of a person's mindset. After examining more than a hundred history texts, one historian concluded that the American Indian has been obliterated, defamed, disparaged, and disembodied. He noted that they are often viewed as subhuman wild beasts in the path of civilization.

A report prepared for the subcommittee by the University of Alaska showed that: 1) 20 widely used texts contain no mention of Alaskan Natives at all; 2) although some textbooks provide some coverage of the Alaskan Eskimo, very few even mention Indians; and 3) many texts contain serious and often demeaning inaccuracies in their treatment of the Alaskan Native. A similar study by the University of Idaho found Indians continually depicted as inarticulate, backwards, unable to adjust to modern Euro-American culture, sly, vicious, barbaric, superstitious and destined to extinction. Minnesota has for years been using an elementary school social studies text which depicts Indians as lazy savages incapable of doing little more than hunting, fishing, and harvesting wild rice.

The president of the American Indian Historical Society told the subcommittee, "There is not one Indian child who has not come home in shame and tears after one of those sessions in which he is taught that his people were dirty, animal-like, something less than a human being."

While visiting the public schools serving Indian children on the Fort Hall Reservation in Idaho, Senator Robert F. Kennedy asked if the school had any books about Indians. After a frantic search in the back closet of the school's library a school administrator came running up to the Senator with his find. It was a book entitled "Captive of the Delawares," which had a cover picture of a white child being scalped by an Indian. When the Senator later inquired whether the culture and traditions of the Indians there were included in the school's curriculum he was informed that "there isn't any history to this tribe."

With attitudes towards Indians being shaped, often unconsciously, by educational materials filled with inaccurate stereotypes—as well as by teachers whose own education has contained those same stereotypes and historical misconceptions—it is easy to see how the "lazy, dirty, drunken" Indian becomes the symbol for all Indians. When the public looks at an Indian they cannot react rationally because they have never known the facts. They do not feel responsible for the Indian because they are convinced that the "savages" have brought their conditions upon themselves. They truly believe the Indian is inferior to them. The Indian is despised, exploited, and discriminated against—but always held in check by the white power structure so that his situation will not change.

At the heart of the matter, educationally at least, is the relationship between the Indian community and the public school and the general powerlessness the Indian feels in regard to the education of his children. A recent report by the Carnegie Foundation described the relationship between white people, especially the white power structure, and the Indians as "one of the most crucial problems in the education of Indian children." The report continued: "This relationship frequently demeans Indians, destroys their self-respect and self-confidence, develops or encourages apathy and a sense of alienation from the educational process, and deprives them of an opportunity to develop the ability and experience to control their own affairs through participation in effective local government."

One means the white power structure employs to limit Indian control, or even participation, is to prevent Indians from getting on local school boards. The subcommittee uncovered numerous instances of school districts educating Indians with no Indian members on the school board. When Ponca City, Oklahoma, Indians tried to crack the white power structure by electing an Indian to the board of an all Indian public school, some were threatened with loss of their rented homes while others were led to believe registration procedures were extremely complicated and would place them in jeopardy of having their land taxed. Chippewas of the Leech Lake Reservation in Minnesota have alleged that their school district has been redrawn to prevent Indians from being elected to the all-white school board. The Mesquakie tribe of Tama, Iowa, send most of their children to South Tama County public school, yet the Indians cannot vote for members of the school board.

History provided several examples of Indian-controlled school systems which have had great success. In the 1800s, the Choctaw Indians of Mississippi and Oklahoma operated about 200 schools and academies and sent numerous graduates to eastern colleges. Using bilingual teachers and Cherokee texts, the Cherokees, during the same period, controlled a school system which produced a tribe almost 100 percent literate. Children were taught to read and write in both their native language and English. Anthropologists have determined that as a result of this school system, the literacy level in English of western Oklahoma Cherokees was higher than the white populations of either Texas or Arkansas.

The Carnegie Report cited an example of the problems Indian parents face in dealing with the power structure. Indians were trying to get a course in Ponca history and culture included in the curriculum of their all-Indian high school. The superintendent's response to their request is explained in the Carnegie report:

> He had reviewed the schedule and found that if the course were taught, the children would be deprived of 54 hours of subjects they needed. Further, the teachers were

doing very well in incorporating Indian culture into their
teaching. Besides, he didn't see the value because this was
"a competitive world and their culture was going to be
lost anyway and they would be better off in the long run
if they knew less of it." He also said that many felt the
theme of the course would be to "teach the children to
hate white people."

One outcome of the Indians' powerlessness and the atmosphere of the white
community in which the Indians attend school is discrimination within the
public schools. Indian students on the Muckleshoot Reservation, in western
Washington, for example, were automatically retained an extra year in the
first grade of their public school. School officials felt that, for Indians, the
first year should be a non-academic, socializing experience. The Nootsack
Indians of western Washington, were automatically placed in a class of slow
learners without achievement testing. The subcommittee found a tracking
system operating in the Nome public schools which several officials described
as highly discriminatory. The system assigned most natives to the lowest level
and most whites to the highest. The school superintendent in Chinle,
Arizona, admitted that his district has a policy of falsifying the Indian
achievement test results because the children were so far behind national
norms that "it just wouldn't look good."

Language is another area in which the Indian is discriminated against in
school. The Bureau of Indian Affairs contends that one-half to two-thirds of
the Indian children enter school with little or no skill in the English
language. Dr. B. Gaarder of the U.S. Office of Education estimated that
more than half of the Indians in the United States between the ages of 6 and
18 use their native tongues. Unfamiliarity of the language of the classroom
becomes a tremendous handicap for the Indian student, and records
indicate he immediately falls behind his Anglo classmates. Most public
school teachers are not trained to teach English as a second language. The
student's position is complicated by the insistence of teachers, who have no
understanding of Indian culture, that he disregard the language spoken by
his parents at home.

The Indian feels like an alien in a strange country. And the school feels it
is its responsibility not just to teach skills, but to impress the "alien" Indian
with the values of the dominant culture. Teachers, textbooks, and curriculums, therefore, are programmed to bring about adoption of such values
of American life as competitiveness, acquisition, rugged individualism,
and success. But for the Indian, whose culture is oriented to completely
different values, school becomes the source of much conflict and tension.
He is told he must be competitive, when at home he is taught the value of
cooperation. At school he is impressed with the importance of individual
success, but at home the value of good interpersonal relations is emphasized.

The teacher complains about him not being motivated. But anthropologist Anne M. Smith asks if he can be expected to be motivated when to do so means rejection of his parents and their teachings, as well as his religion, race, and history.

Condemned for his language and culture, berated because his values aren't those of his teacher, treated demeaningly simply because he is an Indian, the Indian student begins asking himself if he really isn't inferior. He becomes the object of a self-fulfilling prophecy which says "Indians are no good." Study after study shows Indian children growing up with attitudes and feelings of alienation, hopelessness, powerlessness, rejection, depression, anxiety, estrangement, and frustration. Few studies, if any, show the public schools doing anything to change this pattern. The public schools have become a place of discomfort for the Indian student, a place to leave when he becomes 15 or 16. The Indian child comes to believe that "he can only succeed if he were white."

On many occasions in the field, the subcommittee staff members heard Indian children describe themselves as "dumb Indians." "Indians have greater problems because they're real stupid," one student said. Ironically, a majority of white students who have contact with the Oglala Sioux students blamed discrimination on the part of their own ethnic group as the major reason for Indians having problems.

What then happens to the student who is told he is dirty, lazy, and inferior and must undergo school experiences daily which reinforce these attitudes? The statistical data speak for themselves:

> • 87 percent dropout rate by the 6th grade at an all-Indian public elementary school near Ponca City, Oklahoma.

> • 90 percent dropout rate in Nome, Alaska, public schools, with about one-fourth of the students (primarily Eskimo) taking two to three years to get through the first grade.

> • 21 of 28 Indian students in a Washington 8th grade were non-readers; one-third of the 128 Yakima Indians enrolled in 8th grade of a Washington public school were reading two to six grades below the median level; 70 percent Indian dropout rate; average grade was "D" for the Indian senior high students in public school serving Yakima Indians.

> • 62 percent dropout rate in Minneapolis public schools; between 45 and 75 percent statewide dropout rate; 70 percent Indian dropout rate in parts of California.

- 80 percent of the students in three Idaho public school districts, in 1956, dropped out before their class graduated. Seventy-five percent of the native dropouts tested revealed more than enough intelligence to complete high school.

A public school in western Oklahoma with a 25 percent Indian enrollment has been educating Indians for 40 years. During that period, 11 Indians have stayed in school long enough to graduate. Since the 1930s, nine states have assumed total responsibility for the education of their Indians, but data on Indian education from most of these states, as indicated in some of the examples above, is far from impressive. These public schools have indeed failed their Indian constituents.

The question needs to be raised whether public schools are entirely to blame for not solving their Indian education problem. Dr. Leon Osview of Temple University says no. He contends the Federal Government has failed to live up to its responsibilities in providing funds and leadership for assisting public school districts to better understand and meet the special needs of Indian students. How can this leadership be provided? Dr. Osview's report suggests that more than a change of policy will be required. Federal schools must have the quality and effectiveness that will permit them to become centers of leadership for assisting the public schools in meeting the special needs of the Indian children.

Ever since the policy of educating Indians in public schools was adopted it was assumed that the public schools, with their integrated settings, were the best means of educating Indians. The subcommittee's public school findings—high dropout rates, low achievement levels, anti-Indian attitudes, insensitive curriculums—raise serious doubts as to the validity of that assumption.

FEDERAL LEGISLATION

The public school education received by Indian students has been subsidized to some extent by the Federal Government since the 1890s. At that time legislation was passed authorizing the Office of Indian education to reimburse public schools for the extra expense incurred by instructing Indian children. The purpose of the legislation appeared to be two-fold. First, it gave legislative authority to the policy of integrating Indians into white culture, thus establishing the goal of assimilation and the public schools as the vehicle for attempting that goal. Second, it established the precedent of providing subsidies to public schools in order to get them to assume responsibility for Indian education. The Federal subsidy was necessary, both because there was a reluctance on the part of Indians to enter the schools and because the school district was reluctant to assume the extra costs and problems anticipated with Indian students. The subsidy was, in effect, an inducement which the state or school district was almost always willing to take in exchange for providing a chair and a desk in a classroom for an Indian.

The subsidizing approach was formalized in the Johnson-O'Malley Act of 1934, which permitted the Bureau of Indian Affairs to contract with states to provide for the education of Indian students. Indian education was further subsidized in the 1950s with the passage of Public Laws 81-815 and 81-874, impacted aid legislation, which later became applicable to Indians. These three laws provide the basic Federal subsidy for public school education of Indian students.

Public Law 815 In the first fiscal year that section 14, the section applicable to Indians, was in effect, $6.6 million was appropriated for school construction. The following year, 1955, the appropriation was $.4 million. Since that year the appropriation for construction of schools educating Indians has decreased. Because of limited appropriations, requests for 1968 and 1969 under sections 5, 8, and 14 have not been funded. Section 14 has not been funded because the language of the law gives priority in funding to other sections (non-Indian).

Public Law 874 One of the main problems with Public Law 874 has been late funding. Many districts educating Indians, particularly those on Indian reservations, depend on 874 for a substantial part of their budgets. The Ingebretson, North Dakota, school, for example, depends on 874 funds for 74.9% of its operating budget. For Lower Brule, South Dakota, the figure is 63.9%. Late payments to Public Law 874 money mean an excessive hardship to all those districts. The subcommittee has reports from a number of such districts which have indicated that late funding and partial entitlement annually places them in an uncertain position as to whether they will have to reduce their faculties or services mid-year.

Johnson-O'Malley Act Since the act's inception, the number of Indian students in public schools has increased to about two-thirds of all Indian students. Although the act brought about increased enrollment of Indians in public schools, its success in meeting the educational needs of those students is open to serious question. Why hasn't the Johnson-O'Malley Act dealt adequately with the needs of Indian students? The problem lies not so much with the act itself, as with the manner in which it has been interpreted. For though the language of the act is broad, its interpretation has been narrow, and therefore the intent of the legislation has not been realized.

Despite the act's expressed intent to deal only with Indian needs, the Johnson-O'Malley money has been traditionally used by school districts to supplement their general operating budget, thus benefiting all their students.

The Code of Federal Regulations (1958) sanctions this use by stating that JOM funds can be used to meet the financial needs of those school districts which have "large blocks of nontaxable Indians which create situations which local funds are inadequate to meet." The bureau continues to place the tax-exempt status of land as the prime determiner of JOM eligibility rather than educational need.

The JOM money not used for basic support (operation and maintenance) is used to provide lunches, transportation, administrative costs and—occasionally—special instructional services. Twenty to twenty-five percent of JOM expenditures are for school lunches for Indian students, as compared to 3.8 percent of Title I of Elementary and Secondary Education Act expenditures for feeding programs. The Bureau reported in 1969 that it budgeted 30 percent of the funds for "special services." In some states special services mean providing bus service for Indian children. In others it means buying volleyball standards and tumbling pads. Some use it to pay off the mortgage on a bus, increase teacher salaries, or hire attendance officers. In a few cases it is used to hire teacher aides and provide libraries and study halls for Indians. There is no detailed accountability of the use of the money.

Today, 35 years after it was originally adopted, it is still questionable if the Johnson-O'Malley Act is fulfilling the intent of Congress. It is true that more Indians are in public schools, but it is doubtful if the needs of these Indian children are being met any more than they were 35 years ago.

One of the main problems with the act has been the conflict between it and Public Law 874, which provides funds for school districts which educate large numbers of children whose parents live or work on tax-exempt property. Congress never intended that duplicate payments should be made to the same school for the same purpose by two different Federal agencies. But both 874 and JOM do just that. The federal regulation permits such use of JOM money when 874 funds are insufficient for general school operations. Few local administrators are likely to admit they have enough money for normal school operations when they know they can get more, and thus Johnson-O'Malley is continually drained for normal operating budget purposes.

Dr. Alphonse Selinger of the Northwest Regional Educational Laboratory testified before the committee that he encountered at least one principal who admitted giving passing grades to Indian students only to keep them in school so the district could receive JOM money. Officials from two different schools told Dr. Selinger there was very little that they could do for Indian children, so they kept them in the school for the additional funds they brought into the system.

Although Johnson-O'Malley and Public Law 874 serve different functions, Public Law 874 was, and continues to be, interpreted by BIA officials as replacement money for Johnson-O'Malley. The problem with a school district replacing JOM funds with 874 aid is that there is no guarantee the 874 money will be used to benefit Indian students. Such money goes to the school district itself, and any benefit received by Indian children would only be indirect. Johnson-O'Malley funds, though, are suppose to aid only Indian children.

A most important problem with JOM is that, as presently administered, it excludes from participation Indians who have left the reservation. Thousands of such Indians now live in urban areas where Indian children attend public schools. Their needs are being ignored just as much there as in rural areas. In Minneapolis, Minnesota, for example, an estimated 10,000 Indians live in the city. The Indian dropout rate is more than 60 percent. The dropout rate in some California cities approaches 70 percent. Most urban school districts are not eligible for either JOM or 874 because the Indian parents do not live or work on tax-exempt reservations. Thus these Indians are not eligible for the special-needs funds Congress intended for them.

Complaints are innumerable regarding the administration of Johnson-O'Malley. For one thing, the levels of aid are extremely uneven. In 1967-68, Alaska received $690 per JOM pupil while Oklahoma received $37. Arizona received $236 per pupil while neighboring New Mexico received $135. Even within the states the levels vary greatly. In 1966-67, Santa Fe County, New Mexico, received $310 per JOM pupil, while McKinley County (Gallup), New Mexico, received $41.

Johnson-O'Malley is suppose to serve the needs of Indian students, but Indians rarely get an opportunity to decide how the money should be spent. The proposals are usually drawn up by school administrators of white, middle-class backgrounds who direct the money toward general school operations or problem solving techniques which might work for the middle-class student, but not for the Indian. The people who are affected most by the law have little to say about how the money should be used to help their children.

Despite evidence of the failure of public schools to provide Indian students with an adequate education and despite the absence of a commitment by local, state or national authorities to provide Indians with an equal education, the Bureau of Indian Affairs continues its policy of transferring Indians into public schools.

The transfer procedure employed by the Bureau has been discretionary. When the Bureau felt a public school was ready to handle Indian students, the change was effected. The transfer was often a gradual process, involving a phasing out of educational services at the Indian school. No particular criteria appear to be used to determine when a school is ready to accept Indian students. The determination continues to be arbitrarily made by the

Bureau of Indian Affairs. No evaluation of the quality of education in the public school is done before the transfer is effected. The Bureau's only requirement seems to be that the public school has enough space and personnel to handle the additional students.

The Bureau's means of determining when Indians are ready for a transfer is even more puzzling. In the past it appears that the determination was made by the Bureau without consulting with the Indians affected by the change. The Indians were usually informed of the transfer after the decision had been made.

FAILURE OF THE FEDERAL SCHOOLS

The Bureau of Indian Affairs operates 226 schools in 17 states, on Indian reservations and in remote geographic areas throughout the country. Of these, 77 are boarding schools. There are 34,605 American Indian children currently enrolled in BIA boarding schools, 15,450 in BIA day schools, and 3,854 housed in peripheral dormitories while attending public schools with BIA financial support. According to statistics compiled by the BIA in 1968, 82.1 percent of the students enrolled in Federal schools are "Full-Blood" Indians and slightly more than 97 percent of students were one-half or more Indian blood.

A number of witnesses testifying before the subcommittee have suggested that the amount of expenditure per pupil in BIA schools should be doubled or tripled if equality of educational opportunity is to be provided. The ABT report appears to agree with these suggestions, stating: "BIA schools are at this time insufficiently funded to overcome the students' initial difficulties resulting from poverty and cultural barriers. The price of economy is ultimately paid in high welfare payments and reduced revenues."

It should also be noted that the BIA has failed to conduct any meaningful long-range planning, to provide a reliable census of school-age children, or to integrate its planning with other components of reservation development. The results have been substantial numbers of Indian children not in school and many times not even accounted for, severely overcrowded school facilities, large numbers of Alaskan Native children shipped out of the state to Oregon or Oklahoma so that they can receive a high school education, and a variety of unsatisfactory makeshift arrangements (such as the conversion of dormitory space) which must have a deleterious effect on the effective educational program.

The academic performance of students in BIA schools indicates to some degree the magnitude of the problem. Only 60 percent of the Indian students in BIA high schools graduate, compared to a national average of 74 percent. Of the number of students who graduate from high school, only 28 percent enter college, as compared with a national average of 50 percent. Of those Indian students who enter college, only 28 percent graduate. In addition, less than 1 percent of Indian graduate students complete a master's degree.

The Indian student in a BIA school is on the average of 2 or more years behind his non-Indian peers in terms of achievement test scores when he graduates from high school. Thus to bring its program up to national norms the BIA must cut the number of dropouts in half, must double the number of Indian students going on to college, must provide an adequate elementary and secondary education background which will permit a doubling of the number of Indian students graduating from college, and a tenfold increase in the number of Indian students completing a masters degree. Unfortunately, the Bureau of Indian Affairs does not have well specified goals, and has never stated how or over what period of time they feel they can close the gap.

GOALS AND OPERATIONAL PHILOSOPHY

One of the most important findings of the ABT study was the dramatic disparity between the educational goals of the students and the expectations of the teachers and administrators. This is particularly important because educational research has demonstrated that teacher expectations have an important effect on student achievement. The self-fulfilling prophecy of failure seems to be a pervasive element in BIA schools.

The study found that three-quarters of the Indian students wanted to go to college. Most of the students had a reasonable understanding of what college work entailed and 3 percent desired graduate studies at the masters or doctoral level. The students clearly desired a firm grounding in the core subjects of English, mathematics, and science.

In dramatic contrast to the student goals, however, were those of teachers and administrators. When asked to name the most important things the schools should do for the students, only about one-tenth of the teachers mentioned academic achievement as an important goal. Teachers stressed the educational objectives of personality development, socialization, and citizenship. Apparently, many of the teachers still see their role as "civilizing the native." The study also found that "teachers believe in a quiet obsolete form of occupational preparation, for which students show commendable little enthusiasm." One consequence of the unfortunate situation is a serious communications breakdown between student and staff and a serious lack of productive student-staff interactions.

In terms of operational philosophy several other deficiencies were noted. BIA administrators and teachers believe that Indians can chose only between total "Indianness"—whatever that is—and complete assimilation into the dominant society. There seems to be little if any understanding of acculturation processes or the desirability of "combining a firm cultural identity with occupational success and consequent self-esteem." Thus, the goals of BIA education appears to direct students toward migration to a city while at the same time it fails to "prepare students academically, socially, psychologically, or vocationally for urban life. As a result, many return to the reservations disillusioned, to spend the rest of their lives in economic and intellectual stagnation."

QUALITY OF INSTRUCTION

The quality and effectiveness of instructional practices were found very unsatisfactory. For example:

> • The primary in-school cause of the low adequacy achievement levels of Indian students is the inadequacy of the instruction offered them for overcoming their severe environmental handicaps. A great proportion of the teachers in the BIA system lack the training necessary to teach the pupils with the linguistic and economic disadvantages of the Indian child successfully. Only a handful of the Bureau's teachers are themselves Indians, although some bilingual teaching aides are employed. Virtually no non-Indian teachers learn to speak an Indian language, nor are they given formal help to do so. Many tend to take little interest in intellectual and artistic achievement, and therefore fail to stimulate the development of intellectual curiosity and creativity in their pupils.

> • The curriculums used in the Bureau schools are generally inappropriate to the experience and needs of the students. Those for teaching linguist skills are particularly unsuitable, as they fail to respond to the child's unique language problems. Vocational training courses bear little relation to existing job markets. The teaching techniques commonly employed force upon Indian students, a competition alien to their upbringing.

DISCIPLINE—STUDENT LIFE

School environments are sterile, impersonal, and rigid, with a major emphasis on discipline and punishment, which is deeply resented by the students. They find the schools highly unacceptable from the standpoint of emotional, personality, and leadership development. For example:

• Social activities involving both sexes, such as plays, concerts, dances, and social clubs, are relatively infrequent. According to the students, even when they are held they are usually over-chaperoned and end very early. Many teenage students also expressed great frustration with the boredom of weekends in the boarding school dormitories. Teachers and all but a few counselors depart, and almost no social activities are planned; it is hardly surprising, therefore, that students occasionally resort to drinking and gluesniffing in order to relieve their boredom.

• Students complained bitterly of the lack of privacy in the dormitories, of the rigidity of their hours, and of the considerable attention devoted by dormitory staff to inspections and the enforcement of rules and order. At Haskell Institute, students reported that all electric power in the dormitories is turned off at night, to prevent them from reading or listening to the radio. Several students mentioned that they often needed flashlights to complete their reading assignments; they would hide beneath their blankets so as to evade the notice of dormitory aides conducting bed checks.

• Dormitory discipline is often unnecessarily strict and confining. Students in their late teens and early twenties are often forced to conform to rules appropriate for children half their age.

PARENTAL PARTICIPATION AND COMMUNITY CONTROL

The BIA has simply failed in its implementation of the new policy goal of maximizing parental and community participation in the schools in spite of the wishes of the Indian communities.

• Despite a Presidential directive issued more than two years ago, only a few BIA schools are governed by elected school boards.

• The relationship between school staff members and parents is usually too formal and distant. On rare occasions when parents visit their children's school, they often feel unwelcome.

• With few exceptions, the facilities, staff, and equipment of BIA schools are not used as community resources for adult education and other activities.

• Indians participate little or not at all in the planning and development of new programs for Indian education, training, employment, and economic development, despite approval of such participation by the national office of the BIA.

PERSONNEL SYSTEM

One particularly crucial area of concern in the overall effectiveness of the BIA school system lies in the area of personnel recruitment, retention, reward, and utilization. The BIA personnel system contains major deficiencies which undoubtedly have contributed very substantially to all of the other inadequacies already cited.

The turnover rate of teachers is much too high, and often the most ambitious and promising teachers leave the system first. In addition, the civil service status of BIA teachers and staff has severe disadvantages. It is very difficult to reward the outstanding teacher and even more difficult to fire the incompetent. It has been suggested that "teachers' ability to rely on their civil service tenure militates against the total commitment needed from them." They tend instead to provide a minimum of effort and time and "take little interest in the problems of the school and community." Also the rigidity of the civil service system has made it difficult if not impossible to permit Indian tribes and communities some authority over teacher selection and training. Indian communities consider this to be the most critical aspect of their involvement in the school.

ELEMENTARY BOARDING SCHOOLS

Daniel J. O'Connell, M.D., executive secretary of the National Committee on Indian Health, and the Association of American Indian affairs went on record as opposed to the placement of children under the age of 9 in boarding schools as it was a "destructive" practice which resulted in emotional damage to the children. Not long after the first subcommittee hearings, a letter was received from a BIA teacher in one of the largest elementary boarding schools on the Navajo Reservation. It is a very perceptive letter and provided an excellent description of how these schools function.

> I've only had 2 years in teaching here at the Tuba City Boarding School. But I've seen enough here and at schools that I've visited, and talked with enough people from different places to come to some—hopefully accurate—conclusions. I hope they prove to be valid and useful.
>
> One major problem of course, is the boarding school per se. Although the idea of a boarding school, which

draws in students from a broad area, is undoubtedly less expensive and more readily controlled than a large number of small day schools, and offers the students advantages such as a good diet and health and sanitation facilities, the problems that it creates are vast, and require solutions. The problems are often recognized, and are often bemoaned, but little has been done to eliminate them. One of these is distance from the home.

In an age and area which local community interest, involvement, and understanding, in which we are supposed to be building and maintaining a harmony between cultures, we find many schools at such distances from the homes of the students that meaningful contact is difficult to say the least. These distances make meaningful relationships, or even mere visiting, a severe hardship. (For example, the two young boys who froze to death while running away from a boarding school and were trying to get to their homes—50 miles away.) The lack of transportation and the ruggedness of the terrain compound the problem.

As a result, most children on the reservation starting at the age of 6, only see their parents on occasional weekends, if that often. At times parents are usually "allowed to check out their children"—if the child's conduct in school warrants it, in the opinion of the school administration. If he has problems, (i.e. runs away) parents are often not allowed to take him until he has "learned his lesson." This may take up to a month to accomplish. This may tend to cut down on runaways, but it would seem that we should work toward eliminating the cause, rather than punishing the results.

However, these are often the lucky children. I have no evidence of this, except the word of teachers who are directly involved, but I have been told of schools at which parents are not allowed to check their children out on weekends, in order to eliminate runaways (except for emergencies).

When children are taken from their homes for 9 months a year, from age 6 onward, family ties are severely strained, and often dissolved. Even brothers and sisters in the same boarding school rarely see each other, due to dormitory situations, class, and dining hall arrangements. The children become estranged from relatives, culture, and much-admired traditional skills. (For example, few of my students have been able to learn the art of rug weaving, or are familiar with Navajo legends and sandpaintings.)

Yet this could almost be understood if we were replacing it with something strong on which they could build a new life. We are not. We may be providing some opportunities for academic training—but that is all we are doing.

For example, my own school, the Tuba City Boarding School is the largest on the reservation, housing 1,200 elementary students. This alone creates immense problems. I don't believe any public school system in the country would tolerate an elementary school of this size, for the simple reason that the individual student would be lost in the crowd. We have them here, not only for an ordinary school day, but 24 hours, 7 days a week, 9 months a year.

The problems of running any institution of this size are enormous—be it hospital, prison, or whatever. However, when we are involved in what is actually the home situation of young children from another culture, we had best do everything possible to provide a secure, pleasant, stable, and enlightening environment for them. We aren't.

For instance, if day schools are not possible, could we not at least provide some overnight guest facilities for parents who would like to visit their children? Nothing elaborate or expensive would be necessary—a hogan would suffice and could be put together easily by Navajos in the vicinity. Or, a small frame building might be constructed. Yet as far as I know, this is not done anywhere. This might tend to make the school more of a Navajo school, and less a white school for Navajos.

There are many other ways in which the schools could serve. For instance, they could be opened in the evening to provide training, or formal courses, or just things of interest to the people. Areas which require instruction, such as English, or writing, could be taught by the teachers themselves. In many depressed areas, teachers earn extra money by such professional means. Why not here? Also, many talented Navajos might wish to earn extra money by conducting courses in the weaving of quality rugs, or in the teaching of oral English to the people. Consumer and health education could be included, with field trips to make them meaningful. The possibilities are endless. Yet nothing is done in this area.

However, no matter how lacking our program may appear to be, we always manage to consider the academic department to be high quality when we compare ourselves with our dormitory counterpart, the "guidance" department. Herein lies the most serious deficiency of the entire boarding school system, for these people are in charge of children 16 hours a day, 7 days a week, yet they are understaffed, underprogrammed, undersupervised and overextended. For example, each dormitory has only one teacher, and it is extremely difficult to find suitable personnel for these crucial, demanding positions. Yet, even the finest teachers could accomplish little, when they are working with 150 children of a different culture, and are responsible for their care and welfare 7 days a week.

Of course there are aids working with the teachers— usually two, but occasionally only one on duty at a time. However, what with trying to mend clothes, supply linens, check roll, keep order, and bed, there is little time to do more than keep the walls from being pulled down. There is nothing to take the place of the homes they have left behind, or the personal interest and training they would have received from their families. The social relationships and interaction which brings about stability and contentment are denied them.

Even an effective guidance program could not replace that. But the truth is, we don't have an effective guidance program, only a "maintenance" program, due to the shortages of guidance personnel, funding, and planning. This accounts for the high degree of regimented confusion that abounds after the school day ends. Vast blocks of time are filled with boredom or meaningless activity. There are no learning activities, and few recreational or craft areas being worked in.

The children search everywhere for something—they grasp most hungrily at any attention shown them, or to any straw that might offer escape from boredom. You can't help but see it in their faces when you visit the dorm of the younger children. At the older boy's dormitories, they are used to the conditions—you can see that too. They no longer expect anything meaningful from anyone. Many have lost the ability to accept anything past the material level, even when it is offered. Unless you lived with them over a period of time, and see the loneliness and the monotony of daily routine, you cannot appreciate the tragedy of it but it's there.

Because of the shortage of personnel, there is a tendency—a pronounced tendency—to "herd" rather than guide. The boys and girls are yelled at, bossed around, chased here and there, told and untold, until it is almost impossible for them to attempt to do anything on their own initiative—except, of course, to run away.

OFF-RESERVATION BOARDING SCHOOLS

The Bureau of Indian Affairs operates 77 boarding school in all, with a total student population that exceeds 34,000. More than 12,000 students attend the 19 off-reservation boarding schools; approximately 10,000 students are enrolled in the 13 off-reservation schools in which subcommittee staff and consultants have conducted formal evaluations.

The following criteria are used as the basis for admission:

EDUCATION CRITERIA

1. Those for whom a public or federal day school is not available.

2. Those who need special vocational or preparatory courses.

3. Those retarded scholastically 3 or more years or those having pronounced bilingual difficulties.

SOCIAL CRITERIA

1. Those who are rejected or neglected for whom no suitable plan can be made.

2. Those who belong to large families with no suitable home and separation from each other is undesirable.

3. Those whose behavior problems are too difficult for solution by their families or through existing community facilities.

4. Those whose health or proper care is jeopardized by
   illness of other members of the household.

The determination of eligibility of students enrolled under one of the social
criteria is made by Bureau social workers on the student's reservation.
Although parental approval and approval of the reservation superintendent
are also required, social workers usually initiate the application process and
are the primary decision agents. As the evaluation reports make clear, the
student population of the off-reservation boarding schools is one with
special social and emotional problems. The Bureau estimates that 25
percent of the students in these schools are public school dropouts (or
pushouts). Others have accepted boarding school placement as an alterna-
tive to a reformatory.

The lack of appropriate response to social problems is presented by Dr.
Anthony S. Elite in his report of the Phoenix Indian School.

> At the Phoenix Indian School alone, for example, out of
> an enrollment of approximately 1,000 students, over 200
> come from broken homes. Five hundred and eighty
> students are considered academically retarded. There
> are at least 60 students enrolled where there exists a
> serious family drinking problem. From September to
> December of 1967, there were 16 reported cases of
> serious glue sniffing. The school is often pressured into
> accepting students with a history of juvenile delinquency
> and overt emotional disturbance. With this great change
> in the profile of the student body there has not been a
> concomitant change in staffing skilled workers or train-
> ing existing personal to cope with these problems.

If the evaluation teams found the schools' programs sorely in need of
change, their impressions of staff adequacy were hardly more encouraging.
In many cases, neither the quantity nor the quality of personnel was judged
satisfactory. The reports frequently cite insufficient numbers of dormitory
personnel and lack of training for these positions as especially serious flaws.

Perhaps the greatest irony of all is that even as custodial institutions, the
Bureau's off-reservation boarding schools are not satisfactory. Several
reports point to examples of overcrowding in dormitories or classrooms,
of lack of privacy for the students, of inadequate areas for study and
recreation, of unappealing meals, of rules which irritate older students by
their rigid enforcement and inappropriateness to the student's age, and
of punitive discipline. The dormitories are like "barracks"; the living
conditions are "sterile" and "unimaginative" and "institutional"—these
are the descriptions that reappear.

If the boarding schools acted only as custodial institutions, criticism enough could be directed at their failure to educate and at their failing to meet the psychological and social needs of the students as individuals. A strong case can be made, however, that the boarding schools contribute to the students' mental health problems. In testimony before the subcommittee, Dr. Robert Leon reported the following:

> Some of the effects of Indian boarding schools are demonstrated by the very people who are now working in the boarding schools. Many Indian employees, most of whom are guidance personnel, are themselves a product of the Indian boarding school. I have found that some of these people have great difficulty in discussing their own experience as Indian students. Many of them now show what I would call a blunting of their emotional responses. This I would attribute to the separation from their parents and the oppressive atmosphere of the boarding schools.

Another observer, Dr. Thaddeus Krush, reported his "Thoughts on the Formation of Personality Disorder" after a study of an Indian boarding school population. He concluded that the students' "frequency of movement and the necessity to conform to changing standards can only lead to confusion and disorganization of the child's personality. The frequency of movement further interferes with and discourages the development of lasting relations in which love and concern permit adequate maturation." Other mental health experts have expressed similar concerns about the effects of boarding school institutionalization. If they continue to exist, it is painfully obvious that their mission, staffing and program must be freshly tailored to the very special needs of their student bodies.

VOCATIONAL EDUCATION

It was the Bureau relocation program, begun in 1952 that spotlighted the deficiencies in the Bureau high school vocational program. The relocation program was designed to provide the means whereby Indians could leave the economically depressed reservations and go to an urban area where jobs were more plentiful. The Indian family or single adult was transported to certain cities where the BIA had established relocation field offices to receive them. Field office staff provided general counseling to the relocatees and assisted them in finding employment and housing. Financial support was provided until the relocatee was employed and receiving wages. It soon became apparent that the undereducated, poorly trained Indian with his rural background and cultural differences had not been adequately equipped to compete in the labor market or make an adequate social adjustment to his new environment. As a result of these deficiencies, between 1953 and 1957, three out of 10 relocatees returned to the reservation in the same year they had been relocated. There are no statistics which would show how many eventually returned, but the rough estimates run as high as 75 percent.

Although the current philosophy of the Bureau is to prepare students for off-reservation employment, it does "not prepare students academically, socially, psychologically, or vocationally for urban life." It can equally well be said that the limited prevocational program in BIA schools has no relevance to manpower needs or economic development of the Indian community.

HIGHER EDUCATION

There are many reasons why there aren't more Indians in college, and why, once they are enrolled, they are more prone than non-Indians to dropping out. The expectations of teachers, as cited above, are most important. If a teacher doesn't think his pupils are worthy of college, the pupil begins to internalize the teacher's belief and looks upon himself as unfit for college. The subcommittee hearings record several examples of teachers and counselors discouraging Indians from higher education, in some instances, just because they were Indian.

Dr. Lionel H. de Montigny, Deputy Director of the Division of Indian Health in the Public Health Service at Portland, Oregon, reported the following incident in a letter to the subcommittee.

> David Butler, a Makah Indian, wanted to enter college
> with the hope of entering medical school at a later date.
> His local advisers told him that it was out of the question.
> No Makah had ever applied before and he could not be
> expected to make it. He was advised to become a cook.

When many Indians get into a college they find themselves inadequately prepared academically to deal with college work. Most Indians graduate from high school about 2 years behind the average non-Indian high school graduate in the United States. The language difference also serves as a handicap to many Indian students.

The emotional and social adjustment problems the Indian encounters in college also play a part in his inability to succeed in college. Although most college students have problems in this area, studies indicate the problems of Indians to be of a more serious nature. Many are thrown into a new environment with different customs and different values, and they never fully recover from the trauma.

Another contributory cause to the small Indian college enrollment is insufficient funds, especially for clothing and spending money. The research of Artichoker and Palmer found this to be one of the decisive factors in the

Indian's academic failure. Financial difficulties were generally found to be most severe for those who attended colleges at least a year.

Indian students have expressed the desire for college educations. The consistently high dropout rates of Indian students, though, indicate the need for a more adequate education in the preparation for college and a better understanding by teachers, administrators and counselors of the problems and needs of Indian students. A lot needs to be done to upgrade the elementary and secondary education Indians are now receiving. More programs are needed to assist, academically and emotionally, Indian students in college. More scholarships are needed so that Indian students can attend college without financial problems hanging over them.

ADULT EDUCATION

In the past, the Bureau of Indian Affairs has made only token attempts to respond to the need for adult education on Indian reservations. Adult education personnel of the Bureau have been expected to perform such duties as certifying Johnson-O'Malley funds, overseeing boarding school applications, or serving as truant officers or public school relation specialists. The press of these other duties prohibited them from performing much meaningful adult education. Only within the last 2 years has adult education been recognized as a problem with a priority of its own.

The adult education program of the BIA has traditionally defined candidates for literacy training as those having less than 5 years of formal schooling. Comparison with the total society shows that for the 25 and over age group there is a national average of 8.3 percent who had less than five years of schooling (based on the 1960 census). But for the American Indian the rate was three and one-half times that at 27 percent.

Though basic literacy is a prime objective and a need, it is only a beginning. More and more jobs are demanding high school competency. Yet, in the 1960 census it is reported that only 18.5 percent of American Indians over the age of 25 had completed high school. This compared with a national average of 41.1 percent. This clearly dramatizes the need for opportunity for high school equivalency study on reservations.

Although the adult basic education program has been improved and expanded, it is providing only a small fraction of the educational opportunities needed by the adult Indian population. It seems highly unlikely, given the present funding bases, that it can significantly increase its scope.

PART 2: A NATIONAL CHALLENGE—RECOMMENDATIONS

The development of effective educational programs for Indian children must become a high priority objective of the Federal Government. Although direct Federal action can most readily take place in the federally-operated schools, special efforts should be made to encourage and assist the public schools in improving the quality of their programs for Indian children. The United States Office of Education should make much greater use of its resources and professional leadership to bring about improvement in public school education of Indian children.

The costs of improving the education of Indian children are bound to be high. In fact, a truly effective program will require doubling or even tripling the per pupil costs. But, the high educational costs will be more than offset by the reduction in unemployment and welfare rates and the increases in personal incomes certain to follow as a result of effective educational programs.

One of the crucial problems in the education of Indian children is the general relationship between white society and Indian communities. This relationship frequently alienates Indians and Indian communities, dampening both their potential for full self-development and their opportunities for gaining experience to control their own affairs through participation in effective local government.

It is essential to involve Indian parents in the education of their children and to give them an important voice—both at the national and local levels—in setting policy for those schools in which Indian children predominate. Whenever Indian tribes express the desire, assistance and training should be provided to permit them to operate their own schools under contract. A precedent and one model for this approach already exists at the Rough Rock Demonstration School in Chinle, Arizona.

The curriculum in both Federal and public schools serving Indian children should include substantial information about Indian culture and history and factual material about contemporary Indian life. This is important for both Indian and non-Indian children if they are to gain a better perspective and understanding of Indian heritage and current circumstances.

The complexity of the problems associated with cross-cultural education merit substantial research and development and the continuing adoption of promising innovations as they are discovered or developed. The present assumptions underlying the conventional approach of both Federal and public schools have not been valid, and a systematic search for more realistic approaches is clearly in order.

The most important step that can be taken as a matter of national policy and priority is to convert Federal schools in different regions of the country into exemplary institutions which can serve as a resource base and a leadership source for improving Indian education in public schools. They should provide models of excellence in several areas. First, in terms of developing outstanding bicultural, bilingual programs. Second, in terms of the development and utilization of the most effective techniques for educating the disadvantaged student. Third, they should be staffed and operated as therapeutic institutions capable of maximizing the personality development of the Indian child as well as assisting him in resolving his emotional and behavior problems.

In summary, the Federal Government must commit itself to a national policy of educational excellence for Indian children, maximum participation and control by Indian adults and communities, and the development of new legislation and substantial increases in appropriations to achieve these goals.

RECOMMENDATIONS

NATIONAL POLICY

• That there be set a national policy committing the nation to achieving educational excellence for American Indians; to maximum participation and control by Indians in establishing Indian education programs; and to assuring sufficient Federal funds to carry these programs forward.

• That the United States set as a national goal the achievement of the following specific objectives:

> • Maximum Indian participation in the development of exemplary educational programs for Federal schools, public schools with Indian populations, and model schools to meet both social and educational goals.

> • Excellent summer school programs for all Indian children.

> • Full-year pre-school programs for all Indian children between the ages of 3 and 5.

> • Elimination of adult illiteracy.

> • Adult high school equivalency programs for all Indian adults.

> • Parity of dropout rates and achievement levels of Indian high school students and national norms.

• Parity of college entrance and graduation of Indian students with the national average.

• Readily accessible community colleges.

• Early childhood services embracing the spectrum of need.

• Bilingual, bicultural special educational assistance.

• Workable student financial assistance programs at all educational levels.

• Vocational and technical training related accurately to employment opportunities.

• That the funds available for the education of American Indians be substantially increased, and that provisions be made for advance funding of BIA education programs to permit effective planning and recruitment of personnel.

ADMINISTRATION OF INDIAN EDUCATION

• That Indian boards of education be established at the local level for Federal Indian school districts.

• That Indian parental and community involvement be increased.

THE ROLE AND FUTURE OF FEDERAL SCHOOLS

• That the Federal Indian School System be developed into an exemplary system, which can play an important role in improving education for Indian children. Federal schools should develop exemplary programs in at least these three areas:

• Outstanding innovative programs for the education of disadvantaged children.

• Bilingual and bicultural education programs.

• Therapeutic programs designed to deal with the emotional, social and identity problems of Indian youth.

• That the present distribution and location of Federal boarding schools and the pattern of student placement be thoroughly reexamined by the National Indian Board of Indian Education.

• That a special effort be made to disseminate information on loans and scholarships and special programs to Indian students desiring to attend college.

• Colleges and universities should include within their counselor and teacher-training curriculum, courses designed to acquaint future teachers and counselors with the needs, values, and culture of Indian students.

ADULT EDUCATION

• That an exemplary program of adult education be developed which will provide for the following:

> • Basic literacy opportunities to all non-literate Indian adults. The goal should be to wipe out Indian illiteracy.

> • Opportunities to all Indian adults to qualify for a high school equivalency certificate. The goal should be to provide all interested Indian adults with high school equivalency in the shortest period of time feasible.

> • A major research and development program to develop more innovative and effective techniques for achieving the literacy and high school equivalency goals. This would include multi-media instruction and the development of curriculum material that is practical, meaningful and interesting to the adult Indian.

• That the adult Indian education program be effectively integrated with the rest of the BIA education program. The adult education program should as much as possible be placed under Indian control and contribute as well as benefit from the development of Indian controlled community schools.

FEDERAL ROLE AND NON-FEDERAL SCHOOLS

• That Public Law 874 be fully funded.

• That Public Law 815 be fully funded.

• That section 14 of Public Law 815 be declared as deserving of priority funding.

• That each state applying for a Johnson-O'Malley contract should be required to submit a definite plan for meeting the needs of its Indian students.

• That Indians should be involved in the planning, executing and evaluating of JOM programs. A state or district's JOM plan should be subject to the approval of the Indian participants.

• That the expanded contracting authority authorized by the JOM Act's 1936 amendment be utilized for the development of curriculum relevant to Indian culture and the training of teachers of Indian students.

• That tribes and Indian communities should be added to the list of agencies with which the BIA can negotiate JOM contracts and that full use be made of this new contracting authority to permit tribes to develop their own education projects and programs.

• That Indian tribes or communities should approve in a formal referendum the transfer of their children to public schools before such a transfer can be effected.

• That public school districts be required to demonstrate clearly they are ready for the transfer of Indian students by developing programs aimed at meeting the children's special needs and involving the Indian community in the school.[1]

INDIAN SELF-DETERMINATION AND EDUCATION

In 1968 PRESIDENT Lyndon B. Johnson, in a special message to Congress, called for Indian self-determination saying, "Our goal must be ... a policy of maximum choice for the American Indians, a policy expressed in ... self-determination."[1] Two years later President Richard Nixon called on Congress to enact legislation that "would empower a tribe or a group of tribes or any other Indian community to take over the control and operation of federally funded and administered programs," including schools.[2] In 1975, in response to the growing Indian desire for self-determination, Congress enacted the Indian Self-Determination and Education Assistance Act.

With the passage of the act it appeared that a mechanism for tribal control over the educational process had become a reality. Unlike the Buy Indian Act of 1910 (used by some tribes to contract for education programs), which did not allow the Secretary of the Interior to contract away any of his legislatively delegated authority, the Indian Self-Determination Act provided such statutory authorization. However, partially because of the federal trust responsibility, the secretary was empowered to approve or reject tribal contract requests. Consequently, funding and planning of educational programs remained under the purview of the secretary, who retained "the right to decide to his satisfaction, and without consultation" what programs would be funded.

Navajo Attempts to Establish Schools

The desire for Indian self-determination has been nowhere more pronounced than in the field of education. In the 1960s, for example, after passage of the Economic Opportunity Act, the Navajo leaders presented the new Office of Economic Opportunity with a proposal for a tribally controlled educational facility. In 1965, Office of Economic Opportunity funding was set aside to finance the Navajo education demonstration project. The Bureau of Indian Affairs offered the use of its school located at Lukachukai, Arizona, but federal civil service laws required that the school maintain its Bureau-hired teaching staff; this prevented the Navajo Nation from exercising authority over the faculty.

To overcome the problem DINE, Inc. (Demonstration in Navajo Education), was chartered under Arizona law in 1966 to receive funds to provide tribally controlled educational services. That year the Bureau of Indian Affairs turned over to DINE, Inc., a newly constructed school at Rough Rock, Arizona. Because the school was new, DINE, Inc., was able to hire faculty members without regard for federal civil-service restrictions. For the academic year 1966–1967, the school received $636,000 from the Bureau of Indian Affairs and the Office of Economic Opportunity. The first tribally controlled school was established.

The Rough Rock Demonstration School was unique in two respects: It was the first tribally controlled educational facility established since the dissolution of the Five Tribes' educational systems sixty years earlier, and it took a "both-and" educational approach, that is, "students were exposed to important values and customs of both Navajo culture and the dominant society."[3] The school provided instruction in the Navajo language (with English as a second language), established an adult education program, and used community elders to teach children tribal history, traditions, and legends.

After the successful demonstration at Rough Rock, amid increasing calls for self-determination and community control of education, other tribes contracted with the federal government for tribally operated schools.

When President Nixon called for a new policy of Indian self-determination, many Indian communities and tribal groups, although suspicious of a clandestine termination plan, began to assume control over the education of their youth. To encourage them Congress enacted the Indian Education Act in 1972.[4] The law stated that 5 percent of the monies be set aside for Indian-controlled schools. In addition, the law provided grants to Indian tribes, institutions, and organizations, or to state and local agencies, to develop and implement projects to improve educational opportunities for Indian children and to establish adult education programs.

Still, the Indian Education Act left most questions about tribal self-determination unanswered. For example, the law required parents' input but not tribal approval of grants for bilingual and bicultural education programs and for institutions of higher education to train prospective teachers of Indian students. Thus, the law did little but shift the focus of Indian involvement from non-participation to nominal involvement. In 1974 amendments to the Indian Education Act increased the amount set aside from 5 to 10 percent and gave preference to Indians in the awarding of grants. Much like the 1972 law, however, the 1974 amendments did little to promote Indian self-determination, largely because local Indian-controlled school boards took their marching orders from the superintendent, who remained generally implacable in his attitude about education.[5]

Funds Come with Strings Attached

By 1975 there were fifteen tribally operated schools. That year the Indian Self-Determination and Education Assistance Act became law, giving the Bureau of Indian Affairs authority to implement the provisions of the law.[6] Consequently, tribal contractees and bureau contractors have differing views of the law. Tribal contractees perceive the law as giving them the opportunity to determine their own educational programs. Bureau contractors, on the other hand, believe that tribal control means operating bureau facilities under the guidance of the bureau. In the selection that follows, "Self-Determination and American Indian Education: An Illusion of Control," Guy Senese argues that the authority of the Bureau of Indian Affairs to design rules and regulations regarding the contracting process denied Indian communities the power of self-determination over educational processes.

According to Senese, Congress intended to retain certain discretionary authority over the contract schools to prevent total tribal control. By giving the secretary of the interior the power of declination, Congress allowed him to deny or rescind tribal contract requests if he believed the educational criteria were unsatisfactory. Furthermore, bureau control of the disbursement and use of funds prevented tribal communities and organizations from operating schools independently. Central to Senese's argument is his assertion that the act presented the Bureau of Indian Affairs with a conflict of interest: If the Indians succeeded in directing their own educational programs, the bureau would lose its raison d'être.

Self Determination ... an Illusion of Control

In 1975, Indian control of education and economic development was codified through the Indian Self-Determination and Education Assistance Act (PL 93-638). This act provided the legal base upon which to regulate the existing practice of Indian people developing contractual agreements whereby the government would pay the local community to provide a variety of services, schools, clinics, tribal enterprises, public works, legal services, and so forth.

Much of the impact of PL 93-638 fell on the developing institution of the Indian Contract school which, after its start at the Rough Rock Demonstration

School on the Navajo Reservation, had grown considerably to include a number of primary, middle, and high schools and Indian-controlled community colleges. PL 93-638 was greeted with the same laudatory comment as Rough Rock had been in its first experimental months.

Education writers often view PL 93-638 with an optimism uncharacteristic of professionals accustomed to viewing government Indian legislation with a jaundiced eye. Robert Cooper and Jack Gregory wrote that "we now stand on top of the mountain, about to walk down the other side into a valley of sunshine, with a new ray of hope called Indian self-determination." Robert Havighurst, who has written extensively on Indian education policy issues, also concluded that self-determination was a great success and held much promise. He wrote: "All in all, educators and planners in the U.S. can take some satisfaction in having developed, at long last, flexible and effective long-range policies for the Native Americans. Problems are still there, of course, but Native Americans are beginning to feel that they can control their own destiny."

This paper argues that self-determination and community control of education as authorized by PL 93-638 have been severely compromised. Both the language of the law and its implementation severely limit legitimate self-determination. Indeed, the act works as much as a rhetorical device as it does as an instrument to provide real opportunity to run a successful program. It offers Indian people an opportunity to "show" that Indian people can run their own institutions, yet it does not provide the flexibility or resource availability required for the efficient operation of a school. In addition, it allows the Bureau of Indian Affairs (BIA) bureaucracy to maintain indirect control and thereby some of the bureaucratic functions upon which its machinery depends. In PL 93-638, we can see the codification of a series of Indian self-help schemes intended to provide not only the illusion of control but the illusion of competency. Self-help has been reduced to a struggle for survival. Yet the problems endemic to contracting under PL 93-638 have not greatly harmed the rhetoric; rather, they have served to create it.

Basic to the idea of self-determination, as stated early in the body of PL 93-638, once again is the notion of "control." Indian people are to have, through an "orderly transition from federal domination of programs for the services to Indians ... effective and meaningful participation by the Indian people in the planning, conduct and administration of those programs and services." The United States Code of Federal Regulations, which guides the administration and implementation of PL 93-638 contracting policy through a variety of program guidelines (under the authority of federal law), states that "in carrying out its Education mission, the Assistant Secretary of Indian Affairs through the director shall ... ensure that Indian tribes and Alaska Native entities fully exercise self-determination and control in planning, priority setting, development, management, operation staffing, and evaluation in all aspects of the education process." Stated in this way, and carrying such concomitant definition, "control" is equated with power and broad community discretion. Yet analysis of the legislative record shows clearly that this kind of control is severely compromised. Self-contradictory language within the statute and implementation problems which have occurred since its passage both speak to the serious damage done to any legitimate conception of self-determination.

The Bureau of Indian Affairs' interpretation of the meaning of self-determination, and the extent of the control which is conferred through PL 93-638, lies at the root of problems in the implementation of the act. In addition, we can see upon careful examination of the legislative language that with all the purported sharpness of its aim of increased Indian influence, there are key areas which Congress has not allowed to slip from the grasp of the BIA.

The most representative example of the purported legislative intent of PL 93-638 is found in the form of the community-controlled Contract school. For it is here that the greatest expression of Indian control of education was to be located. Implementation and contract compliance problems for these schools have multiplied and caused great difficulty for Contract school communities as a result of this language. Bureau education policy and procedure related to school contracting have ranged, in general, from obfuscation and inertia to administrative sabotage. Indian control of education, basic to the legal and historic meaning of self-determination, has been hamstrung by the high degree of discretion that the BIA still exercises under PL 93-638. Its authority to decline contract applications is extensive and allows for little redress. Distribution and amount of funding are persistent problems, which places Contract school operations in jeopardy time and time again. Payroll, hiring, job, and supply security are a constant worry and a drain on administrative energy and time. Finally, there are serious problems with the amount and quality of technical assistance for contracted operations which PL 93-638 says will be provided to the tribe/community by the bureau.

These difficulties suggest a reevaluation of the problem of conflict of interest in which the bureau may interpret any successful contracted operation as another example that the BIA itself is unnecessary. Any notion of self-determination which has more than rhetorical intent and which has legitimate self-rule at its root implies at least that tribal entities and communities would be taking responsibility now for program inauguration, continuation, and progress. These problems would act, at least partially, without dependence on bureau control and thus would work to lessen the need for the bureau to act in its traditional patronizing capacity.

On January 5, 1975, following a string of legislative moves directed toward increased self-determination through community control, the passage of PL-93-638 signaled a supposed milestone in the move toward self-determination for Indian people. Title I of this law simply "provided for maximum Indian participation in government programs for Indian people."

Though it has been hailed as a new direction in Indian policy, self-determination requires a closer examination. Robert Roessel, who helped plan Rough Rock and acted as its first director, warned in 1978 ... that "the method the BIA uses in allocating funds to support contract schools makes only the strongest and most fearless communities want to enter such a financially uncertain funding arrangement. There is no doubt that there would have been many more contract schools on the Navajo reservation if the method of funding such schools had been adequate and certain!"

Counter to these warnings and other systematic problems, which will be cited later, the rhetoric of self-determination in the text of PL 93-638 virtually rings with the promise of increased Indian control over the planning and administration of contracted operations. It is purposed to be an act

> to provide maximum Indian participation in the Government and education of the Indian people; to provide for the full participation of Indian tribes in programs and services conducted by the federal government for Indians and to encourage development of human resources of the Indian people; ... to support the right of Indian citizens to control their own educational activities; and for other purposes.

The Act claims to be recognition that "parental and community control of the educational process is of crucial importance to the Indian people." Further:

> The Congress hereby recognizes the obligation of the United States to respond to the strong expression of the Indian people for self-determination by assuring maximum Indian participation in the direction of education as well as other federal services to Indian communities so as to render such services more responsive to the needs and desires of those communities.

With the passage of PL 93-638, the rhetoric of self-determination closed like a steel trap upon the imagination of contemporary writers and policy makers in American Indian affairs. It has closed with as much power upon the Indian communities which have tried to create programs workable in the best spirit of self-determination.

The analysis contained here will be restricted to an examination of educational programs under the purview of PL 93-638 and concurrent BIA regulations regarding the contracting with the federal government of education services by Indian communities and tribes.

By taking a first glance at the statements of purpose which form the first part of the text of the act, it would seem that this legislation was a revolutionary step away from government paternalism. A brief analysis of the specific provisions which follow in the text, as well as the documentary and testimonial record surrounding the statute's implementation, suggest that this, clearly, was not the case.

DISCRETION, DECLINATION, FUNDING, AND CONFLICT OF INTEREST

Discretion

Problems with the meaning of self-determination were not lost on those who reviewed Senator Henry Jackson's Senate Bill 1017, which preceded PL 93-638. The bill came under immediate fire for being unlikely to achieve the purpose for which it was apparently designed—increased local control. Funding and planning were kept under the purview of the Interior Department and the Department of Health, Education and Welfare (HEW). These agencies retained control through the judicious application of their "discretionary" power throughout the planning, procurement, and operation stages of a contracted school operation. Congress received testimony from legal consultant Michael Gross during hearings on S. 1017. He argued that "the provisions of this bill would work to entrench and strengthen present systems for educating Indians rather than reform them." He continued on to cite the problem as it centered upon the notion of discretionary power—control of funds and incipient conflict of interest: "It must be recognized that the BIA's infrastructure has an interest diametrically opposed to Indian self-determination, for the latter will inevitably mean placing administration of Indian programs in Indian hands, thus making the BIA's overblown bureaucracy largely superfluous." Gross went on to note that trying to implement legitimate self-determination through the Secretary of Interior's discretion is likely to produce precisely the opposite effect than that intended. Instead of giving Indians control over their lives, the language quoted in the bill will probably serve to preempt the self-determination policy by giving "hostile elements in the Federal government control over the pace and characteristics of its implementation."

The "Congressional Findings" and "Declaration of Policy" sections which form part of the preface to Titles I and II of the act as it finally took form, give the impression that control over Indian education will take a dramatic turn; that control will clearly now be directed by Indian people rather than the BIA. Yet the broad discretion which remains with the Interior Secretary later in the text of the act works to belie the early promises. The act reads that "the Secretary may decline to enter into any contract requested by an Indian tribe if he finds that: (1) the service to be rendered to the Indian beneficiaries of that particular program or function contracted will not be satisfactory." Thus, the Secretary retains the right to decide to his satisfaction, and without consultation, except such as shall remain advisory on the part of the contractee, what are the dimensions and characteristics of a fundable program. This is clearly far away from a notion of self-determination which included the right for Indian people to decide which program will be supported and which will not. While the preface of the act argues that the government will actively encourage self-determination, this discretionary power only outlines criteria for discouragement—criteria provided by the Interior Secretary through the BIA.

This federal discretionary power expressed a lack of responsible negotiation which lies at the heart of a true contract. Mel Conasket, then president of the National Congress of American Indians, elaborated on this problem in 1977 when he testified at the Oversight Hearings on PL 93-638 that "according to the Indian Self-Determination Act, a negotiation process between an agency and a tribe is required. In reality negotiation never actually occurs because most programs have predetermined budget. … Funding levels are not negotiated." Wayne Holm, director of the Rock Point Community School, which began contract operations shortly after Rough Rock in a community thirty miles to the north, testified that BIA discretionary power was strengthened by PL 93-638, making it more difficult for smaller communities to contract than had been the case prior to the act.

In the development of this legislation, one clear case points to a successful attempt by the BIA to strengthen and consolidate its discretionary power. In the 1973 hearings on S. 1017, Commission of Indian Affairs Morris Thompson attempted to work language into the bill which would greatly increase the discretionary power of the BIA over contracting procedures. Section 106(d) of the bill and the present statute provided that a contracting body may retrocede the program to the government should it find itself unable to carry out its programs. Thompson referred to this provision as it stood as "indirect" and argued for a more "explicit" approach. He wanted to add a new section (109) which would allow the Secretary to rescind a contract "in any case where he found that a tribe was operating a program so as to endanger the health, safety or welfare of any persons or so as to demonstrate gross fiscal negligence or mismanagement." Although he added that he was "primarily referring to contracts with HEW in the health field," the language as it is found now in Section 109, makes no stipulation as to the limit of its intent. Indeed, one could not argue against the sense of terminating a contract whose operation endangers health, safety, or welfare. However, since there is no clarifying language in the law, the interpretation of danger here is left entirely up to the Secretary, or more specifically, to his contract officers in the field. Furthermore, Section 109 now reads that in such cases the Secretary should, under regulations provided by him (the Secretary) and after notice and a "hearing," have the discretion to terminate the contract immediately. This provision was developed without local participation in the decision except in the form of a "hearing." It appears to limit effectively the scope of community control by virtually excluding Indian participation in a retrocession, except a retrocession initiated by the Secretary, and then places Indian communities in an "advisory" rather than a bargaining capacity.

The broad discretionary power invested in the Secretary of the Interior is evidence that Congress was less interested in a definition of self-determination which mandates self-government and more interested in allowing contracting to take shape without greatly altering the power and influence of the BIA. One of the other ways this power is exercised is in the criteria developed upon which an attempt to contract may, with broad powers retained in the Interior Department, be declined.

Declination

PL 93-638, Title II, Part A, section 202 (sec. 4) reads:

> The Secretary of the Interior shall not enter into any contract for the education of Indians unless the prospective contractor has submitted to, and has had approved by the Secretary of the Interior, an education plan, which plan, in the determination of the Secretary, contains educational objectives which adequately address the educational needs of the Indian students who are the beneficiaries of the contract.

In this way the educational criteria for the establishment of an Indian-controlled school must be criteria which are acceptable, not necessarily to Indian parents and educators, but to the Secretary of the Interior and the BIA. Yet, in the implementation hearings of 1977, Senator Melcher of the Senate Select Subcommittee on Indian Affairs inquired about the extent to which services delivery could be checked in the field. Replying to this, LaFollete Butler, acting director of the commissioner's self-determination staff, said: "Senator, the difficulty we have is that the contract proposal is often a great deal different than the operation the Bureau has. ... So the standards and criteria for the program operation are really the tribe's. Whether or not the results will be better than an operation by the Bureau under its standards and criteria would be very difficult to arrive at."

There are several problems here. First, the claim by Butler that declination and evaluation criteria are explicitly "the tribe's" is not to be found in PL 93-638. Rather, these guidelines exist in the Code of Federal Regulations which, though growing out of the law, are subject to periodic revision without legislative review. The Code of Federal Regulations is a published set of documents that federal agencies use to implement the statutory mandate of Congress. These regulations are voluminous, usually covering hundreds more pages than the statutes from which they derive their authority. They are developed within agencies such as the BIA and as such are often more reflective of the needs of a particular agency, and are more susceptible to alteration, than the statutes themselves. Indeed, they are the interpretation of the letter and spirit of Congressional intent and subject to easier review and alteration than statutes, and since they are the handbook by which the agency administers the programs, they are extremely important documents. They carry much of the real weight of the law between their covers.

Relegation of this mandate to maximize Indian criteria for program quality to the flexible code of Federal Regulations is reflective of the lack of confidence in self-determination. Furthermore, a violation of the code is not a violation of the law; it is rather simply a disregard for another administrative regulation whose enforcement is overseen by BIA administrators, not Congress. The power of declination criteria in the law lies firmly in the hands of the Secretary of the Interior. The criteria, as seen in the law and not the code, are more clearly those of the Secretary, not the tribes' and communities'—the beneficiaries of self-determination.

Declination of contracts has, however, been the exception rather than the rule. The bureau declination authority has been exercised largely in cases where the Commissioner's office has decided that insufficient funds were available for the proposal. While not stated in the legislation as a declination issue, "insufficient funds" has been used as a criterion for declination. Again, the determination of sufficiency or insufficiency is made solely under the authority of the Commissioner's office. Community/tribal involvement is not a part of the decision.

Still, the declination threat is always there. According to testimony submitted by Virgil Kills Straight, Secretary of the Little Wound School Board in Kyle, South Dakota, "BIA personnel are advocates for the government in terms of negotiating for the government and determining declination issues." Again, according to Wayne Holm of Rock Point School:

> (While) PL 93-638 went a long way in reducing the number of reasons why the Bureau could decline to contract ... as part of a trade-off, however, they appeared to raise the requirements for an initial proposal. ... New Boards must either start at the place it has taken existing boards several years to arrive at, or ... decide contracting is simply too complicated and too risky. Too many boards have decided just that.

Funding

The control, amount, and disbursement of funds to contract school operations are serious obstacles to legitimate community control. One of the most serious roadblocks in the path of a contracted program exists in the inability of the BIA to disburse funds in a timely manner such as might encourage the operation of orderly administrative procedures. Funds are not provided by advance payment each contract period. Rather, operations proceed on a cost-reimbursable basis. Thus, any delay in the process of administering payments at the agency, area, or bureau level results in a shortfall of cash at the site. A problem at any level can result in frozen paychecks, late bills, default, and any number of distribution problems which keep staffing and supply in a constantly tenuous position. Community schools are often forced to run their accounts from the authority of letters of credit while waiting for reimbursement.

The problems faced by Contract schools in receiving funds are built with a purpose into PL 93-638. Section 106 reads that payments may be made either in advance or by reimbursement, as the Secretary "deems necessary to carry out the provisions of this act." Yet the Secretary would have no real authority to pay in advance and must choose the cumbersome reimbursement method if he is to honor the intent of the next line of the statute. It reads: "The transfer of funds shall be scheduled consistent with program requirements and applicable Treasury regulations, so as to minimize the time elapsing between the transfer of such funds from the U.S. Treasury and the disbursement thereof by the tribal organization." This provision was included in the act on the recommendation of the Comptroller General in order to minimize the interest which would be lost to the Treasury by delaying payment of contract support funds until the last possible moment before the tribe or community must distribute its own payments. This is clearly a provision pursuant to more general governmental contracting guidelines which state: "The government's basic policy in procuring property and services is to do so in a manner calculated to result in the lowest ultimate overall cost to the government."

Thus, in the spirit of "maximum participation," Indian communities are also allowed to participate maximally in the effort to save the government interest money. This comes, unfortunately, at the expense of running their schools with convoluted accounting and a constant risk of default and closure. The alleged "self-determination" has been won at the price of administrative anxiety, staff insecurity, and low morale. In the "Oversight Hearings," Wayne Holm commented on this problem. "Contract schools are already rather precarious places to work. Many good people are reluctant to work at a Contract school, not because of the generally lower salaries, but because of real or potential problems in getting paid."

However, insufficient funds are clearly as great a problem as their insecure disbursement periods:

> The BIA budgeting process takes care of raises and promotions for BIA administered programs but makes no provision for tribally contracted programs.

Finally, the control of funds has been a key problem affecting self-determination for Indian people through contract operations. Former Navajo Tribal Chairman Peter McDonald has said plainly that Congress should "get serious about self-determination or let's not pretend anymore. If you want to enable us to try to do our own thing and take the risk that we may succeed, then provide the money without the strings." Clearly, the lack of meaningful input on BIA budgeting by tribes for contract support is evidence of the weakness of the claims for self-determination.

Conflict of Interest

Complaints about problems related to PL 93-638 implementation have come from all corners of Native America. Writers sound a central theme concerning conflicts of interest between the tribes and the BIA over the implementation of this act. One of the loudest complaints centers on the lack of bureau accountability for the use of money earmarked for the provision of technical assistance to the tribes for contract operations. Too often this money goes toward the hiring of more bureau employees, and too much is being spent on the operations at the area, not the local level, the complaint being that the area (large BIA administrative district) is "too distant and too ignorant of most tribes' concerns to provide the kind of technical assistance (they) need." Contract operations that run through the few scattered area offices cannot be as responsive as the local agency. For example, the area offices in Phoenix and Albuquerque, while supporting Navajo regional affairs, are far removed from the localities and special problems with which these localities must deal.

Much of the strength of PL 93-638 clearly is used to shore up the bulwarks of BIA control. Tribes who contract a program that is operated in an identical manner to the bureau-operated program it is "replacing," that displaces no bureau personnel, and that operates so as to have the bureau run the program while working within predesigned BIA budgetary guidelines at the level of funding determined by the bureau, have contracted the type of program most likely to succeed.

The meaning of control has been severely compromised in the operations of what self-determination has come to mean through the codification and implementation of PL 93-638. Speaking for the Navajo Tribal Council, Tribal Chairman McDonald claimed: "The Self-Determination Act gave to the self-same bureaucrats whose conspicuous failure had led to the Act, the responsibility for determining how tribes might try to accomplish what these same officials had already failed at. Thus, those with a proven record of failure were to judge and 'guide' those who would try to succeed." Certainly, there is a problem when an agency is put in charge of the program which would, should it succeed, spell the beginning of the end of that same agency. The bureau sees no self-interest in increased self-determination by the tribes, if by self-determination we mean increased local control of programs. However, [some] have argued ... [that] the BIA has chosen to interpret the intent of PL 93-638 such that minimal damage will be done to the extensive control of the BIA. Two major reasons exist for the failure of self-determination to confer increased local control:

> 1. The flexibility that the Act brings to contracting with tribes involves preserving substantial federal discretion to refuse to contract and to renege on contracts; and

> 2. the Bureau interprets the reference to "trust responsibility" in the law as a mandate not to delegate any of its powers to regulate tribal resources.

The Secretary of the Interior is given the power to refuse to contract if, in the opinion of the Secretary, "adequate protection of trust resources is not assured." Yet the fog shrouding the meaning of "trust resource" is thick indeed. While Indian people generally want their treaty-bound trust resources protected, there is no clear agreement on the meaning of this concept, despite the attempts—beginning in 1975—of the American Indian Policy Review Commission to define the limits of "trust." The issue is clouded in controversy, its meaning varying with the interpretation of the current administration in Washington.

The fact, however, that tribes are concerned that the government keep its promise to hold its resources in trust to protect natural and, some argue, human resources from harm, abuse, or neglect raises serious questions about the ultimate legitimacy of a policy of self-determination interpreted fully as the operation of self-rule, community control, and legitimate sovereignty. This definition runs perhaps the risk of abrogating the federal responsibility to provide services for the protection of the trust. All of the issues raised here have profound consequences, not only for the interpretation of the meaning of self-determination but the concept of "trust" which lies at the foundation of relationships between the United States government and American Indians.

Returning to self-determination, however, we see that Indian leaders have disagreed on whether the concept is in itself an abrogation of the trust responsibility. Some will argue for more control over funding and administration of the contracted programs and, while loudly decrying the problems of PL 93-638 implementation, stand firmly by the concept of self-determination as a step in the right direction. "Self-determination," through whatever means it is expressed or implemented, has, for many Indian people, become a welcome addition to the policy language. Perhaps they believe that the rhetoric will harden into something tangible; that the betrayal of faith in legitimate sovereignty and self-rule will one day fade away. They believe, perhaps, that the concepts of community control, self-rule, and sovereignty will be one day fully realized in a subtle balance, with respect to the crucial and sacred treaty agreements which established the present trust accord, and that self-determination will one day be raised from its present status as a vocabulary work. Indeed, the Acting Director of the Association of Navajo Community Controlled Schools testified: "We must constantly fight to maintain community control efforts, because we strongly believe in self-determination. It is not a fad with us. It is here to stay."

Yet the Indian educators and tribal leaders cited here are joined in a chorus indicting the language and especially the implementation of PL 93-638. There are always, however, disagreements within Indian communities as to the dangers inherent in the intent of any Indian policy legislation. Any turnback of responsibilities of Indian education, welfare, and resource development has been seen by some as the beginning of a new move to abrogate treaty-bound trust responsibilities and terminate federal reservation status once Indians have assumed sufficient control. Others have resisted contracting local operations because these tribal members were also BIA employees. People have feared loss of jobs when "massive RIF (reduction in force) meetings were held by BIA agency offices when tribal contracting of services became imminent." For some, the concept "self-determination" has become the battle cry of the beginning of a great new era of local control. For most, PL 93-638, which is the vehicle that carried the concept into the policy arena, is the beginning of a new series of problems in the long history of government Indian misadventure.

Self-determination has been used most often with an emphasis on its rhetorical rather than its realistic possibilities. It has continually worked as a part of attempts to signify the separateness, indeed the claimed state sovereignty of groups and peoples within nations. More often than not, the cry for self-determination arose from the throats of those bereft of the benefit of political recognition and legitimate sovereignty. It did not appear often in the parlance of those describing a state of legitimate sovereignty already enjoyed. Self-determination is best understood in the language of the politically and jurisdictionally undernourished.

If we view the Indian Self-Determination and Education Assistance Act in light of a definition of self-determination which works to maximize Indian community self-government and local control, we can begin to understand the support of those who value this as a fundamental human right. Many of those who supported this law were working to retain power for Indian people which had previously been usurped and held by the federal government through the Bureau of Indian Affairs. Self-determination is a part of the long and convoluted history of "reform" which had sent United States policy toward Indian people through a series of convulsions. Yet most of the conventional literature explaining Anglo-Indian sociopolitical history argues that major changes in Indian policy have come as a result of the real or perceived need of policymakers and opinion leaders to redress the purported wrongs perpetrated by the then current policy. Still, "All major Congressional Indian programs, however well intentioned, have increased the power of the BIA. Each increase in the power of the Bureau has increased Indian welfare."

It is common for policymakers and opinion leaders to be critical of programs and for these criticisms to emerge later in the shape of program alterations or full-scale reform. It is less common for those who are interested in, and who write about, Indian social and education policy to place criticism at the doorstep of reform itself. Yet, bound by administrative precedent and an overweening bureaucratic posture aligned for self-preservation, self-determination through PL 93-638 has become a design for stunted community control, marred by administrative intransigence.

Some may view a move toward Indian self-determination through the implementation of PL 93-638 as the beginning of an attempt to terminate federal trust dependent status or may see it as a hope, a beginning of a new, stronger era for tribal and Indian community sovereignty. Yet, whatever the dreams of reformers or the nightmares of the reformed, the policy of self-determination grinds on.

Clearly, many of those struggling to realize self-determination through community control of education are aware of the reasons for the weaknesses of this movement. Yet, as it remains, supposedly out on the slim, bright halo around the dark head of Native American Schooling, the faltering programs and failing schools are, unlike the control they purport to represent, no illusion at all.[7]

TRIBALLY CONTROLLED COMMUNITY COLLEGES

IN THE MID-1960s, as the desire for Indian self-determination grew, a movement to establish Indian-controlled community colleges commenced. These colleges perpetuated tribal culture and focused on the needs of the Indian community, both of which were the beneficiaries of benign neglect in other educational institutions. Tribally controlled community colleges are recent arrivals in the field of higher education in the United States: there are twenty-four tribally controlled community colleges in the country, sixteen of which are located in Montana, North Dakota, and South Dakota.

History of Higher Education for Indians

Efforts to provide higher education to American Indians date back to the seventeenth and eighteenth centuries, when colleges such as Harvard, Dartmouth, and William and Mary educated a small number of American Indians. Harvard College, for example, was established in 1636 to provide for "the education of the English and Indian youth in knowledge and Goodness."[1] Furthermore, when Dartmouth College was established in 1769 its goal was to "teach Indian boys to read and write ... and especially to teach them thoroughly the catechism and the principles of the Christian religion."[2]

Like most other non-Indian-controlled educational endeavors, higher education usually denigrated Indian culture. Many students were faced with the choice of accepting the "white man's ways," at the expense of their traditional culture or retaining their traditional culture and values, which often led to increased hostility from the white world. By the late nineteenth and early twentieth centuries, higher education was foreign to most American Indians, although some Native Americans, such as Dr. Charles Eastman, were highly educated.

The Meriam Report urged the Bureau of Indian Affairs to "encourage promising Indian youths to continue their education beyond the boarding school and fit themselves for professional, scientific and technical callings."[3] To implement such an undertaking, the Meriam Report recommended that scholarships and student loans be made available to American Indians interested in attending college. Despite these recommendations most Indians prior to World War II placed a low value on higher education.

Postwar Efforts

After World War II many returning American Indian war veterans began to realize that higher education was necessary to tribal survival; that is, they saw education as a tool to protect tribal integrity and rights.

The higher education programs of the postwar era were markedly similar to those of the prewar era—assimilationist. In 1962 Dr. G. D. McGrath, commenting on Indian students in higher education, concluded that cultural values were crucial in explaining the poor academic performance of Indian students.[4] A related obstacle was the language handicap. In light of these issues—and the desire for Indian self-determination in education—several tribes chartered their own community colleges in the 1960s and early 1970s.

The movement toward tribally controlled community colleges began in earnest with the establishment of the Navajo Community College in 1969. Other tribes chartered community colleges under the 1965 Higher Education Act, which earmarked specific funds for tribal community colleges. With the passage of the 1978 Tribally Controlled Community College Assistance Act, a method of federal support for higher education in tribally controlled colleges was established.[5]

Islands of Hope

With the passage of the Tribal College Act, an island of cultural hope was preserved in a sea of educational despair—at least while Congress provided adequate support for the tribally controlled schools. True to form, Congress did not sustain adequate funding.

In the fall of 1989, after a two year study of tribally controlled community colleges, the Carnegie Foundation for the Advancement of Teaching issued a special report entitled *Tribal Colleges: Shaping the Future of Native America*. The report presents several themes, including the federal government's benign neglect of Indian-controlled higher education. Despite the lack of support, the report concluded, tribal colleges are significant institutions that seek to rebuild the heritage of Native Americans by instilling pride and self-respect. Tribal colleges act as cultural translators, which, according to the report, allows the colleges to be the vanguards of a cultural renaissance. In a larger context, tribal colleges can serve as an example of renewal to a national education system that is desperately in need of direction and purpose.

Tribal Colleges: Shaping the Future of Native America

Twenty years ago in Arizona, Native Americans created a new institution— the first tribally controlled college. Today twenty-four higher learning institutions, founded and controlled by Indians, are serving Native communities from Michigan to Washington state. While most of these colleges are no more than a decade old—a blink in time for higher education—they have undergone dramatic growth, expanding and gaining recognition in spite of conditions others would regard as impossible.

Viewed by numbers alone, tribal colleges add up to only a small fraction of the total higher education picture—the equivalent perhaps of a small branch of a single state university. But using conventional yardsticks to measure these colleges misses the significance of their work. Tribally controlled colleges can be understood only in the historical context of Indian education and in the spiritual role they play in bringing renewal to their people. When viewed from these perspectives, tribal colleges assume a mission of great consequence to Native Americans and to the nation.

Tribal colleges are truly community institutions. After years of brutal physical hardships and disorienting cultural loss, Native Americans—through the tribal college movement—are building new communities based on shared traditions. They are challenging the conditions that plague their societies and continue to threaten their survival. At the heart of the tribal college movement is a commitment by Native Americans to reclaim their cultural heritage. The commitment to reaffirm traditions is a driving force fed by a spirit based on shared history passed down through generations, and on common goals. Some tribes have lost much of their tradition, and feel, with a sense of urgency, that they must reclaim all they can from the past even as they confront problems of the present. The obstacles in this endeavor are enormous but, again, Indians are determined to reaffirm their heritage, and tribal colleges, through their curriculum and campus climate, are places of great promise.

If we have learned anything from our relationship with the American Indian, it is that people cannot be torn from their cultural roots without harm. To the extent that we fail to assist Native Americans, through their own institutions, to reclaim their past and secure their future, we are compounding the costly errors of the past.

Tribal Colleges: A New Era The story of the Native American experience has been described, almost always, in the language of despair. Indian life is filled with images of poverty, and the government policy has consistently been called a failure. We often speak of "the plight of the Indians" and conclude with resignation that little can be done. But there is in fact a lot that can be done. We report here on some of the great beginnings that have been accomplished for the Indians themselves, and offer recommendations for support that should be offered to help assure their continued support.

At the heart of the spirit of renewal among the Indians is a network of Native American colleges providing education and community service in a climate of self-determination. Although the oldest tribal college was started just two decades ago, these fledgling institutions are creatively changing the educational and social landscape of the reservations. Today, these institutions have a full-time equivalent enrollment of more than 4,400 students and serve over 10,000 Native American individuals.

The challenges these institutions confront cannot be overstated. A typical tribal college necessarily charges low tuition but lacks a tax base to support the full education costs. Meanwhile, the limited federal support these colleges receive—the backbone of their funding—fails to keep pace with their enrollment growth. Classes at tribal colleges frequently are held in shabby buildings, even in trailers, and students often use books and laboratory equipment that are embarrassingly obsolete. At the same time, the colleges are educating many first-generation students who usually have important but competing obligations to their families and local communities.

Tribal colleges also offer vital community services—family counseling, alcohol abuse programs and job training—with little financial or administrative support. Successful programs frequently end abruptly because of budget cuts. Considering the enormously difficult conditions tribal colleges endure, with resources most collegiate institutions would find unacceptably restrictive, their impact is remarkable. It became unmistakably clear during our visits that, even as they struggle to fulfill their urgent mandates, tribal colleges are crucial to the future of Native Americans, and of our nation.

First, tribal colleges establish a learning environment that encourages participation by and builds self-confidence in students who have come to view failure as the norm. The attrition rate among Indian students, at both the school and college levels, greatly exceeds the rate for white students. Isolated by distance and culture, many have come to accept that they cannot complete school. College seems to many Native Americans an impossible dream. Tribal colleges offer hope in this climate of despair.

Second, tribal colleges celebrate and help sustain the rich Native American traditions. For many Americans, Indian culture is little more than images of tepees, peace pipes, and brightly colored rugs. But in many reservation communities, traditional cultural values remain a vital part of the social fabric. Tribal languages are still spoken, and traditional arts and crafts and spiritual beliefs are respected.

While non-Indian schools and colleges have long ignored Indian culture, tribal colleges view it as their curricular center. They argue that it is through a reconnection to these longstanding cultural skills and beliefs that Indians can build a strong self-image and participate, with confidence, in the dominant society. Each of the tribal colleges offers courses, sometimes taught by tribal elders, in native language, story-telling, history, and arts.

Third, tribal colleges provide essential services that enrich the communities surrounding them. These colleges are, in the truest sense, community institutions. Located on reservations, nearly all colleges offer social and economic programs for tribal advancement. Some offer adult education, including literacy tutoring, high school equivalency programs, and vocational training. Others work cooperatively with local businesses and industries to build a stronger economic base.

Fourth, the colleges are often centers for research and scholarship. Several have established cooperative programs with state universities to conduct scientific research, while others sponsor seminars and studies about economic development needs. To cite just one measure of achievement, twelve of the colleges are now fully accredited and eight others are now candidates for accreditation, a remarkable feat considering how young the colleges are and how thoroughly they have been scrutinized by the regional accrediting agencies, as well as by federal administrators and auditors.

These institutions have taken on a breathtaking array of responsibilities. As they move beyond their infancy, successes are now clearly visible; their value is well documented. But recognition and acceptance happen despite the federal government's benign neglect and a lack of national awareness of their merits. Relative to enrollment, federal support to tribal colleges has, in fact, declined for nearly a decade. Private support, while expanding, cannot fill the gap. Even with a twenty year history, the tribal colleges are known to only a few Americans, and they continue to be ignored by much of the higher education community. ...

Tribal Colleges: A Study of Survival In 1911, an Indian named August Breuninger proposed the creation of an Indian university that would focus on Native American culture and be connected to an Indian museum. In a letter outlining his proposal, Breuninger argued that such an institution would both create opportunity for Indians and demonstrate the vitality of Indian culture.

> A university for Indians is the greatest step we educated
> Indians could make in uniting our people. It would
> eliminate the general conception—that an Indian consists
> of only feathers and paint. It would give us a better
> influence with the rising generation, by setting out our
> character in such a conspicuous manner as to be observed
> and imitated by them.

Advocates of an Indian-controlled college were not looking to retreat from the modern world; rather, the goal was to foster a more successful path for native people toward participation as equals in the larger American society. It was not surprising, though, that the strict assimilationists of the period opposed such efforts. For example, Richard Pratt, head of the Carlisle Indian School, was convinced that Indian-controlled education would work against the integration of Indians into American society. In his eyes Indian culture was, by definition, a hindrance to advancement.

Against this prevailing attitude, proposals for native colleges continued to be made periodically for another half century, with little result. It was not until 1968 that the politics, philosophical arguments and pragmatic need all came together on the Navajo Reservation, and the first tribally controlled college was at last founded. The impetus for the creation of the Navajo Community College came directly from the Indians themselves. The college was established with the aid of various grants, and two years later received support from Congress in the Navajo Community College Act. From this beginning followed the founding of more colleges. A critical piece of legislation to which most of the later tribal colleges owe their existence was the Tribally Controlled Community College Assistance Act of 1978.

In recent years, many non-Indian colleges and universities have become more hospitable—and at least eighty-five have organized Indian studies programs. Nevertheless, mainstream institutions are not able to serve well the diverse community needs that have become the special focus of tribal colleges, and the success rate of non-Indian colleges is not praiseworthy. In fact, close to 90 percent of Native Americans who enter such colleges eventually drop out.

Those who are part of Native American communities accept the fact they do not live in isolation, but they are no longer willing to be led by the government. Instead, Native Americans want skills to determine their own future. It is within this context that tribal colleges should be viewed—not as a retreat from the dominant white society, but as a route for Indian people to reach greater equality and more constructive interchange with the larger world.

A Place for Traditional Culture Tribal colleges, in sharp contrast to past federal policies, argue that there is still a central need for traditional culture.

Indeed, they view traditional culture as their social and intellectual frame of reference. These institutions have demonstrated eloquently that the traditional Indian cultures, rather than being disruptive or irrelevant, are supportive and nurturing influences on Indian students.

Individuals firmly rooted in their own heritage can participate with more confidence in the complex world around them. In this way, tribal colleges are "cultural translators," according to a counselor at one Indian college. "Many students need to learn how to fit into the twentieth century and still be a Chippewa," he said.

While American education policy towards Indians has matured considerably since the first students were enrolled, it was not until Indians themselves became participants in determining their future that true advancement and productive interaction began. Tribal colleges are a major part of this trend and their success in the future will, in a very real way, assure the continued emergence of a dynamic and self-sustaining Indian population.

Educational Philosophy and Curriculum All Indian-controlled colleges share a common goal of cultural understanding and tribal development, but there is diversity in educational philosophy from college to college and each curriculum reflects the priorities of that tribe. Each focuses on the needs of its own community and provides opportunity for students who choose to remain on the reservation.

A native studies program is a significant feature of all tribal colleges. Some students concentrate on native culture; others take courses in tribal languages, art, history, society, and politics, for personal understanding. Many colleges infuse a Native American perspective throughout the college and the curriculum. Navajo Community College, for example, has structured its campus and programs to reflect the traditional emphasis on the four compass points and values attached to each. Turtle Mountain Community College seeks to insert an Indian perspective in all of its courses.

In addition, most colleges offer a broad curriculum that provides a firm and rigorous general education. Not merely centers of vocational education, they provide a full range of academic courses that challenges what one tribal college president called the "good with their hands syndrome." Two of the colleges—Sinte Gleska and Oglala Lakota—have developed baccalaureate degree programs, and Sinte Gleska now has a master's degree program in education. While such a development is not likely to become universal among the tribal colleges, there is increasing interest in moving to the baccalaureate level to accommodate the genuine needs that exist.

Enrollment Tribal college enrollments vary greatly, the number for a given college depending on the age of the institution and the size of the community it serves. None of the colleges is large. Navajo Community College remains the largest with well over a thousand students. Oglala Lakota College in South Dakota has also grown to over a thousand. Most other institutions' students number in the hundreds, and a few of the smallest have a hundred or less. Added together, Indian-controlled colleges enrolled about 4,400 full-time equivalent students in 1989. This figure represents a dramatic growth since 1981, when 1,689 students were enrolled.

The Students Most students enrolled at tribal colleges live within the reservation boundaries. They tend to be considerably older than those at non-tribal institutions, and most are women. Frequently, they are the first in their families to attend college. The average income, for students and their families, is far below the national average, so most require federal assistance.

Because of restricted funds, tribal colleges do not have good data gathering procedures that would provide a full profile of their students. We found, however, that each institution has a remarkably similar story to tell. At Fort Berthold College, the average student's age is 33. Single women with children dominate the enrollment. The average at Little Hoop Community College is twenty-nine. Ninety percent of its students are first generation college students. About 35 percent of students at Standing Rock College are married and over half were unemployed the year before they enrolled.

Tribal colleges do not drain students away from distant non-Indian colleges. Instead, they provide an opportunity to those who frequently are unable or unwilling to leave their community. Other students come to the tribal colleges after failing at a non-Indian college. Still others see tribal colleges as a valuable stepping stone between high school and a non-Indian college. While little overall information is available here, our site visits confirmed the assertion made by faculty and administrators that the tribal colleges act as a bridge between the Indian and Anglo worlds. Students looking for greater emotional and academic support can turn to a tribal college, after a negative experience elsewhere, rather than simply dropping out of higher education. Similarly, students lacking confidence can take a few classes or complete an Associate of Arts degree before transferring to a four year, non-Indian institution.

The majority of students who enter degree programs at most tribal colleges do not complete them. Many have poor academic preparation, they feel the pressure of family obligations and they live in communities with no tradition of formal education. These barriers are significant, and finding ways to overcome such roadblocks is a challenge these colleges have accepted. But it is also true that because of their unique role as community centers, tribal colleges serve a significant number of tribal members who wish to take only a few classes for personal enrichment or in preparation for transfer to another college.

Faculty Most faculty at tribal colleges are non-Indian. This is in contrast to the dominance of Native Americans in the administration and student body. While tribal colleges are eager to include more Native American instructors, the truth is, because of failed policies of the past, the number of available Indian teachers is small. Many white instructors are, however, familiar with the tribal community and sensitive to the needs of the students. Some arrive from outside the reservation, expecting to stay for only a short time. But many others call Indian Country their home and are fully accepted by the students and the larger communities.

A special group of tribal college instructors has little formal mainstream education, but is respected for its knowledge of traditional arts, history, philosophy, or language. Indian elders are often appointed as instructors in tribal classes or, as at Salish Kootenai College, serve as authenticators of what is taught in the native studies department. In this arrangement, instructors of Indian language and culture, along with the content of their courses, are certified by these tribally recognized experts.

There is considerable concern at tribal colleges over the high turnover rate of faculty and staff. Isolation and low pay conspire to limit the tenure of instructors, who frequently have enormous teaching loads but earn much less than their colleagues at non-Indian community colleges. The financial and, occasionally, the political pressures of the presidency work against stability in that post as well.

Many colleges do, however, enjoy stable administration, and the transition in the leadership at others has tended not to be disruptive. This has been the case, in part, as a result of frequent meetings among presidents at leadership seminars—now formalized under a policy institute. These sessions promote stability and professionalism among those who lead these institutions within the American Indian Higher Education Consortium. In addition, cooperative programs in leadership training and faculty development have built a sense of purpose and direction.

Physical Facilities Physical facilities at tribal colleges vary greatly from campus to campus. Navajo Community College has the largest campus, with dormitories, classrooms, and recreation facilities all surrounding a glass-walled administration building reminiscent of the traditional Navajo home, the hogan. Salish Kootenai has a small but elegant campus built in a pine grove beneath the mountains of western Montana. Space is at a premium, but offices and classrooms are comfortable and well-equipped. In contrast, Oglala Lakota College operates a decentralized system on the large but sparsely populated Pine Ridge Sioux Reservation.

Elsewhere, colleges have made innovative use of donated space. Little Big Horn College, for example, houses its administration, library, and science department in an old tribal gym. Half a mile away, a sewage treatment plant has been turned into a science laboratory. Salish Kootenai held classes in the tribal jail in the early years, and the Sinte Gleska College's administrative offices are housed in an old Bureau of Indian Affairs building that was once condemned. Rarely do tribal colleges have sports facilities, student centers, or cafeterias, and money to construct such facilities is not in sight. "Getting by" is all that most tribal colleges can currently hope for.

The Need for Funding The greatest challenge to tribal colleges is the persistent search for funding. Indeed the ability to secure adequate financial support will determine if several of the colleges continue to exist. Most of the nation's community colleges are supported through local tax dollars; tribal colleges are not. Because their students live in poverty-ridden communities, tuition must be kept low. Few tribal colleges have local benefactors, and regionally based foundations are scarce in areas where most of the colleges are found. As a result, all must look for support beyond reservation boundaries if they are to survive. They exist on a collection of grants, gifts, and federal appropriations that are unpredictable and frequently threatened.

Financial support provided by the federal government is especially vital. Navajo Community College benefited from federal aid in its early years and today receives approximately $4 million dollars annually through the Navajo Community College Act. In addition, most of the other colleges owe their very existence to the Tribally Controlled Community College Act of 1978 and its annual appropriation that has now reached $8.5 million. This funding, first sought by the older colleges in 1972, is critical for each of the tribal colleges in existence today. The available funds are distributed according to each college's Indian student count. Only Navajo Community College is funded according to need rather than enrollment.

The impact of the tribally controlled college legislation cannot be over-stated. Before the 1978 act, there were only a handful of Indian colleges. After its passage, the number grew to twenty-four in little more than a decade. For most colleges, this aid is essential for their survival; some institutions depend on it to meet 80 percent or more of their annual operational and capital expenses. College presidents are increasingly alarmed, however, that federal funding is not keeping up with the growth in tribal college enrollment. Congress authorized $4,000 per student in the original legislation—an authorized level that has since been increased to nearly $6,000—but the amount actually released has become only progressively smaller. In 1980, for example, $5 million in federal money was distributed under the Tribally Controlled Community College Act, providing about $3,000 per student. This year the appropriation climbed to $8.5 million, but the amount generated for each student declined to $1,900! In effect, tribal colleges are being penalized for their own success.

Clearly, the tribal colleges face many serious challenges. The need to build a stable administration, meet the educational needs of an underserved population and secure a diverse financial base is a test for every college. But while tribal colleges work with greater uncertainty and fewer resources than most non-Indian college administrators could even image, the dominant mood remains one of optimism and success.

The Tribal Colleges in Context Tribal colleges play an important role in their local communities. But for the potential of these institutions to be fully understood, we must place them in the context of the larger Indian movement now building. There is a movement among Native Americans even more sweeping in its significance than the New Deal reforms. It's a movement that is resilient because it is self-directed. For the first time since becoming wards of the state 150 years ago, American Indians are building institutions and developing skills to control their own lives, a strategy that can, they believe, outlast Washington's shifting political winds.

Today's era of Indian self-determination reveals that constructive change in Indian society can occur when it is self-directed. Freed from aggressive abuse and misdirected intervention and ready to assert their cultural uniqueness in their own ways, American Indians are feeling a new spirit of opportunity and hope in many of their reservation communities. Tribal leaders are defining priorities of their own, and American Indian communities are combining, by their own choice, the values of two worlds—Indian and Anglo. While acknowledging that Indian society cannot retreat from the non-Indian culture, Native Americans have also reaffirmed those traditions and values that have sustained Indians for generations.

The emerging consensus is that you can be a lawyer and dance a pow-wow. "Cultural adaptation and change can take place if it is not forced and if there is a free interplay of ideas between cultures," according to researcher Jon Reyhner. In advocating self-determination in Indian education, he declared: "Indian education must be a synthesis of the congruent strengths of the dominant and tribal cultures rather than a process of erasure of the Indian culture and the transference of American culture."

The impact of the current Indian movement is not just philosophical or legal, illustrated by the highly publicized claim of a legal right included in several treaties between the United States and these sovereign Indian nations. The influence of the movement is also inward, touching the quality of life on the reservation, providing tangible impact on the lives of Indian people. And the reinforcement of native culture has become a crucial part of this new movement.

Native Culture: A Force for Change Anglo leaders of the past saw Indian culture as an annoying barrier to change. Today most leaders, both within and outside Indian society, recognize just that the opposite is true. Rather than being a hindrance, traditional culture is an important force for constructive change. But for much of white society, Indian culture still means little more than stereotypic childhood images of feathered Indians on the warpath. Native Americans are often seen as people of the past, identified by the artifacts they left behind. And in Indian Country today—the vast empty expanses of America's West where many reservations are found—these images are exploited for the tourist trade.

But beneath the surface, there are still the bonds of shared values and heritage that sustain Indian communities. Increasingly Native Americans are learning this lesson of self-identity, in a true renaissance of traditional culture. Albert White Hat, an instructor at the Rosebud Sioux Community College, stated: "We're trying to bring a positive image back. We're telling the young people that they can be proud of who they are and what they are. They don't necessarily have to wear a feather to be an Indian, but what is inside—how they look at themselves—is what's important. You know, traditions can be carried on whether you wear blue jeans or traditional costumes."

Economic Empowerment While cultural integrity is at the heart of Native American self-determination, tribal leaders are also concerned about enhancing economic opportunity within the reservation communities. This is a formidable assignment. Many reservations exist in isolated, depressed regions with no natural economic base. Poverty remains the dominant condition, and many Indian communities are among the poorest in the nation. South Dakota's Rosebud Reservation, for example, has much in common with many Third World countries. Unemployment is estimated to be about 80 percent. Similar conditions exist at the nearby Pine Ridge Reservation and on reservations elsewhere. Even in more "affluent" Indian communities, unemployment is more than 50 percent.

Through cultural integrity, economic development, and social responsiveness, Native Americans are accepting responsibility for needs that were once either ignored or left to the federal government. Moreover, the movement, though still young, is already offering evidence that it can promote real change. A word of caution, however: self-determination does not mean an end to the federal government's trust responsibility. Most reservations have not seen such economic transformations. Poverty remains a grim reality in most Indian communities. Often established in barren regions, most reservations do not, alone, have the resources needed for a second economy. The social and economic gains in some Indian communities must not be seen as an excuse to diminish federal and private assistance.

In the end, the issue is empowerment. No longer pawns, Native Americans are demonstrating that they should decide their own fate. This empowerment should be seen as a legal right and also as the best way to achieve greater opportunity for Native Americans. Indians themselves must determine the direction of their lives and the values they will hold as their own. Toward this end, government remains an essential partner, but no more.

Colleges that Build Communities Native Americans are constructing new and more supportive communities, and tribes are working to preserve the traditional values of their cultures. The Indians, having experienced the loss of so much of what bonds a society, feel an urgency to rediscover and rebuild. Strengthening their communities depends on retrieving and preserving traditions which have come close to extinction. The need for social bonding is deep-rooted and is one shared by all societies. Tribal colleges are working, not to return to the past, but to see the past as the foundation for a better present and a sounder future. In this way, reconciliation with the Native American heritage is as essential to Indian culture as an understanding of Jeffersonian thought is to Anglo-American culture.

In Indian society, as well as in the non-Indian world, education plays a central role in this search for interaction. According to Native American historian Jack Forbes, Indian-controlled colleges can fulfill the same cultural and social role in their communities that white-controlled colleges have traditionally provided in theirs. Tribally controlled colleges, in fact, are among the most successful examples of institutions that are rebuilding shared traditions. Like their community college counterparts across the United States, tribal colleges are expected to serve the needs of both individuals and communities. What we found remarkable is that while most of these institutions have existed for only a decade or less, they already provide their tribal societies with unity and human understanding that much of American society is still seeking.

Tribally controlled colleges are, at first glance, a study in diversity. Curricula, teaching styles, and campus architecture mirror the surrounding tribal cultures, each college possessing a unique character. Some focus on general education, others emphasize vocational training. A few have campuses that would be the envy of any small rural college, while others offer classes in mismatched trailers. Beyond the differences, all tribal colleges share common goals. They seek to strengthen respect for their cultural heritage, create greater social and economic opportunities for the tribe and its members, and create links to the larger American society. The watchword at Indian colleges is not simply education, but empowerment.

All tribal colleges seek first to rebuild, among students, an understanding of their heritage, and in some settings this has been a particularly challenging task. On many reservations, native beliefs, language, and traditional arts were not strong. Values once shared through a rich tradition of storytelling were not being preserved—traditional culture existed to a large degree only in textbooks, while Anglo values remained alien and unaccepted.

Tribal colleges are in the vanguard of a cultural renaissance in all of their communities. Courses in Native American culture are centerpieces. On the Sinte Gleska College campus, for example, the Lakota studies department offers classes in Sioux history, oral literature, Lakota thought, and a four course language sequence. "Today we drive cars, live in houses, and wear modern clothes," reflected Native Studies director Albert White Hat. "But we still speak our language and sing our songs. We are struggling to survive."

At Lac Courte Oreilles Ojibwa Community College in Wisconsin, courses in native studies include traditional clothing styles, music, and dance. Continuing education courses at Oglala Lakota College include "How to set up a Tipi," quillwork, and preparation of traditional Indian foods. Northwest Indian College offers canoe carving, woodwork, and Indian knitting—skills unique to its tribal culture.

Even on reservations where traditional beliefs have not been so severely challenged, an emphasis on cultural integrity remains the foundation. Students learn firmly that who they are and what they believe has great value. Rather than being a disorienting experience for Indian students, college represents a reinforcement of values inherent in the tribal community. Courses in Indian culture are not just an area of study. They are the bridge to tribal unity and individual pride.

Contrast this to the typical Native American experience in non-Indian-controlled institutions both in the past and now. While a handful of students has been able to overcome the cultural barriers, many have felt inferior and alienated. Researcher Danielle Sanders reported, for example, that much of what Indians find in non-Indian educational institutions "runs contrary to the social norms, self-perceptions, and expected behaviors that they have learned at home and that have been reinforced in their own cultural community." Tribal colleges seek to eliminate this discontinuity between the classroom and life outside. Gerald Slater, Vice President at the Salish Kootenai campus, added: "Forced assimilation has resulted in a lack of respect for Indians and their ways. Now people are realizing that these ways are good. They're different, but there is nothing wrong with them. There is a sense of pride and dignity that comes with it."

Myrna Chief Stick, a part-time instructor at Salish Kootenai spoke of the "self-respect, dignity, and honesty" that traditional culture provides. "Through the work of the tribe and the college," she says, "tribal members are starting to identify these values for themselves. In the last four or five years, people are becoming more aware than they have been in years."

Classes in Native American culture offer a bridge to the past—and to the future, too. A student in a Coyote Stories course said: "I think that's why I took it," she said. "A lot of our elders and a lot of our old people who told these stories are now dead. Their children and grandchildren don't know them. I'd like to be able to pass them down."

What we found is that tribal colleges seek to integrate traditional values into all aspects of the institution. All activities within these colleges are expected to be connected seamlessly to the community. At Little Big Horn College in Montana, the need for courses in traditional culture is less urgent. In this community, the tribal culture has remained strong. Instead, traditional culture is felt in how the affairs of the college are conducted. Each department tries to integrate Indian thought into its activities and much of the work is focused on adapting the curriculum to Crow values and individual needs.

Other colleges offer their own innovative ways to bridge the gap between Indian thought and Western education. Turtle Mountain Community College in North Dakota, for example, does not offer a separate native studies program. Instead of isolating courses in Indian thought from the rest of the curriculum, Turtle Mountain injects an Indian perspective into all of its classes and programs. In this way Indian values and history are not just one area of possible study, but theoretically are part of all that the college does.

Social science departments at tribal colleges have been especially creative in offering traditional Indian perspectives. Texts that treat Native Americans with respect are used and supplemented with additional books and articles that explain the Native American experience. For example, the study of family life would treat not only Anglo social structures, but also the Indian family's distinctive structure. Literature and history courses at tribal colleges are equally successful in including an Indian perspective. Even biology and geology classes have tapped into this integrative goal by including the study of local plants and exploring with students how the region's rolling topography was formed.

But it is clearly more difficult to find a cultural-community connection to mathematics and the physical sciences. For some professors in these areas, the best solution has been to make the subjects as intellectually and emotionally accessible as possible. As at Turtle Mountain Community College, the Indian influence is not always noticeable in the material, but in how the material is taught. Sister Margaret Pfeifer, a math instructor at Turtle Mountain, believes students are best able to succeed when the air of academic competition is replaced by greater cooperation, a philosophy that is more in line with Indian society, where family obligations are stressed over individual advancement.

Navajo Community College has been working not only to find culturally appropriate teaching methods, but also to pattern the college's larger academic structure after Navajo beliefs. While individual courses are not being transformed, academic disciplines are being structured around the

Navajo culture's traditional emphasis on the four compass directions. The academic disciplines of religious studies, physical education, language and aesthetics all mold into a single category of attributes inherent in the east: knowledge that prepares people to make decisions. The west, meanwhile, focuses on the social well-being of the tribe. Within this category, the disciplines of sociology, history, and government fit comfortably. Other areas of study are linked to the north and south.

The college itself is located in the very center of Navajo land, and the campus layout is modeled after the four directions, all within a larger circle. While not all of this symbolism may be useful to students trying to pass an algebra exam, the larger message is hard to miss. The college exists within the larger Navajo experience. It is an integral part of traditional tribal culture.

We were greatly impressed during our study by the distinctiveness and vision of tribal colleges. Here, within the Indian community, there is an authentic effort to blend education and tradition. But what of the results? At many of the campuses, student retention remains a problem. Many students leave long before graduation and the reasons are not difficult to find. First, there is a climate of failure surrounding education. While estimates vary from tribe to tribe, Native Americans drop out of secondary schools at significantly higher rates than all other racial and ethnic groups. It has been estimated that no more than 55 percent of Indian students graduate from high school, and for those who do finish school, the level of academic preparation is often poor. Students therefore come to college with poor academic preparation and low self-esteem, and many come with the expectation of failure. The goal of every tribal college is to overcome these barriers.

Tribal college presidents told us they do not expect all students who enter to leave with a diploma. Some students arrive intending to take introductory courses before transferring elsewhere. Others take selected courses for personal enrichment, not a diploma. Another group "stops-out," entering and leaving multiple times before completing a degree.

Success stories are nevertheless impressive. Problems not withstanding, tribal colleges are beginning to bring a spirit of renewal to people in their communities. There are already a cadre of tribal college graduates who have succeeded academically and gone on for further study or found meaningful work. Before the founding of Sinte Gleska College on the Rosebud Reservation, there was only a handful of Indians working as teachers in the reservation public schools. Today there are thirty-four. Other examples tell a similar story:

> • On the Pine Ridge reservation, Oglala Lakota College,
> in recent years, has increased the number of Native
> American teachers from one to nearly a hundred.

- Dull Knife Memorial College in Montana has, in its short history, graduated 315 certificate and associate students. In a recent survey of its graduates, the college found that half of those who completed a two-year degree went on for further study, while 70 percent of the graduates of a certificate program pursued more education.

- Sisseton-Wahpeton Community College has graduated 113 associate of arts students. A 1988 study found that 91 percent were fully employed in a four-year institution. Three have earned a master's degree and one has completed a doctoral degree.

- Turtle Mountain Community College found that 28 percent of its vocational education graduates transferred to a four-year college and, overall, more than 70 percent found jobs immediately after graduation.

- At Standing Rock College, a total of 228 students graduated between its founding in 1976 and 1986. Moreover, while the reservation unemployment rate is about 80 percent, less than 5 percent of the college's graduates are known to be unemployed or not attending another institution of higher learning.

At first glance these numbers appear small. In the larger American society the impact of a few hundred college graduates is difficult to see. But on the reservations with populations that range from three to eight thousand, the impact of new-found knowledge and expertise is pervasive. But the benefits of tribal colleges go far beyond job placement, as important as this is. In small communities, graduates can advance all of tribal society, and their value as role models is substantial. Graduates who remain on the reservations after graduation offer the seeds of social stability, economic growth, and future leadership. These tribal colleges offer more than a degree; they are the key to a healthy culture.

It must also be noted that the contribution of the colleges and their students goes far beyond the boundaries of their reservations. By offering services—ranging from day care and GED testing to alcohol counseling and literacy tutoring—tribal colleges have become a powerful, often the most powerful, social force in their communities. Indeed, on some reservations, the college is the only institution—government or tribal—that is examining all community needs, and working to provide real solutions. Graduates with knowledge and skills enrich all of American society. The country as a whole could learn from the tribal college's ability to connect to its society.

As the United States looks to rebuild a commitment to service and renewal, it could do no better than to examine the most dynamic and successful tribal colleges. Through the emphasis on traditional culture, social responsibility and economic development, these institutions have become the single most important force in their nations. In the end, college officials insist, all of American society benefits.

Recommendations: A Strategy for Excellence We applaud tribal colleges for their often heroic accomplishments. The educational and cultural contributions of these institutions, often achieved under difficult conditions, is enormously impressive. Tribal colleges are giving hope to students and bringing new life to their communities. But with all of their accomplishments, tribal colleges urgently need help. They are, we believe, ready to move into an exciting new era, but reaching their full potential will require significant support from both the public and private sectors. The goal must be to assure that by the year 2000, the network of community-based tribal colleges created by Native Americans, colleges that offer quality education to their students and bring a spirit of renewal to their nations, is funded, expanded, and flourishing.

First, we urgently recommend that the federal government adequately support tribal colleges by providing the full funding authorized by Congress. Specifically, we recommend that the $5,820 authorized per student be appropriated and that, from this point on, federal appropriations keep pace with the growth of Indian student enrollment.

Second, we urge that the libraries, science laboratories, and classroom facilities at tribal colleges be significantly improved through the federal government appropriations. We also propose that foundations help improve facilities at tribal colleges. This is an urgent need that cannot wait much longer for resolution. We do not propose spacious facilities for these institutions. All we call for are spaces that would bring dignity to tribal colleges and greater effectiveness to learning.

Third, we urge that connections between tribal colleges and non-Indian higher education be strengthened. Specifically, we recommend that four-year institutions work with tribal colleges for the transfer of credit and the development of cooperative degree programs. The center for Native American Studies at Montana State University estimates that graduates from tribal colleges are at least twice as likely to succeed in a non-Indian college as Indian students who did not first study at a tribally controlled institution. This early evidence suggesting that tribal colleges can have a crucial impact is encouraging, since Indians traditionally have had among the highest non-completion rates of any college population.

Fourth, we recommend that programs linking tribal colleges to their communities be significantly increased.

Fifth, we recommend that tribal colleges expand their important role of preserving the languages, history, and cultures of the tribes. The history of education for Native Americans in this country has been marked by the suppression of the rich heritage of the tribes. One of the important missions of the tribal colleges is to preserve for Indians their great heritage, for purposes of identity, self-esteem, and cultural enrichment.

Sixth, we recommend that state governments more adequately support tribal colleges. We urge especially that the states target funds for community service programs. We recommend that state and local governments join with tribal colleges in partnerships for community development and educational excellence. An expanded cooperative effort between tribal colleges and government officials can improve the quality of education and the breadth of services at every college.

Seventh, we recommend the establishment of a comprehensive program for faculty development at tribal colleges. All colleges need programs to enrich faculty and build leadership at the administrative level. At tribal colleges, these needs are especially acute, since these institutions are young, operate under difficult conditions, and are often isolated.

Eighth, we propose that foundations collaboratively support the Tribal College Institute, which is designed to strengthen administrative leadership in Native American higher education. Future leaders must be developed within the Indian community.

Ninth, we recommend that the national awareness and advocacy programs for tribal colleges be strengthened. Specifically, we recommend that private philanthropies collaborate to provide, for three years, support for a Washington D.C. office with a full-time director. Increased public awareness means better public policy, and there simply must be an increased understanding of the role tribal colleges play in Native American communities and in society at large.

Finally, we recommend that the newly established tribal college endowment be supported to increase the fiscal base and bring long-term stability to these institutions. American higher education discovered long ago that quality cannot be achieved if an institution is forced to live from hand to mouth, with no stability in support. Endowments have become crucial in integrating long-range planning, cushioning unanticipated budget shortfalls, and increasing the stability of the institution. Further, Title III of the Tribal College Act provides for federal matching funds for endowment purposes. We urge that Congress commit itself to the building of long-term financial stability for tribal colleges through this important authorization.

Conclusion During the Carnegie Foundation's two-year study of tribal colleges, we became convinced that the idea of Indian-controlled higher education is both valid and long overdue. We also concluded that the growing network of tribally controlled colleges offers great hope to the Native American community and the nation as a whole.

At the same time, we saw problems. Tribal colleges have distressingly inadequate facilities, poor salaries, understaffed academic programs, and frequently they encounter divisive politics. Graduation, continued education, and employment rates are not all well documented. The need for sound research is urgent. All of this was noted in our visits.

As a movement, however, tribal colleges are an inspiration. These institutions are creating opportunity for Native Americans who, for more than three hundred years, suffered shameful misunderstanding and abuse. Tribal colleges offer hope. They can, with adequate support, continue to open doors of opportunity to the coming generations and help Native American communities bring together a cohesive society, one that draws inspiration from the past in order to shape a creative, inspired vision of the future.[6]

14

CONCLUSION

THE HISTORY OF education among American Indians in many respects constitutes miseducation. Indeed, past educational efforts seem to indicate that education has been designed more to acculturate than to educate. In this process, traditional Indian educational practices and educational values were subjected to mainstream Anglo-American educational philosophies. Consequently, the Indian educational process has often denigrated Indian culture, assuming that Indians had no system of education and no culture worth preserving. Not surprisingly, many American Indians have taken a perfunctory view of American education.

The American Indians' educational experience over the past several centuries has been, according to Diane Ravitch, a history of educational failure: "Where educational oppression of a minority was blatant and purposeful, as in the case of the American Indians, the policy was a disaster which neither educated nor assimilated."[1] Delores Huff has written that the history of Indian education, as it was influenced by Euro-American educational values, has been fraught with erroneous assumptions. "For centuries," Huff wrote, "Indians have told Bureau personnel what was needed ... yet the objective of the Bureau has always been to assimilate the Indians into the non-Indian society, using the education system, while the Indian has resisted assimilation, and therefore education, in order to maintain some semblance of cultural integrity."[2]

The American colonies tried—largely unsuccessfully—for more than a century and a half to incorporate the Indian population into the transplanted European educational system. In the eyes of the colonists, if the Indians could not or would not change—and the colonists fully expected the Indians to accept the more "civilized" educational system—it was the Indians who failed. Indians who did not change were considered an impediment to progress and subject to possible extermination. But even those Indians who chose to accept the new values and cultural characteristics were not fully accepted by the non-Indian world.

The educational process among the Indian tribes was at one time controlled by tribal leaders, and the education imparted to the tribal youth reflected the cultural needs of the tribes. In this process, elders were respected for their knowledge and children received a personalized education that was suited to the cohesion of the tribe and reflected the values necessary for tribal identity. In the post-European-contact era, several tribes made exceptional adaptations to the Euro-American educational system. Particularly significant were the school systems developed and controlled by the Cherokee and Choctaw nations, which together operated over 200 schools and academies. The Choctaw and Cherokee developed schools that not only incorporated tribal values and needs, but also included the core of an American education. Both tribes were well aware of the need to send their youth to higher institutes of education outside of the Indian Territory to protect the rights of the tribes.

To speed the assimilation of Indian children into American culture, the federal government began educating Indians in boarding schools in the 1870s. There was no bigger champion of the new system of education than Captain Richard Henry Pratt, whose educational philosophy was built around military discipline and the premise of taking Indian children to "civilization." Consequently, Indian children were taken away from their home environment and culture and transported hundreds, and in some cases thousands, of miles away to federal boarding schools. At these highly institutionalized schools students were often taught obsolete vocations and a new set of social and cultural values. Traditional language, custom, dress, and family values were subverted, often by force, to be replaced by a new set of values. Such a system of education dominated the Indian educational scene for nearly fifty years.

Even nineteenth-century conservative reformers admitted that the white man has often been the reason for the educational failure of the American Indians. The Board of Indian Commissioners wrote in 1869 that:

> The white man has been the chief obstacle in the way of Indian civilization. The benevolent measures attempted by the government for their advancement have been almost uniformly thwarted by the agencies employed to carry them out. The soldiers, sent for their protection, too often carried demoralization and disease into their midst. The agents, appointed to be their friend and counsellor, frequently went among them only to enrich themselves in the shortest possible time, at the cost of the Indians. The general interest of the trader was opposed to their enlightenment as tending to lessen his profits. Any increase in intelligence would render them less liable to his impositions. The interpreter knew that if they were taught, his occupation would be gone. The more submissive and patient the tribe, the

greater the number of outlaws infesting their vicinity; and all these were the missionaries teaching them the most degrading vices of which humanity is capable. If in spite of these obstacles a tribe made some progress in agriculture, or their lands became valuable from any cause, the process of civilization was summarily ended by driving them away from their homes with fire and sword, to undergo similar experiences in some new locality.[3]

In the post–Civil War years, the federal government attempted to prevent the abuses of the unscrupulous Americans who exploited the Indians. The answer, the federal government promised, was to remove the Indian agencies from the hands of politicians who were motivated by personal gain and turn them over to religious denominations.

The new system of agency control was just as objectionable as the system it replaced. Under the auspices of religious organizations, much of the Indian's culture was irrevocably harmed. Religious tolerance, despite a constitutional guarantee, was almost universally non-existent, as tribes were subjected to the religious persuasion of the agency authority. Less than thirty years later, when some Indian tribes desired to have some religious instruction as part of the educational process, Congress prohibited all sectarian education among the Indians. Only with a Supreme Court ruling did Indian tribes recapture their constitutionally protected right of religious freedom.

In 1928, the Meriam Report was published. Perhaps the most significant result of the report was a new philosophy that encouraged the use of reservation day schools which allowed Indian children to attend school on or near their reservation communities.

Margaret Szasz, writing on the history of Indian education, succinctly illustrated why the new Bureau philosophy continued to fail Indian students: "The efforts of the Bureau in the 1930s to teach some Indian culture in the federal schools, while much better than the previous approach, did not begin to solve the problems of adjustment for a disoriented Indian child. A course in silverwork or in Indian history did not answer the child's question: 'Who am I'?"[4]

Although Indian students had been placed in public schools since the late nineteenth century, the movement was greatly heightened in the 1930s with the passage of the Johnson–O'Malley Act, which authorized the Secretary of the Interior to contract with states for the education of Indian students. The purpose was to completely integrate Indian students into mainstream society. Many public schools however, seemed more interested in receiving federal subsidies for Indian education than in actually educating Indians. Once in the public schools, the values and attributes of mainstream society were once again impressed upon the Indians. Indians were depicted as "savages" without a history and culture of their own. A recent article has described the educational alienation experienced by many Indian students:

> Indian youth become lost in their two worlds when they begin to experience the dominant culture and begin to develop an awareness of the differences that exist between their Indian community and the larger dominant society. Generally, the heavy exposure crests at the on-set of the teens. Through observations and interactions with non-Indians, different expectations are placed upon their behavior. JoAnn Kessel demonstrates quite vividly that these observations and external expectations place a heavy burden on Indian youth and as a result of cultural conflicts Indian youth develop negative coping patterns and behaviors. ... As a result, Indian youth begin to incorporate the dominant culture attitude that Indian cultures are inferior. This leads to feelings of inferiority, adaptations of dysfunctional attitudes, values, and behaviors. Behaviorally, Indian youth begin to act inferior and adopt stereotypical behavior, primarily because they see no solution to being able to live in the world of the dominant culture while retaining their Indianness.[5]

By the mid-twentieth century, Congress had had its fill of cultural pluralism. In 1944, the House Select Committee on Indian Affairs recommended the "final solution" to the Indian problem: a return to the pre-Meriam Report days of complete integration of the Indians. Real progress, the committee noted, could only be made if Indian children were once again taken away from their homes and placed in off-reservation boarding schools. The goal of such a policy was to make Indians better Americans rather than better Indians.

Along with the termination of some federal services for Indians, the federal government implemented a relocation program designed to remove Indians from their reservation communities and relocate them to urban areas. Federal Impacted Aid funds were also made available to local school districts. By providing federal subsidies based on "federal impact areas" rather than race, the federal government sought to end Indian-only Johnson–O'Malley funding and remove itself from the field of Indian education. Throughout the 1950s numerous federal schools were closed and students were transferred to public schools.

When the Navajo Tribe requested additional schools for their youth in the late forties, the federal government appropriated money for fewer than one-half of the requisite schools. The remainder of the need was tied to the relocation project, which was heavily encouraged among the Navajo. As a result, thousands of Navajo children remained out of school as late as the 1970s.

In 1969 the Kennedy Report noted that the educational policy not only remained assimilationist in nature but also brought "disastrous effects on the education of Indian children." In effect, the government schools had become "battlegrounds" where Indian children attempted to protect their integrity and identity as individuals by defeating the purposes of the school.

In the early 1970s, in response to the Indian desire for self-determination, Congress enacted several educational laws designed to grant the Indian people greater control over their own destiny. The Indian Education Act of 1972 and the Indian Self-Determination and Education Assistance Act of 1975 were designed to encourage greater Indian participation in the educational process, and to provide for special Indian education programs such as bilingual and bicultural education. Yet, despite the passage of such acts, the concept of Indian self-determination was left unresolved. The educational system has for the most part remained in the hands of the Bureau of Indian Affairs rather than the tribes'.

American Indians have made numerous attempts to adapt mainstream education to their needs and values. The construction and operation of Indian controlled community colleges is perhaps the prime example of such adaptation. Such tribal colleges did not become a reality until the 1960s when Navajo Community College became the first Indian-controlled community college in the United States. Tribally controlled colleges are significant in that they actively seek to rebuild Indian communities and reassert tribal identity.

The desire for self-determination among American Indian tribes has been nowhere more pronounced than in the field of education. Not surprisingly, tribally controlled educational facilities allow Indian tribes to incorporate tribal values, attitudes, and perspectives into the education of their youth, thereby enhancing Indian self-identity and pride. In 1979 Roger Buffalohead, then chairman of the Indian Studies Department at the University of Minnesota, noted the significance of Indian identity when he wrote:

> Every Indian child has an inherent right to achieve a sense of self-realization within the context of his or her cultural understanding ... [and] every school system must respect that right while providing and enabling Indian children and youth to use education as a vehicle for developing to their fullest potential as individuals and as members of the local community, the tribe, the nation, and the world of which they are a part.[6]

American Indians do not envision a return to the past when they seek to determine the educational future of their children; instead, tribal leaders and members envision an education that will not only prepare their children for the future but also instill pride and identity in their Indianness. Tribally controlled education seeks to preserve and rebuild the heritage of American Indians. By not educating Indian children through a process that is unique to the tribal groups, American education may well remain a foe to many Indians. The sentiment of a nineteenth century American philanthropist may be true today.

As I have gone back to the days of John Eliot, I have asked why should it take so long, this work of educating Indians. ... Sometimes I think it is because we have had not only to educate the Indian but to educate the white man. The two have had to go hand in hand, and the education of the white man has been the more difficult task.[7]

Until American Indians are allowed to provide their youth with a culturally relevant education, many may continue to view education with a jaundiced eye. Morgan Otis wrote in 1972:

In effect, the Indian has rejected the American educational system because it first rejected him: Indians have desired education, but within a system that includes the home and community in the educational process. It is through this process that Indian children learn their tribal language, custom, tradition, religion, and philosophy. If the Native American Indian appears to be apathetic about supporting the efforts of his children to succeed in school, it is not because of hostility to the educational process, but rather because of his rejection of the narrowness of the system that controls the education process.[8]

ENDNOTES

Introduction

1. William Hedgepath. "America's Indian—Reawakening of a Conquered People." *Look* 34:11 (June 2, 1970): 36.
2. Gerald Wilkenson. "Educational Problems in the Indian Community: A Comment on Learning as Colonialism." *Integrateducation*, Horace Mann Bond Center for Equal Education, University of Massachusetts 19:1–2 (January 1982): 49.
3. Kennedy Report. Senate Subcommittee on Indian Education. *Indian Education: A National Tragedy—A National Challenge.* 91st Congress, 1st Session, 1969, S. Rept. 501 (serial 12836): 9.
4. Ibid.

Chapter 1

1. George Bird Grinnell. *The Cheyenne Indians: Their History and Ways of Life.* New York: Cooper Square Publishers, 1962, p. 102. (Original edition: Yale University Press, New Haven, Connecticut, 1923.)
2. George C. Sibley to Thomas L. McKenney, October 1, 1820, in Jedidiah Morse, *A Report to the Secretary of War of the United States on Indian Affairs.* New York: A. M. Kelley, 1970, p. 207. (Original edition: S. Converse, New Haven, Connecticut, 1822.)
3. Kennedy Report. Senate Subcommittee on Indian Education. *Indian Education: A National Tragedy—A National Challenge.* 91st Congress, 1st Session, 1969, S. Rept. 501 (serial 12836):140. (Original: Benjamin Franklin. *Two Tracts, etc.* Philadelphia, 1794, pp. 28–29.)
4. John C. Cremony. "The Apache Race." *Overland Monthly* 1 (September 1868): 207.
5. Charles Eastman. *Indian Boyhood.* New York: McClure, Phillips and Company, 1902.
6. Ibid., pp. 49–60.

7. Don C. Talayesva. *Sun Chief: The Autobiography of a Hopi Chief.* New Haven, Connecticut: Yale University Press, 1942, pp. 51–52.
8. Eastman, *Indian Boyhood,* pp. 86–89.
9. John G.E. Heckewelder. *History, Manners, and Customs of the Indian Nations Who Once Inhabited Pennsylvania and the Neighbouring States.* Philadelphia: The Historical Society of Pennsylvania, 1876, pp. 113–17.
10. Abraham Eleaser Knepler. "Education in the Cherokee Nation." *Chronicles of Oklahoma* 21 (1943): 378–401.
11. Grinnell, *The Cheyenne Indians,* pp. 103–24.

CHAPTER 2

1. Final Report to the American Indian Policy Review Commission, Task Force Five: Indian Education. *Report on Indian Education.* Washington, D.C.: Government Printing Office, 1976, pp. 24–26.
2. Ibid., pp. 26–27.
3. Abridged from Alice Fletcher. A report prepared in answer to Senate Resolution of February 23, 1885. *Indian Education and Civilization.* 48th Congress, 2d Session, SED 95 (serial 2264). Washington, D.C.: Government Printing Office, 1888, 75-102.
4. Ibid., pp. 77–78.
5. Ibid., pp. 78–80.
6. Ibid., p. 83.
7. Ibid., p. 84.
8. Ibid., pp. 86–88.
9. Ibid., p. 91.
10. Ibid.
11. Fletcher, *Indian Education and Civilization,* pp. 94–96.
12. Ibid., pp. 97–103.
13. Ibid., p. 99.
14. Ibid., p. 105. See also Task Force Five, *Report on Indian Education,* p. 28.
15. Task Force Five, *Report on Indian Education,* p. 28.

CHAPTER 3

1. Treaty with the Creek Nation of Indians, Article 7, 12 February 1825, 7 Stat. 237.
2. Treaty with the Choctaw Nation of Indians, Article 2, 20 January 1825, 7 Stat. 234.
3. Treaty with the Delaware Nation, Article 6, 17 September 1778, 7 Stat. 13. Treaty with the Cherokee Nation, Article 12, 28 November 1785, 7 Stat. 18.
4. "An Act to Regulate Trade and Intercourse with the Indian Tribes, and to Preserve Peace on the Frontiers," Section 3, 19 May 1796, 1 Stat. 469. See also act of 3 March 1799, Article 3, 1 Stat. 743, and act of 30 March 1802, Section 3, 2 Stat. 139.
5. "An Act to Provide for the Government of the Territory Northwest of the River Ohio," Northwest Ordinance of 1787, Article 3, 13 July 1787, 1 Stat. 50.

6. Treaty with the Oneida, Tuscarora, and Stockbridge Indians, Article 3, 2 December 1794, 7 Stat. 47.

7. Treaty with the Kaskaskia Tribe of Indians, Article 3, 13 August 1803, 7 Stat. 78.

8. Treaty with the Kiowa and Comanches, Article 7, 21 October 1867, 15 Stat. 581; Treaty with the Cheyenne and Arapahoe Tribes of Indians, Article 7, 28 October 1867, 15 Stat. 593; Treaty with the Ute Indians, Article 8, 2 March 1868, 15 Stat. 619; Treaty with the Different Tribes of Sioux Indians, Article 7, 29 April 1868, 15 Stat. 635; Treaty with the Crow Tribe of Indians, Article 7, 2 May 1868, 15 Stat. 649; Treaty with the Northern Cheyenne and Northern Arapahoe Tribes of Indians, Article 4, 10 May 1868, 15 Stat. 655; Treaty with the Navajo Tribe of Indians, Article 6, 1 June 1868, 15 Stat. 667; Treaty with the Eastern Band of Shoshonees and the Bannack Tribe of Indians, Article 7, 3 July 1868, 15 Stat. 673.

9. "Report of the Indian School Superintendent." In Commissioner of Indian Affairs, *Annual Report*. Washington, D.C.: Government Printing Office, 1885, p. xxviii.

10. Ibid., p. xxxiii.

11. "An Act Making Appropriations for the Current and Contingent Expenses of the Indian Department," 3 March 1871, 16 Stat. 566.

12. Vine Deloria, Jr. *A Legislative Analysis of the Federal Role in Indian Education.* Unpublished report prepared pursuant to a contract from the U.S. Office of Education, Department of Health, Education, and Welfare. Washington, D.C.: Government Printing Office, 1975, pp. 39–71.

CHAPTER 4

1. Abraham Eleazer Knepler. "Education in the Cherokee Nation." *Chronicles of Oklahoma* 21 (1943): 395.

2. "An Act Making Provision for the Civilization of the Indian Tribes Adjoining the Frontier Settlements," 3 March 1819, 3 Stat. 516.

3. Abridged from Martha E. Layman, Ph.D. dissertation. *A History of Indian Education in the United States.* St. Paul: University of Minnesota, 1942, pp. 159–314.

4. Wilcomb E. Washburn. *The Indian in America.* New York: Harper and Row, 1975, p. 120.

5. Layman, *A History of Indian Education in the United States*, pp. 159–314.

CHAPTER 5

1. Indian commissioner John Q. Smith compiled statistics on the number of agencies administered by various religious groups and the number of Indians served by these agencies. The results are given in the following table. The Methodists had the most agencies serving the greatest population: fourteen agencies serving 54,473 Indians. It is interesting to note that the Baptist agencies numbered only five but the number served totaled 40,800. In 1876, when this census was taken, Catholics

were in the middle range in terms of the number of agencies and population served.

Religious Groups	Agencies	Indians
American Board of Commissioners	1	1,496
Baptist	5	40,800
Catholic	7	17,856
Christian	2	8,287
Congregational	3	14,476
Dutch Reformed	5	8,118
Episcopal	8	26,929
Hicksite Friends	6	6,598
Lutheran	1	273
Methodist	14	54,473
Orthodox Friends	10	17,724
Presbyterian	9	38,069
Unitarian	2	3,800

(Source: Commissioner of Indian Affairs, *Annual Report,* Washington, D.C.: Government Printing Office, 1876, p. 318.)

2. Commissioner of Indian Affairs, *Annual Report,* Washington, D.C.: Government Printing Office, 1874, p. 193.
3. Commissioner of Indian Affairs, *Annual Report,* Washington, D.C.: Government Printing Office, 1892, pp. 177–178.
4. Ibid., p. 178.
5. Commissioner of Indian Affairs, *Annual Report,* Washington, D.C.: Government Printing Office, 1899, p. 18 (Table 8).
6. Francis Paul Prucha. *The Churches and the Indian Schools, 1888–1912.* Lincoln: University of Nebraska Press, 1979, p. xii.
7. Board of Indian Commissioners, *Annual Report,* Washington, D.C.: Government Printing Office, 1892, pp. 62–63.
8. Ibid., pp. 63–65.
9. Board of Indian Commissioners, *Annual Report,* Washington, D.C.: Government Printing Office, 1894, pp. 43–44.
10. Board of Indian Commissioners, *Annual Report,* Washington, D.C.: Government Printing Office, 1893, pp. 112–14.
11. Prucha, *The Churches and Indian Schools,* p. 61.
12. Commissioner of Indian Affairs, *Annual Report,* Washington, D.C.: Government Printing Office, 1906, pp. 52–53.
13. "Letter of William Moody to President Theodore Roosevelt," 4 January 1906. General records of the Department of Justice, National Archives, Record Group 60, File 2290-02. For a detailed discussion of the attorney general's report see Prucha, *The Churches and Indian Schools,* pp. 116–22.
14. *Reuben Quick Bear v. Leupp* 210 U.S. Reports 50.

CHAPTER 6

1. Abraham Eleaser Knepler. "Education in the Cherokee Nation." *Chronicles of Oklahoma* 21 (1943): 378.

2. Treaty with the Cherokee Nation, 2 July 1791, 7 Stat. 39.
3. Treaty with the Choctaw Nation of Indians, 20 January, 1825, 7 Stat. 234.
4. Treaty with the Choctaw and Chickasaw Nations, 27 June 1855, 11 Stat. 611.
5. Treaty with the Creek Nation, 7 August 1856, 11 Stat. 699.
6. Treaty with the Cherokee Nation, 19 July 1866, 14 Stat. 799.
7. Kennedy Report. Senate Subcommittee on Indian Education. *Indian Education: A National Tragedy—A National Challenge.* 91st Congress, 1st Session, 1969, S. Rept. 501 (serial 12836): 25.
8. Abridged from Helen M. Scheirbeck, unpublished Ph.D. dissertation. *They Ran Their Own Schools: Education in the Five Civilized Tribes, 1819–1915*, pp. 18–51, pp. 83–130.
9. Kennedy Report, pp. 19–20.

CHAPTER 7

1. Senate Committee on Indian Affairs. *Tuberculosis Among the North American Indians: Report of a Committee of the National Tuberculosis Association.* 67th Congress, 4th Session. Washington, D.C.: Government Printing Office, 1923, p. 97.
2. Public Health Service. *Contagious and Infectious Diseases Among the Indians.* 62d Congress, 3d Session, 1913, S. Doc. 1038.
3. American Red Cross. "A Study of the Need for Public-Health Nursing on Indian Reservations." Reproduced in Senate Subcommittee of the Committee on Indian Affairs, *Survey of Conditions of the Indians in the United States: Hearings Before a Subcommittee of the Committee on Indian Affairs.* 70th Congress, 2d Session, part 3, 1929.
4. Board of Indian Commissioners, *Annual Report*, Washington, D.C.: Government Printing Office, 1888, pp. 5, 59.
5. Commissioner of Indian Affairs, *Annual Report*, Washington, D.C.: Government Printing Office, 1885, pp. cviii–cxiii.
6. Board of Indian Commissioners, *Annual Report*, Washington, D.C.: Government Printing Office, 1889, pp. 82–83.
7. Elaine Goodale Eastman. *Pratt: The Red Man's Moses.* Norman: University of Oklahoma Press, 1935, pp. 221–25, 227–32.
8. Senate Subcommittee of the Committee on Indian Affairs. *Conditions of the Indians.* 71st Congress, 2d Session, part 18, 1932, pp. 81–84.
9. Ibid., part 4, 1929, pp. 1600–1607.
10. Ibid., pp. 1608–15.
11. Frances Leupp. *The Indian and His Problem.* New York: Scribner's, 1910, pp. 115–23, 129.

CHAPTER 8

1. Francis Paul Prucha. *The Great Father: The United States Government and the American Indians*, abridged edition. Lincoln: University of Nebraska Press, 1984, p. 286.
2. Angie Debo. *A History of the Indians in the United States.* Norman: University of Oklahoma Press, 1970, p. 284.

3. Lewis Meriam. *The Problem of Indian Administration.* Meriam Report. Baltimore: Johns Hopkins Press, 1928.

4. Ibid., p. 7.

5. Ibid., pp. 314–40, 346–429.

CHAPTER 9

1. Treaty with the Navajo Tribe of Indians, Article 6, 1 June 1868, 15 Stat. 667.

2. Commissioner of Indian Affairs, *Annual Report,* Washington, D.C.: Government Printing Office, 1946, p. 357.

3. House Select Committee on Indian Affairs. *An Investigation to Determine Whether the Changed Status of the Indian Requires a Revision of the Laws and Regulations Affecting the American Indians.* 78th Congress, 2d session, 1944, H. Rept. 2091 (serial 10848): 9.

4. Ibid.

5. George A. Boyce. *When Navahoes Had too Many Sheep in the 1940s.* San Francisco: The Indian Historian Press, 1974, pp. 192–93.

6. George Sanchez. *The People: A Study of the Navajoes.* U.S. Department of the Interior, U.S. Indian Service, 1948.

7. George A. Boyce. "First Report on Education to the Navaho Indian Tribe." In *Navajo Service* (March 1945). See also Boyce, *When Navahoes Had too Many Sheep in the 1940s,* pp. 143–91.

8. Senate Committee on Indian Affairs. *Navajo Indian Education: Hearings Before the Committee on Indian Affairs.* 79th Congress, 2d Session, 1946, pp. 2–5.

9. Senate Subcommittee of the Committee on Interior and Insular Affairs. *Rehabilitation of the Navajo and Hopi Indians: Hearings Before a Subcommittee of the Committee on Interior and Insular Affairs.* 80th Congress, 2d Session, 1948, pp. 428–34.

10. Ibid., pp. 482–85.

11. Ibid., pp. 189–97, 216.

12. Ibid., pp. 306–8.

13. Kennedy Report. Senate Subcommittee on Indian Education. *Indian Education: A National Tragedy—A National Challenge.* 91st Congress, 1st Session, 1969, S. Rept. 501 (serial 12836): 160.

CHAPTER 10

1. "Report of the Superintendent of Indian Schools." In Commissioner of Indian Affairs, *Annual Report,* Washington, D.C.: Government Printing Office, 1894, p. 341.

2. Ibid.

3. Final Report to the American Indian Policy Review Commission, Task Force Five: Indian Education. *Report on Indian Education.* Washington, D.C.: Government Printing Office, 1976, p. 59.

4. Commissioner of Indian Affairs, *Annual Report,* Washington, D.C.: Government Printing Office, 1909, pp. 84–85.

5. "An Act Authorizing the Secretary of the Interior to Arrange with States

or Territories for the Education, Medical Attention, Relief of Distress, and Social Welfare of Indians, and for other Purposes." Johnson–O'Malley Act, 16 April 1934, 49 Stat. 1458.

6. Margaret Connell Szasz. *Education and the American Indian: The Road to Self-Determination, 1928–1973.* Albuquerque: University of New Mexico Press, 1977, pp. 89–105, pp. 181–87.

CHAPTER 11

1. Abridged from Kennedy Report. Senate Subcommittee on Indian Education. *Indian Education: A National Tragedy—A National Challenge.* 91st Congress, 1st Session, 1969, S. Rept. 501 (serial 12836): ix–xiii, 21–136.

CHAPTER 12

1. Lyndon B. Johnson. "Special Message to the Congress on the Problems of the American Indian: The Forgotten Americans," 6 March 1968. In *Public Papers of the Presidents of the United States: Lyndon B. Johnson, Containing the Public Messages, Speeches, and Statements of the President, 1968–1969,* Book 1. Washington, D.C.: Government Printing Office, 1970, pp. 335–44.

2. Richard M. Nixon. "Special Message to the Congress on Indian Affairs," 8 July 1970. In *Public Papers of the Presidents of the United States: Richard M. Nixon, Containing the Public Messages, Speeches, and Statements of the President, 1970.* Washington, D.C.: Government Printing Office, 1971, pp. 564–76.

3. Robert Roessel, Jr. "An Overview of the Rough Rock Demonstration School." *Journal of American Indian Education* 7 (3 May 1968): 6.

4. "Indian Education Act," [P.L. 93–318], 23 June 1972, 86 Stat. 337.

5. Vine Deloria, Jr. "Token Indian, Token Education: Indian Traditions versus the Federal Grant." *Four Winds: The International Forum for Native American Art, Literature, and History* 6 (Winter 1980): 29.

6. "Indian Self-Determination and Education Assistance Act," [P.L. 93–638], 4 January 1975, 88 Stat. 2203.

7. Guy Senese. "Self-Determination and American Indian Education: An Illusion of Control." *Educational Theory* 36, no. 2 (Spring 1986): 153–164.

CHAPTER 13

1. Alice Fletcher. A report prepared in answer to Senate Resolution of February 23, 1885. *Indian Education and Civilization.* 48th Congress, 2d Session, SED 95 (serial 2264). Washington, D.C.: Government Printing Office, 1888, p. 53.

2. Ibid., p. 54.

3. Lewis Meriam. *The Problem of Indian Administration.* Meriam Report. Baltimore: Johns Hopkins Press, 1928, p. 35.

4. G. D. McGrath. "Higher Education of Southwestern Indians." *Journal of American Indian Education* 7 (n.d.): 61

5. "An Act to Provide for Grants to Tribally Controlled Community Colleges and for Other Purposes." [P.L. 95–471], 17 October 1978, 92 Stat. 1325.

6. The Carnegie Foundation for the Advancement of Teaching. *Tribal*

Colleges: Shaping the Future of Native America. Princeton, New Jersey: Princeton University Press, 1989, pp. xi–6, 23–87.

CHAPTER 14

1. Diane Ravitch. "On the History of Minority Group Education in the United States." *Teacher's College Record* 78 (December 1976): 219.
2. Delores Huff. "Educational Colonialism: The American Indian Experience." *Association Bulletin of Harvard Graduate School of Education* 42 (Spring–Summer 1976): 3.
3. Board of Indian Commisioners, *Annual Report,* Washington, D.C.: Government Printing Office, 1885, p. 8.
4. Szasz, p. 78.
5. "Cultural Aspects of Working with American Indian Youth," *Indian Child Welfare Digest* (Aug-Sept 1989), p. 6.
6. Margot M. LeBrassuer and Ellen S. Freark. "Touch a Child—They Are My People: Ways to Teach American Indian Children." *Journal of American Indian Education* 21 (May 1982): 7.
7. Board of Indian Commissioners, *Annual Report,* Washington, D.C.: Government Printing Office, 1897, p. 54.
8. Morgan Otis. "Indian Education: A Cultural Dilemma." In *The American Indian Reader,* ed. Jeannette Henry. San Francisco: The Indian Historian Press, 1972, p. 72.

BIBLIOGRAPHY

American Red Cross. "A Study of the Need for Public-Health Nursing on Indian Reservations." *Survey of Conditions of the Indians in the United States.* Hearings Before a Subcommittee of the Committee on Indian Affairs. 70th Congress, 2d Session, part 3, 1929.

American State Papers: Indian Affairs. Volume I, Government Printing Office, 1832.

Board of Indian Commissioners, *Annual Report.* Washington, D.C.: Government Printing Office.

Boyce, George A. "First Report on Education to the Navaho Indian Tribe." *Navajo Service* (March 1945).

————. *When Navahoes Had too Many Sheep in the 1940s.* San Francisco: The Indian Historian Press, 1974.

The Carnegie Foundation for the Advancement of Teaching, *Tribal Colleges: Shaping the Future of Native America.* Princeton, New Jersey: Princeton University Press, 1989.

Commissioner of Indian Affairs. *Annual Report.* Washington, D.C.: Government Printing Office.

Cremony, John C. "The Apache Race." *Overland Monthly* 1 (September 1868).

"Cultural Aspects of Working With American Indian Youth," *Indian Child Welfare Digest* (August–September 1989).

Debo, Angie. *A History of Indians in the United States.* Norman: University of Oklahoma Press, 1970.

Deloria, Vine, Jr. *A Legislative Analysis of the Federal Role in Indian Education.* Washington, D.C.: Government Printing Office, 1975.

————. "Token Indian, Token Education: Indian Traditions versus the Federal Grant." *Four Winds: The International Forum for Native American Art, Literature, and History* (Winter 1980). Austin, Texas: Hundred Arrows Press, 1980, pp. 24–30.

Eastman, Charles. *Indian Boyhood.* New York: Dover Publications, Inc., 1971 edition.

Eastman, Elaine Goodale. *Pratt: The Red Man's Moses.* Norman: University of Oklahoma, 1935.

Final Report to the American Indian Policy Review Commission, Task Force Five: Indian Education. *Report on Indian Education.* Washington, D.C.: Government Printing Office, 1976.

Fletcher, Alice. A report prepared in answer to Senate Resolution of February 23, 1885. *Indian Education and Civilization.* 48th Congress, 2d Session, SED 95 (serial 2264). Washington, D.C.: Government Printing Office, 1888.

Grinnell, George Bird. *The Cheyenne Indians: Their History and Ways of Life.* New York: Cooper Square Publishers, Inc., 1962.

Heckewelder, John G.E. *History, Manners and Customs of the Indian Nations Who Once Inhabited Pennsylvania and the Neighboring States.* New York: Arno Press and *New York Times,* 1971 edition.

Hedgepath, William. "America's Indians—Reawakening of a Conquered People." *Look* 34:11 (June 2, 1970).

Huff, Delores. "Educational Colonialism: The American Indian Experience." *Association Bulletin of Harvard Graduate School of Education* 42 (Spring–Summer 1976).

Johnson, Lyndon B. "Special Message to the Congress on the Problems of the American Indians: The Forgotten Americans," (March 6, 1968). *Public Papers of the Presidents of the United States: Lyndon B. Johnson, Containing the Public Messages, Speeches, and Statements of the President, 1968–1969.* Book 1. Washington, D.C.: Government Printing Office, 1970.

Knepler, Abraham Eleazer. "Education in the Cherokee Nation," *Chronicles of Oklahoma* 21 (1940).

Layman, Martha E. Unpublished Ph.D. dissertation. *A History of Indian Education in the United States.* University of Minnesota, 1942.

LeBrasseur, Margot M., and Ellen S. Freark. "Touch a Child—They Are My People: Ways to Teach American Indian Children." *Journal of American Indian Education* 21 (May 1982).

Leupp, Francis. *The Indian and His Problem.* New York: Scribner's Sons, 1910.

McGrath, G. D. "Higher Education of Southwestern Indians." *Journal of American Indian Education.* Phoenix: Arizona State University, 1974.

Meriam, Lewis. *The Problem of Indian Administration.* Meriam Report. Baltimore: John Hopkins Press, 1928.

Moody, William. Letter to President Theodore Roosevelt, January 4, 1906. General Records of the Department of Justice, National Archives, Record Group 60, File 2290-02.

Morse, Jedidiah. *A Report to the Secretary of War of the United States on Indian Affairs.* New York: A. M. Kelly, 1970.

Nixon, Richard M. "Special Message to the Congress on Indian Affairs." *Public Papers of the Presidents of the United States: Richard M. Nixon, Containing the Public Messages, Speeches, and Statements of the President, 1970.* Washington, D.C.: Government Printing Office, 1971.

Otis, Morgan. "Indian Education: A Cultural Dilemma." *The American Indian Reader.* San Francisco: The Indian Historian Press, 1972.

Prucha, Francis Paul. *The Churches and the Indian Schools, 1888–1912*. Lincoln: University of Nebraska Press, 1979.

———. *The Great Father: The United States Government and the American Indians*, abridged edition. Lincoln: University of Nebraska Press, 1984.

Public Health Service. *Contagious and Infectious Diseases Among the Indians*. 62d Congress, 3d Session, S. Doc. 1080, Washington, D.C.: Government Printing Office, 1913.

Ravitch, Diane. "On the History of Minority Group Education in the United States." *Teacher's College Record* 78 (December 1976.).

Reuben Quick Bear v. Leupp. 210 U.S. Report 50-82.

Roessel, Robert, Jr. "An Overview of the Rough Rock Demonstration School," *Journal of American Indian Education* 7 (May 3, 1968).

Sanchez, George. *The People: A Study of the Navajoes*. U.S. Department of the Interior, U.S. Indian Service. Washington, D.C.: Government Printing Office, 1948.

Scheirbeck, Helen. Unpublished Ph.D. dissertation. *They Ran Their Own Schools: Education in the Five Civilized Tribes, 1819–1915*.

Senese, Guy. "Self-Determination and American Indian Education: An Illusion of Control." *Educational Theory* 36 no. 2 (Spring 1986).

Statutes at Large of the United States of America, 1789–1873. 17 vols. Washington, D.C., 1850–1873.

Szasz, Margaret Connell. *Education and the American Indian: The Road to Self-Determination 1928–1973*. Albuquerque: University of New Mexico Press, 1977.

Talayesva, Don C. *Sun Chief: The Autobiography of a Hopi Chief*. New Haven, Connecticut: Yale University Press, 1942.

U.S. Congress. House. House Select Committee on Indian Affairs. *An Investigation to Determine Whether the Changed Status of the Indian Requires a Revision of the Laws and Regulations Affecting the American Indians*. 78th Congress, 2d Session, 1944, H. Rept. 2091, (serial 10848).

U.S. Congress. Senate. Committee on Indian Affairs. *Navajo Indian Education: Hearings Before the Committee on Indian Affairs*. 79th Congress, 2d Session, 1946.

U.S. Congress. Senate. Committee on Indian Affairs. *Tuberculosis Among the North American Indian Tribes: Report of a Committee of the National Tuberculosis Association*. 67th Congress, 4th Session. Washington, D.C.: Government Printing Office, 1923.

U.S. Congress. Senate. Subcommittee of the Committee of Indian Affairs. *Survey of Conditions of the Indians in the United States: Hearings Before a Subcommittee of the Committee of the Indian Affairs*. Part 4, 1929 and part 18, 1932.

U.S. Congress. Senate. Subcommittee of the Committee on Interior and Insular Affairs. *Rehabilitation of the Navajo and Hopi Indians: Hearings Before a Subcommittee of the Committee on Interior and Insular Affairs*. 80th Congress, 2d Session, 1948.

U.S. Congress. Senate. Committee on Labor and Public Welfare. Subcommittee on Indian Education. *Indian Education: A National Tragedy—A National*

Challenge. Kennedy Report. 91st Congress, 1st Session, 1969, S. Rept. 501 (serial 12836).

Washburn, Wilcomb E. *The Indian in America.* New York: Harper and Row, 1975.

Wilkenson, Gerald. "Educational Problems in the Indian Community: A Comment on Learning as Colonialism." *Intergrateducation,* Horace Mann Bond Center for Equal Education. University of Massachusetts 19:1–2 (January 1982).

INDEX